CAMBRIDGE TEXTS IN THE HISTORY OF POLITICAL THOUGHT

Fichte: Addresses to the German Nation

This is the first translation of Fichte's *Addresses to the German Nation* for almost 100 years. The series of fourteen speeches, delivered whilst Berlin was under French occupation after Prussia's disastrous defeat at the Battle of Jena in 1806, is widely regarded as a founding document of German nationalism, celebrated and reviled in equal measure. Fichte's account of the distinctiveness of the German people and his belief in the native superiority of its culture helped to shape German national identity throughout the nineteenth century and beyond. With an extensive introduction that puts Fichte's argument in its intellectual and historical context, this edition brings an important and seminal work to a modern readership. All of the usual series features are provided, including notes for further reading and a chronology.

GREGORY MOORE is lecturer in German at the University of St Andrews. He previously taught at the University of Wales Aberystwyth, and was Junior Research fellow at Sidney Sussex College, University of Cambridge. He is Secretary of the Friedrich Nietzsche Society.

CAMBRIDGE TEXTS IN THE HISTORY
OF POLITICAL THOUGHT

FICHTE
ADDRESSES TO THE GERMAN NATION

CAMBRIDGE TEXTS IN THE HISTORY
OF POLITICAL THOUGHT

Series editors

RAYMOND GEUSS, *Professor of Philosophy, University of Cambridge*
QUENTIN SKINNER, *Professor of the Humanities, Queen Mary, University of London*

Cambridge Texts in the History of Political Thought is now firmly established as the major student textbook series in political theory. It aims to make available to students all the most important texts in the history of Western political thought, from ancient Greece to the early twentieth century. All the familiar classic texts will be included, but the series seeks at the same time to enlarge the conventional canon by incorporating an extensive range of less well-known works, many of them never before available in a modern English edition. Wherever possible, texts are published in a complete and unabridged form, and translations are specially commissioned for the series. Each volume contains a critical introduction together with chronologies, biographical sketches, a guide to further reading and any necessary glossaries and textual apparatus. When completed, the series will offer an outline of the entire evolution of Western political thought.

For a list of titles published in this series, please see end of book.

FICHTE: ADDRESSES TO THE GERMAN NATION

EDITED WITH AN INTRODUCTION AND NOTES BY

GREGORY MOORE
University of St Andrews

CAMBRIDGE
UNIVERSITY PRESS

CAMBRIDGE
UNIVERSITY PRESS

University Printing House, Cambridge CB2 8BS, United Kingdom

One Liberty Plaza, 20th Floor, New York, NY 10006, USA

477 Williamstown Road, Port Melbourne, VIC 3207, Australia

314-321, 3rd Floor, Plot 3, Splendor Forum, Jasola District Centre, New Delhi - 110025, India

103 Penang Road, #05-06/07, Visioncrest Commercial, Singapore 238467

Cambridge University Press is part of the University of Cambridge.

It furthers the University's mission by disseminating knowledge in the pursuit of education, learning and research at the highest international levels of excellence.

www.cambridge.org
Information on this title: www.cambridge.org/9780521448734

© In the translation and editorial matter Cambridge University Press 2008

First published 2008

A catalogue record for this publication is available from the British Library

Library of Congress Cataloging in Publication data
Fichte, Johann Gottlieb, 1762–1814. [Reden an die deutsche Nation. English]
Fichte : Addresses to the German nation / edited with an introduction and notes by Gregory Moore.
p. cm. – (Cambridge texts in the history of political thought)
Includes bibliographical references and index.
ISBN 978-0-521-44404-0
1. Germany – Politics and government – 1806-1815. 2. Education and state – Germany. 3. National characteristics, German. I. Moore, Gregory. II. Title.
DD199.F413 2008
320.540943
2008026932

ISBN 978-0-521-44404-0 Hardback
ISBN 978-0-521-44873-4 Paperback

Contents

Contents

Acknowledgements

I should like to thank Daniel Breazeale for advice in matters of translation, Quentin Skinner and Raymond Geuss for their helpful comments on the introduction, and Richard Fisher for his forbearance during the protracted gestation of this project.

Introduction

At noon on Sunday, 13 December 1807, Johann Gottlieb Fichte stood before an expectant audience in the amphitheatre of the Berlin Academy of Sciences and began the first of a series of fourteen weekly lectures known as the *Addresses to the German Nation*. A year before, Prussia, the last German state left standing against Napoleon, had been brought to its knees, its armies routed at the Battle of Jena. As the French advanced unopposed towards Berlin, Fichte fled the city, following the king and his government east to Königsberg. Now, after a Carthaginian peace had stripped Prussia of her rank as a major European power and reduced her to a satellite of the Grand Empire, Fichte returned to the occupied capital, traumatised, yet convinced it was his duty to mobilise a defeated people and urge their spiritual renewal. It was a course of action not without danger. Recalling the fate of Johann Palm, a Nuremberg book-dealer executed by the French for printing a seditious pamphlet, Fichte wrote: 'I know very well what I risk; I know that a bullet may kill me, like Palm; but it is not this that I fear, and for my cause I would gladly die.'[1] Over the sound of the drums of French troops marching in the streets outside, he began to speak ...

This story, told and retold throughout the nineteenth century and beyond, has helped win for the *Addresses* a privileged place in histories of nationalism as well as in nationalist histories of Germany. Claimed by liberals and conservatives, socialists and fascists alike, Fichte's best-known work has come to be seen as a definitive statement of romantic or 'messianic' nationalism. Although he may not have been the first

---

[1] *GA* iii/6, p. 213. (For abbreviations see p. xlv).

xi

theorist of the nation, or even the first spokesman for the unity of his country, his ideas about the relationship between language and identity, his portrait of the German character and its mission in the world, his vision of education as the means of moral regeneration, would shape German self-understanding for the next 150 years. Yet the *Addresses* owe their influence and reputation not only to *what* Fichte said but *how* he said it. Kant's self-anointed successor and – in his own eyes, to be sure – the leading thinker of the day, he appeared before his audience not merely as a philosopher. Just as he intended, some hailed him as a German Demosthenes, others saw in him a new Luther – ensuring that his words, a mixture of prophetism and polemic, eloquence and abstraction, long echoed in the German cultural imagination, recalled in both victory and defeat. Even if the *Addresses* are, inescapably, a response to a particular moment of historical crisis for a particular people, they yet have a broader significance. For Fichte also appeals, indirectly at least, to all of humanity, whose freedom, he believed, can be realised only by patriotism standing proxy for the idealism so disastrously lacking in the modern world.

The state of the nation

The very title of Fichte's work is a calculated provocation to his audience. When he delivered the *Addresses*, 'Germany' did not exist as anything more than a vague geographical expression. There was no unitary German state. Nor was it by any means clear – even to the inhabitants of central Europe – whether there was such a thing as a 'German nation'. How would one define its properties? What did it mean to be 'German'? These are the questions that Fichte sets out to answer.

In 1808 'Germany' referred to a collection of forty-one separate territories: Prussia, Austria and the various members of the Confederation of the Rhine, who owed their allegiance, and in some cases their crowns, to France. Even this was a great simplification of the situation prevailing at the close of the eighteenth century, before the revolutionary wars and Napoleon's redrawing of the map of *Mitteleuropa* (greeted, one presumes, with some relief by professional cartographers). Hundreds of duodecimo states, free cities and ecclesiastical possessions were scattered across the landscape in bewildering profusion. Many of these dominions were themselves broken up by a number of internal civil, legal and fiscal boundaries; some were not made up of contiguous pieces, but joined only by their ruler's personal authority; others had to tolerate enclaves of autonomous power within their borders. 'German' politics was a hopelessly complicated affair with conflicting jurisdictions, uncertain sovereignties and perpetual peacelessness. Holding most, but not all, of these units together, at least in theory, was the Holy Roman Empire of the German Nation, an entity that traced its ancestry back to the partition of the Carolingian Empire in 843. As Voltaire acidly but truthfully observed, it was neither holy nor Roman nor an empire. Nor, one might add, was it exclusively German. The King of England was a member as Elector of Hanover, the King of Denmark as Duke of Holstein, the King of Sweden as Lord of Pomerania, while Belgium participated as a dependency of the House of Habsburg. The empire included substantial French, Italian and Polish minorities, and many German-speaking communities lived outside its formal frontiers. The 'nation' its name referred to was not, then, a homogeneous ethnic group or the common people, but rather the *Adelsnation* or political elite of the *Reich*.

The gravitational pull of the imperial constitution had grown steadily weaker since the Peace of Westphalia in 1648 and the beginning of the internecine struggle between the two largest German powers, Austria and Prussia. In the absence of a strong centralised government, a capital city, or even a single currency, a sense of unity was hard to establish: the Holy Roman Empire was simply too diffuse. But if German political identity was fragile, there were some attempts to foster a *cultural* identity. The first of these was undertaken during the Reformation period. Already humanist scholars, following the rediscovery of Tacitus' *Germania* (AD 98) in the middle of the fifteenth century, had claimed to find in this idealised portrait of tribal society a catalogue of supposedly 'Teutonic' virtues that were still imprinted on the national character many hundreds of years later. Honesty, courage, honour, love of liberty – these were the traits that distinguished the German-speaking peoples even now from the decadent Latin countries (or *die Welschen*, the collective name given to the French and Italians). Martin Luther saw his own struggle against papal power as a continuation of an ancient desire for self-determination: he invoked the Cheruscan chieftain Arminius, who had won a crushing victory at the Battle of Teutoburg Forest in AD 9, as a symbol of Germany's renewed campaign against the corrupting influence of Rome. Just as momentously, Luther's translation of the Bible laid the foundations of a modern standard variety of German on which a secular public sphere began to build in the eighteenth century. This was essentially a literary culture, composed of readers and writers who were joined through an ever-expanding network of publishers, periodicals and lending libraries, reaching beyond territorial and social barriers, linking German speakers from Cologne to Königsberg, the Elbe to the Alps. It was, its champions hoped, the basis for a truly national community, one rooted in indigenous traditions and free from the oft-decried German tendency to ape foreign fashions and taste (*Ausländerei*). But this culture touched only a small minority of central Europeans in the eighteenth century: it was national in aspiration but not in fact. Nevertheless, it marked the emergence of what Friedrich Meinecke would later call the German *Kulturnation*.

Patriotism flourished, but it was of a local variety (*Heimatliebe*; *Schollenpatriotismus*). One's 'fatherland' was not the decrepit and often invisible Empire – which by the eighteenth century was more often than not an object of derision – but the principality or duchy, the city or even rural commune in which one lived. Prussians could and did take pride in the achievements of Frederick the Great, Austrians in their country's hereditary clout and influence, Danzigers in the history of the Hanseatic League. Even so, patriotic allegiances could be transferred without difficulty: Thomas Abbt, Swabian by birth, wrote *On Dying for the Fatherland* (1761) with Prussia in mind. As the novelist Christoph Martin Wieland pointed out in the 1790s, devotion to a larger 'Germany' was difficult to find. 'I see Saxon, Bavarian, Württemberg, and Hamburg patriots,' he wrote, 'but German patriots, who love the entire *Reich* as their fatherland ... Where are they?'[2]

Widespread provincialism co-existed with the enlightened cosmopolitanism espoused by many of the intellectual class. Excluded from power and responsibility, they felt that they had more in common with reformers and scholars in other lands than with their own countrymen and preferred to regard themselves as citizens of the worldwide republic of letters, an imaginary space where free-thinkers could exchange ideas for the good of humanity. This simultaneously internationalist and parochial outlook could not survive for long in the turmoil of the revolutionary age. The mass mobilisation of a citizen army had defended France against a coalition of foreign troops; but when this unprecedented military force went on the offensive from 1792, it would, by sweeping away the feudal structures of the Holy Roman Empire, reshape

---

[2] Wieland, 'Über teutschen Patriotismus. Betrachtungen, Fragen und Zweifel', in *Werke*, vol. 3 (Munich: Hanser, 1967), pp. 744–54 [p. 750].

the German political landscape also. The French revolutionary armies acted as undertaker to the old *Reich* and midwife to German nationalism: the humiliation of defeat and resentment at the treatment of the occupied German lands, first under the Directory and later under Napoleon, fostered a new solidarity rooted in shared suffering and adversity. Of even greater importance was a shift in the meaning of the term 'nation' itself, most obviously and consequentially under the influence of Johann Gottfried Herder. Where Karl Eugen, Duke of Württemberg, had once echoed Louis XIV when he contemptuously declared 'I am the fatherland', Herder viewed the nation as co-extensive with the people or *Volk*, the totality of a given cultural and ethnic community and not merely the privileged members of the *Adelsnation*.[3] The *Volksnation*, the German answer to the civic nation of the French, was increasingly seen to have an identity distinct from feudal or state institutions. And it is this *Nation*, the German people as a whole, to which Fichte's *Addresses* are directed.

The philosophy of freedom

Fichte's own 'dearly beloved' fatherland was Saxony.[4] Born in 1762, the son of a lowly though literate weaver, he was rescued from a life of provincial obscurity by an aristocratic patron eager to fund the education of so precociously gifted a child. After leaving Pforta, the same boarding school that would later produce Nietzsche, Fichte studied theology with the aim of becoming a pastor – a well-trodden path for talented but unmonied children of the *Reich*. Kant, Herder, Schelling, Hölderlin and Hegel all travelled the same road. Forced by his straitened circumstances to leave university without graduating, Fichte, like so many of his colleagues, earned his crust while waiting for a pastorate by working as a private tutor to various wealthy families in the furthest-flung corners of the German-speaking world. Such tutors were treated as little more than indentured servants, though they were expected to possess the social graces necessary to cultivate gentlemen, and the humiliation of this experience instilled in Fichte a lasting distaste for lackeydom and the frivolity of the *beau monde*.

---

[3] Joachim Whaley, 'Reich, Nation, Volk. Early Modern Perspectives', *Modern Language Review*, 101 (2006), 442–55.

[4] *GA* III/1, p. 385.

Fichte's material hardship during these years was compounded by a spiritual crisis. He found himself reluctantly persuaded by the determinism then fashionable in Germany, and associated with Spinoza and certain thinkers of the French Enlightenment: the idea that human beings were not exempt from the laws of the physical universe; that their desires, actions and thoughts could be explained as necessary consequences of physiological, psychological or environmental factors. Though compelling, such a position was deeply troubling, especially for someone preparing to dedicate his life to the Church, for it seemed to leave no scope for agency or choice. Fichte found a way out of this impasse when he stumbled on Kant in 1790. Kant's reconciliation of freedom and determinism, his bifocal view of man as having both an empirical self subject to natural causation and a transcendental self that enjoyed untrammelled moral autonomy, led Fichte to experience, as he put it, a 'revolution' in his thinking.[5] He had found a new vocation.

He began by anonymously publishing an essay so thoroughly Kantian that it was widely assumed to have been written by Kant himself (*Attempt at a Critique of All Revelation*, 1792), but from the first Fichte was chiefly preoccupied by the critical philosophy's political and moral implications as well as its metaphysical significance. In 1793 he issued two works occasioned by the recent upheavals in France: a brief pamphlet entitled *Reclamation of the Freedom of Thought from the Princes of Europe Who Have Oppressed it Until Now* and the longer and unfinished *Contribution to the Rectification of the Public's Judgement of the French Revolution.* Fichte was not alone among German writers and intellectuals in welcoming the outbreak of revolution in France. Unusual, though, was his devotion to the cause even at a point when the Revolution had begun to devour its children and when many of his initially sympathetic compatriots – including Klopstock and Schiller, who had been made citizens of the Republic in 1792 – had turned away in fear and disgust. Choosing this moment to enter an impassioned and eloquent plea on behalf of the Revolution and to elucidate its underlying theoretical premises would earn him a reputation as a German Jacobin and trouble-maker.

'We carry our charter of freedom, given and sealed by God, deep in our bosom', Fichte declared in *Contribution*.[6] No external authority can bind the individual save that to which he freely gives his consent in a

---

[5] Ibid., p. 190.   [6] *GA* I/I, p. 266.

contractual arrangement with others: he is beholden only to the Kantian moral law within him. This absolute autonomy – our freedom of will, which releases us from the necessity of the natural world; our freedom of thought, which raises us above the mechanical association of ideas in animals – is expressed in and through certain inalienable rights: our right to say and think and do whatever we want, so long as it is in accord with our conscience; those rights whose abolition would infringe on the principle of moral self-sufficiency and human dignity. It is these rights that absolutist regimes seek to suppress: in imposing their arbitrary will on others, tyrants rob their subjects of their freedom and thus of their very humanity. And it is in defence of these rights, Fichte concludes, going where Kant had feared to tread, that a citizen is empowered to terminate his contract with the state; that revolution is then always justified, indeed a duty. For a people can never abdicate its right to liberty and self-realisation.

The same cause of freedom that moved him to champion the French Revolution later stirred his patriotic appeals for German unity. It also inspired his philosophy proper. Called to the University of Jena on the strength of his reputation as a leading interpreter of Kant, he set to work overthrowing orthodoxies old and new. Fichte once famously claimed that it was while writing about the Revolution that he received the 'first hints and intimations' of his principal work: the *Wissenschaftslehre* (*The Science of Knowledge*), which he originally published in 1794 but continued to revise until his death in 1814. A highly abstract inquiry into the source, limits and objects of human knowledge, the *Wissenschaftslehre* is an attempt to go beyond the compromises of Kant's epistemological dualism and ultimately to reconceive the nature of philosophy itself.

Fichte had come to appreciate that any account of knowledge that allowed it to be conditioned by entities external to the mind was an obstacle to the complete vindication of human autonomy. For Fichte, only a philosophy that started from the spontaneously self-positing I as the ground of all possible experience was entitled to call itself the 'first system of freedom', which led him to claim of the *Wissenschaftslehre*: 'Just as France has freed man from external shackles, so my system frees him from the fetters of things in themselves.'[7] Hence there were two ways of looking at matters, according to Fichte. Either one subscribes to 'idealism' or to

---

[7] *GA* III/2, p. 298; *Early Philosophical Writings*, trans. Daniel Breazeale (Ithaca, NY: Cornell University Press, 1988), pp. 385–6.

'dogmatism'. Either one sees the world as contingent on the mind and thus under the sway of the moral will and adaptable to its ends, or one does not. Either one is deeply convinced of the reality of human freedom and resolved to preserve that freedom in all that one undertakes, or one is not. Thus, the kind of philosophy one chooses 'depends on what kind of person one is',[8] and has a profoundly practical significance. The idea of being a mere appendage of nature, acted upon rather than acting and forever governed by forces beyond one's control, possessed a certain allure for many who were by no means averse to regarding themselves as helpless, passive objects rather than as self-determining subjects. Fichte suggests that there is perversity or cowardice or simple laziness in upholding such a view: it encourages supineness, the abdication of responsibility for one's own affairs and those of others, and the view that the status quo is unalterable. The conviction of man's transcendental freedom, however, produces sovereign individuals and gives them the strength to win their political liberty too. This opposition between the idealist and dogmatic philosophical standpoints Fichte would later reformulate in the *Addresses* as the difference between German and 'foreign' modes of thought.

Philosophy and the public sphere

'I wish not merely to think, but to act', Fichte told his fiancée in 1790.[9] Those words, written when he was an obscure and penniless private tutor on the geographical and social margins of the German-speaking world, point already to his long-held ambition to close the gap between philosophy and everyday life that had opened up through the professionalisation of the discipline in eighteenth-century Germany. During the period from 1794 to 1799, when he held the chair of philosophy at the University of Jena, Fichte searched for ways to reach beyond the academy and influence a broader public sphere. This required first and foremost a recasting of the role of the scholar in society, a role that would not be limited to the purely scientific or theoretical realm. More than any other group the scholarly class had a duty to the commonwealth: they were a vanguard elite that determined the evolution of culture, supervising and co-ordinating humanity's progress towards perfection,

---

[8] *GA* I/4, p. 195. [9] *GA* III/1, p. 72.

ever seeking new means to develop its potential. Consequently, Fichte was adamant that the philosopher must apply his insights to the actual events and problems of his own age. These were not empty words for Fichte: he practised what he preached. In the *Foundation of Natural Right* (1796/7) he showed that even as forbiddingly abstruse a work as the *Wissenschaftslehre* could serve as a basis for a theory of human rights and international law. He repeated the trick for morality in his *System of Ethics* (1798). Though he drifted away from the uncompromising individualism expressed in his writings on the French Revolution, his demands for political reform were no less radical or utopian: in *The Closed Commercial State* (1800) he argued for an early variant of *dirigiste* socialism. Most importantly and characteristically, whilst at Jena he began to lecture not only to his students and colleagues but to a wider audience as well. Forced to resign his chair at Jena after charges of atheism were brought against him, he was granted permission to settle in Berlin where, lacking an institutional base, he repackaged the *Wissenschaftslehre* in a 'popular' form that could be understood by educated laymen. Hence most of his major works after 1800 – *The Vocation of Man* (1800), *The Characteristics of the Present Age* (1804) and *The Way Towards the Blessed Life* (1806) – were originally delivered as public talks. By all accounts an inspirational speaker, equally at home behind the pulpit and the lectern, Fichte was suspicious of the written word and the power of the new literary market place to debase the discourse of civil society. If reading was, as he believed it to be, an essentially passive and solitary occupation that failed to stimulate independent thought, then he would revive the rhetorical character of ancient Greek philosophy; his oratory was designed to engage both the heart and the mind, to persuade his listeners as well as to move them to action.

When war broke out against France in 1806, Fichte offered his services first as a tribune, then as chaplain with the Prussian troops, promising to elucidate the deeper meaning of the battle and speak 'swords and lightning bolts';[10] he outlined his 'Addresses to German Warriors' only for the government to turn him down. When hostilities resumed in 1813 he again approached the authorities with a similar proposal; after being politely refused once more he joined the newly levied militia (*Landwehr*). In this sense at least, the *Addresses to the German Nation* do not represent a departure from Fichte's usual procedure: they are, rather, only the most

---

[10] *GA* II/10, p. 80.

conspicuous example of his attempts to shape national life, indeed to bring a truly national life into being for the first time.

Rebirth of a nation

Fichte begins his *Addresses* by announcing that he intends to view recent events within the framework of the philosophical eschatology he had outlined in *The Characteristics of the Present Age*, a series of seventeen lectures delivered three years previously. There he asserted that the human race is governed by the unfolding of a providential 'world-plan' that prescribes advancement towards ever greater freedom and rationality. From this premise he deduced five necessary epochs in history, sketching a kind of pilgrim's progress of Reason, a five-act drama that coincides with the five stages of Christian theology, stations on man's circuitous journey from a paradise unearned to a paradise regained.[11] The first era was a period of noble savagery ('the State of Innocence'), followed by an age of absolutism predicated on unconditional obedience to authority ('the State of Progressive Sin'); the third, the present age, was characterised by arid intellectualism, empty freedom and unrestrained licentiousness ('the State of Completed Sinfulness'); the fourth embraced truth as the highest of all things (the 'State of Progressive Justification'); and, having now apprehended the laws of Reason, in the fifth and final phase ('the State of Completed Justification and Sanctification') humanity would begin consciously and freely to build a social order based on these foundations, 'until the Race become a perfect image of its everlasting archetype in Reason; – and then shall the purpose of this Earthly Life be attained, its end become apparent, and Mankind enter upon the higher spheres of Eternity'.[12] The *Addresses* are explicitly advertised as a sequel to this earlier work and signal from the outset Fichte's determination to see the French invasion not only as a moment of national crisis for 'Germany', but also as a seismic shift of universal significance.

Prussia's collapse seemed to confirm Fichte's diagnosis of the present age as one of complete sinfulness. The Germans had brought moral and military catastrophe on themselves because they – the population as a

---

[11] M. H. Abrams, *Natural Supernaturalism: Tradition and Revolution in Romantic Literature* (London: Oxford University Press, 1971), p. 218.
[12] *CPA*, p. 9.

whole and not just the rulers – had suicidally developed their complacent materialism to its utmost degree, thereby allowing this 'realm of self-ishness' to be swept away by Napoleon's all-conquering armies. The collapse of the old regime had brought the third epoch of history to an abrupt and (Fichte admits with untypical modesty) completely unforeseen close. Having exhausted its capacity for decadence, Germany stood, abased and defeated, on the threshold of a new era. But in order to cross over, it would have to be born again – undergoing not only political but spiritual renewal. It must recognise its helplessly corrupt state, cast off its old divided self and fashion a new identity: 'we must become on the spot what we ought to be in any case, Germans'.[13]

How does one become German? This requires an act of the imagination. As Fichte well knew, he was addressing a German nation that did not yet exist: his actual audience in Berlin was a small and unrepresentative group of the Prussian educated elite. In other words, his discourses are proleptic: his aim was to paint a picture of German identity, to present a vision of what Germans have been, are and yet might be, so that his listeners might transform themselves into the model citizens of his fancy. They would prove their Germanness by refusing, like Fichte, to acknowledge regional and class differences, by demonstrating the unity which he evoked and claimed to be already existing (at least latently), by having the courage to act.

Crucially, though, Fichte does not stop there. It is not the fate of Germany alone that hangs in the balance. By enacting their nationhood, by awakening to the potential that lies therein, the Germans will redeem not only themselves but the whole world, leading the way into the next epoch of history. The German nation will be pioneers of a truly rational social order. 'If you sink,' Fichte accordingly warns at the end of his Fourteenth Address, 'all humanity sinks with you.' This messianic zeal seems at first sight a long way from his earlier defence of the French Revolution. But on closer inspection it is not. We have already seen that Fichte clung to his hopes in France for much longer than many of his compatriots. As late as 1799 he could write: 'It is clear that from now on only the French Republic can be the fatherland of the man of integrity, that only to it can he devote his energies; for from now on not only the dearest hopes of humanity but even its existence depend upon its

[13] See below, p. 155.

victory.'[14] Later that same year he even welcomed the prospect of French intervention in German politics. What changed? Not Fichte – he remained faithful to the ideas of 1789. He did not turn his back on the Revolution; the French did. The key to his thinking can be found in an illuminating passage from *The Characteristics of the Present Age*: the 'fatherland of the really educated Christian European' is 'in each age that European state which leads in culture'. But what if the 'sun-loving spirit' had forsaken France because 'light and justice' were no longer at home there?[15] And they weren't. The Republic, on whose behalf Fichte had once pledged to work, had given way to a sham monarchy bent on conquest for its own sake. Accordingly, he formed a quite visceral hatred of Napoleon, the man who had betrayed the cause, and whom, refusing to recognise his imperial dignity, he insisted on calling 'the nameless one': Fichte certainly did not share Hegel's admiration of the self-crowned Emperor. To his mind, the French had ultimately shown themselves to be unworthy of their appointed role in spreading the evangel of freedom. Perhaps it was now once again the turn of the Germans; perhaps they, the descendants of Arminius and Luther, could succeed where the French had failed and bring the Revolution to completion.

Nor did Fichte see his conversion to the cause of German patriotism as a disavowal of the cosmopolitan principles espoused in his earlier writings. His nationalism – unlike that of later pan-Germans – ultimately rested on the confidence that love of fatherland need not be narrow, selfish and particular, but was compatible with a wider devotion to humanity, which otherwise would remain a bloodless abstraction. This notion is first expressed in *Philosophy of Freemasonry* (1802) and again in *Patriotism and its Opposite*, a dialogue written in 1806, just before the Battle of Jena. There Fichte observes that, if cosmopolitanism is 'the will that the purpose of life and of man be reached in all humanity', then patriotism is 'the will that this purpose be reached first of all in that nation whereof we are members'.[16] But here is the typically Fichtean twist: because the goal of humanity can be advanced only by 'science', and only the Germans have begun to possess such science (through Fichte's own *Wissenschaftslehre*), only Germans while serving their country can simultaneously work for humanity as a whole.

[14] *GA* III/3, p. 349.   [15] *CPA*, p. 240.   [16] *GA* II/9, p. 399.

The idea of a people's calling or election is as old as nationalism itself. English Puritans in the seventeenth century reckoned themselves the vessels of divine grace and the Commonwealth a new Jerusalem. The westward expansion of the United States was enshrined in the doctrine of Manifest Destiny. The French revolutionaries likewise believed, especially after 1792, that it had fallen to them to liberate not just the *patrie* but the whole earth by exporting their ideals abroad. For Fichte, though, the special task of the Germans will not be accomplished by victory on the battlefield. The war of arms is over, he tells his audience; now begins the war of principles, morals, character, a war to end all wars: 'Yours is the greater destiny, to found the empire of spirit and reason, and to annihilate completely the crude physical force that rules the world.' This was a campaign which, with the heavy artillery of the *Wissenschaftslehre*, Germany was well equipped to win.

Even Fichte's conviction that Germany had a mission, one overwhelmingly spiritual in nature, was neither new nor uncommon amongst the German intelligentsia in the early years of the nineteenth century.[17] It served as a point around which the concept of the nation could crystallise, giving meaning to a specifically German identity for the first time. But it also served as wish fulfilment in an age when the country's fate was in the hands of foreign powers. Indeed, Germany's very impotence in the absence of a unified state was seen as a virtue: by remaining aloof from international politics, the German people had shown themselves, in Hölderlin's words, 'poor in deeds but rich in thought' – something that seemed to be borne out by the extraordinary efflorescence of German literature and philosophy at the close of the eighteenth century. Schiller spoke of his compatriots' peculiar moral grandeur: their lot was not 'to triumph with the sword' but to be a storehouse of civilisation and knowledge; as the Germans found themselves at the geographical centre of Europe, so they were 'the heart of humanity'. And while every nation had its day on the stage of history, 'the day of the German is the harvest of all Time'. Yet though Fichte was by no means the first to expound Germany's manifest destiny of the spirit, no one, to be sure, articulated this creed as forcefully, systematically and eloquently as he did.

---

[17] See Aira Kemiläinen, *Auffassungen über die Sendung des deutschen Volkes um die Wende des 18. und 19. Jahrhunderts* (Helsinki: Finnish Academy of Science and Letters, 1956).

Language and the inner frontier

The basis of German uniqueness, Fichte claims, is language. As he freely admits, this was hardly a novel insight. Language and identity had long been linked in the German historical imagination. This was unsurprising, given that the German tongue was the one thing that united a population divided by religion, politics and class: a fact already recognised in the eleventh-century *Annolied*. Ever since the Thirty Years War, scholars and writers such as Opitz, Thomasius, Leibniz, Gottsched and Campe had laboured to build the cultural nation from the ground up by reforming the vernacular, increasing its expressive potential, and asserting it against Latin in the universities and French in the salons. Moreover, Herder had recently argued that language was the pre-eminent vehicle of the national spirit (*Volksgeist*), a theory apparently supported by Schlegel's pioneering researches into the relationship between Sanskrit and Indian philosophy. For Fichte, language constitutes what he calls the inner frontier, the original and 'truly natural' borders of nations, often ignoring and cutting across the recognised limits of existing states. The dotted lines separating Prussia from Saxony on a map were accidental, ever-changing, merely political. Similarly, the Rhine could be bridged; but the linguistic boundaries separating the Germans from the French were absolute, eternal and impermeable.

What is language? Fichte rejects the dominant Enlightenment view of language as an entirely arbitrary system of signs. Words are not conventional tokens; Fichte holds that a fundamental law governs why a particular sound and no other represents an object or idea in language, for the latter is an elemental force, the spontaneous eruption of human nature. All languages are therefore varieties of a hypothetical protolanguage, which, under the pressure of assorted external influences on the organs of speech, was diverted down particular phonetic and lexical paths. As the primordial tongue split off into different groups, so too did humanity: with new dialects nations are formed. A people, then, is a linguistic community, one that continues to speak and develop, to preserve and expand the language it has inherited from the previous generation. Even though after some centuries have passed a group can no longer understand the idiom of their ancestors (as modern Germans can no longer easily understand medieval German), their language remains

xxiv

fundamentally the same, because at any one time its speakers have never ceased to understand one another.

In all languages words are first coined to describe the physical world. But the time comes in a people's intellectual growth when it must reach beyond the mundane and attempt to grasp what is inherently intangible: the realm of abstract thought. Concepts can therefore be represented only indirectly, by means of a symbol (*Sinnbild*), a metaphorical equation of the sensuous and the supersensuous. The very word 'idea', Fichte explains, illustrates how this operation works: the Greek *eidos* originally designated an object of sight. An idea, then, is something we 'see' in our mind's eye. That is to say, the meanings of a language's conceptual vocabulary are all ultimately embedded in concrete experience. Since different linguistic communities have different ways of understanding and describing the sensible world, indeed since the horizons of that lived world are different for each people, one language's metaphor, let alone its entire symbolic system, will not always be comprehensible to speakers of another. Language is hence rooted in its native culture (to use the organic imagery that Fichte himself favours); it cannot be transplanted into foreign soil. In the end, Fichte is interested in language less as a means of describing reality than as the medium of a specific 'national imagination', of the outlook, manners and values particular to a subgroup of humanity, which accompanies even the individual's attempts at self-expression 'into the inmost recesses of his mind as he thinks and wills'.[18]

Fichte does not stop at saying that Germans constitute a nation by virtue of their language and the distinctive mentality manifested therein. He goes further: the Germans *alone* among modern Europeans have preserved their linguistic and cultural identity throughout history; German *alone* is an 'original language', one that has been continuously spoken over countless millennia, never becoming fossilised but always diversifying. Fichte's argument here rests on the assumption that all (Western) European peoples are descendants of the various ancient Teutonic tribes. While the forebears of the Germans remained in their homeland, the Franks, Goths, Burgundians, Langobardi and so on migrated into Roman territory, conquered the local population but, crucially, became assimilated to its culture and gave up their mother tongue. The language they adopted, Latin, was a superficial and artificial

---

[18] See below, pp. 56, 58.

acquisition, because they inherited a semantic universe that was irreducibly foreign to their own experience. Latin may have gradually metamorphosed into French, Spanish and Italian, but whatever the conquerors added was grafted on to an idiom that was closed to them. Hence the Romance languages, their glittering appearance notwithstanding, are dead at the root: they have been cut off from the stream of life.

German, by contrast, like Greek before it, has developed without interruption from the origin of language as a natural force; it is a dialect, no matter how distantly related, of the Adamic vernacular. Only in German does the evolutionary chain of sensible and supersensible signification appear transparent and necessary, because every word corresponds to the people's own observations and nothing is of foreign provenance – a comically myopic claim given the importance of such Latin-derived terms as *Vaterland* (a calque on *patria*), *Nation* and even *Germane* to Fichte's argument.[19] Only in German are the resources for poetic invention and philosophical inquiry constantly being renewed and enriched. Only the Germans, therefore, have the right to call themselves a people – an entity that Fichte understands first and foremost as characterised by its discursive practice, formed by an unbroken series of inherently democratic communicative acts. The deracinated French are not a true nation because they have lost their language and their soul; they are foreigners because they have become estranged not only from the Germans but from themselves. They have no identity.

Once again: a dead language means that a culture is dead. And a dead culture is, ultimately, how Fichte defines 'foreign' – or everything that is antithetical to a German identity. Perhaps 'identity' is the wrong word: what makes the Germans German is the same dynamism, an openness to change, that distinguishes their language. Foreignness and Germanness are not, at least in the first instance, ethnic categories: present-day Germans, Fichte is at pains to point out, have by no means a nobler pedigree than other branches of the Teutonic family tree. These terms describe not descent, but a moral attitude, a world view. To be un-German means, at bottom, to believe that all is fixed, final and settled

[19] David Martyn, 'Borrowed Fatherland: Nationalism and Language Purism in Fichte's *Addresses to the German Nation*', *Germanic Review* 72 (1997), 303–15.

without the prospect of change – a perspective imposed by the constraints of one's lifeless language. This way of looking at things – that is, frivolously, derivatively, superficially – can influence every form of discourse, from science to politics and history. For example, Fichte rails against the dominant 'foreign' (or 'dogmatic') philosophy of materialism, which reduces the universe to clumps of atoms acted on mechanically by the forces of Newtonian physics: a vision of a dead and barren nature that merely resides in equally dead and barren minds. German (or 'idealist') philosophy apprehends life in its restless flux and variety, going beyond mere appearance to open up vistas of infinite possibility. A true German cannot perceive reality in any other fashion (contemporary 'Germans' who do not – Schelling, for instance – have been infected with the foreign spirit); indeed, the German language is uniquely able to grasp the slipperiness of Being: and it is no coincidence that the *Wissenschaftslehre* was written in German. Whereas foreign societies grind down their masses in the clockwork apparatus of the modern bureaucratic state, a German polity obtains its legitimacy from the people, and would seek to beget both patriotic citizens and proud human beings. Foreigners see the development of the race as locked in an endless cycle of rising and falling civilisations; but the German makes history, not merely repeating what has been and gone before, but producing something entirely new and without precedent. In short, to be German means to be capable of spiritual freedom, a freedom that is guaranteed by the purity of one's language. And this division between the free and unfree, the German and the foreign, is the deepest fault-line cleaving Europe in two.

Heaven on earth

A people is not just a group that shares a language spoken continuously since its first emergence. Fichte insists that the nation is a given manifestation of the divine, of the realm of pure thought, of original life. It is the totality of that group's spiritual being, the repository of innumerable individual and collaborative acts of creation that shape and reshape it constantly, a body politic and a soul politic, a self-generating and self-perpetuating culture that, in the minds of its members, dwells simultaneously in the past, present and future. As such, the nation, like religion, answers a basic human need: the desire for transcendence, for eternity, the impulse to leave behind some trace of one's existence in this world and not just in the world to come. Through the nation we can achieve immortality; it is the kingdom of heaven on earth.

The recognition of this fact – and the affirmation of the singularity of one's people – is what Fichte calls patriotism or love of fatherland. Love of fatherland means embracing the nation as the vesture of the eternal. It is this promise of everlasting life that inspires men to die for their country, but in the current era only the Germans are capable of such self-sacrifice and such idealistic fervour (or rather, they will be, once they have heard Fichte's message). For only they have a fatherland and are a people in this 'higher sense of the word'. Only they can behold the nation as both terrestial and divine, universal and particular. Only they have a national character: that is, constantly represent to themselves their specificity, actively constitute their own identity by lending visible form to the imageless flow of primordial becoming. Just as the neo-Latin peoples have no mother tongue, so they have no fatherland: they are orphans of the spirit.

Love of fatherland requires an entirely different order of emotional investment than mere civic pride and constitutional patriotism. For that reason it must become the guiding principle of any future German state (or states: nowhere in the *Addresses* does Fichte demand the political union of Germans). The function of the state is to provide for the material welfare and prosperity of its citizens, to ensure law and order, and guarantee their rights and liberties. But all this, Fichte declares, is only a prerequisite 'for what love of fatherland really desires: that the eternal and the divine may flourish in the world and never cease to become ever more pure, perfect and excellent'.[20] And, because these legal and economic goods are not the acme of a people's collective aspirations, they can be sacrificed for a greater goal: the preservation of the nation itself and its freedom. Just as the individual can gamble his own life, so the nation can stake the very existence of the state in defence of its most cherished ideals.

As the means of securing a German identity, of safeguarding the distinctiveness of the nation, love of fatherland serves a higher human purpose. Fichte offers this sort of patriotism as an antidote to the various 'selfish' ideologies prevalent in modern international relations. The first is the post-Westphalian dogma of the balance of power in Europe, which posits a state system in which Germany acts as the fulcrum, but is required to remain impotent and divided so as not to upset the

[20] See below, p. 105.

delicately poised equilibrium. This arrangement is inherently unstable, a kind of armed peace, and not the lasting harmony of a new moral arrangement such as Fichte demands. The second is world trade, which hampers the ability of states to determine their own internal affairs, and the rapacious acquisitiveness of colonialism. Finally, Fichte inveighs against the Napoleonic attempt to re-establish a 'universal monarchy', which, like the Roman Empire and the medieval Catholic Church before it, results in a typically 'Latin' negation of plurality and the imposition of a monolithic culture. These doctrines are a two-dimensional version of cosmopolitanism, or its alienated double, which precisely by short-cutting, undermining or flattening particular nations conflicts with the loftier interests of humanity. (Already, Fichte's nationalism, like later strains, emerges as a response to anxieties about the global flow of capital and the homogenising tendencies of supranational political institutions.) In *The Closed Commercial State* Fichte had argued for the necessity of economic autarky: political autonomy was only possible when the state becomes self-sustaining; it must therefore opt out of its trade links and diplomatic ties with other states. A similar emphasis on cultural autonomy underpins the *Addresses*. Humanity, Fichte writes, is the product of the simultaneous but independent self-realisation of discrete cultures: its essence is expressed only in the natural and inevitable differences between individuals and agglomerations of individuals – of nations, in other words. 'Only as each of these peoples, left to itself and in accordance with its peculiar quality, develops and takes shape, and as every individual among that people, in accordance with this common quality as well with as his own, develops and takes shape, is the appearance of divinity reflected in its proper mirror, as it should be.' It is hence a sacred task to preserve the diversity of national character, for only in difference can we find the guarantee of the 'present and future dignity, virtue and merit' of nations.[21]

Educating the nation

The renewal of the nation will not be achieved by political means alone. Modern humanity is so thoroughly corrupt, Fichte believes, that we must start all over – this really is a year zero – and create an entirely new order of things. This is only possible by introducing comprehensive improvements to the system of education and by putting our hopes in the next

---

[21] See below, p. 172.

generation. 'Only that nation which has first of all solved the task of educating the perfect human being,' he avers, 'will also solve that of the perfect state.'[22] Once this programme has been successfully implemented at the national level, it can be spread elsewhere and help humanity to realise its vocation: a society based on reason and freedom.

The basic principles of this education are, as Fichte frankly concedes, borrowed from the Swiss pedagogical reformer Johann Heinrich Pestalozzi (1746–1827), although the wider aims and applications Fichte envisages for them are entirely his own. After making an intensive study of Pestalozzi's writings during the winter of 1806–7, Fichte came to the conclusion that, without fully appreciating it, this provincial school-master had discovered 'the true medicine for sick humanity' and, revealingly, 'also the only means of making it capable of understanding the *Wissenschaftslehre*'.[23] Like Rousseau before him, Pestalozzi wanted to establish a method of teaching that was sympathetic to the individual child's natural psychological development. As he argued in his major work *How Gertrude Teaches Her Children* (1801), the young ought not to be overtaxed with rote learning and complex concepts, but were instead to be encouraged by stimulating their self-activity – a key term for Pestalozzi as it was for Fichte. Starting with intuitive observation (*Anschauung*) and practical tasks, with the child pursuing his own interests and drawing his own conclusions, instruction would proceed only gradually to abstract ideas so that the child's own powers of seeing, judging and reasoning were unfolded. Moreover, the training of the intellect was to be undertaken simultaneously with the cultivation of the moral and sensitive faculties: there was to be harmony between head, hands and heart.

Fichte, too, bemoans the shortcomings of the prevailing system of education: it has been one-sided and inadequate, nurturing only part of the child rather than forming well-rounded human beings. The new education, by contrast, would be moral and ultimately religious: it must succeed in producing self-governing individuals who are inwardly and fundamentally good, who desire and do the right thing unpromptedly, unhesitatingly, resolutely, with no prospect of material reward and heedless of utilitarian calculations. This kind of moral autonomy – predicated on a firm will, a good will in the Kantian sense – education hitherto has singularly failed to inculcate. Fichte is sure it can best be arrived at

---

[22] See below, p. 81.   [23] *GA* III/6, p. 121.

not by exhortation or pious homilies but indirectly, by unshackling the human being's innate drive to independent thought – his capacity to project images that do not merely replicate the existing world of sense but prefigure alternative and as yet only ideal structures of being. Hence, following Pestalozzi, Fichte insists that his proposed scheme of education will not teach pupils what to think but how to think. More important than the memorisation of bare facts is the child's self-activity and the pleasure in learning for its own sake that this inspires: for this spontaneity and the attendant feeling of love – the same love that is the essence of patriotism – are for Fichte the *sine qua non* of the moral subject. Indeed, the true aim of education is, by enabling this mental activity, to prepare the pupil to create for himself an image of the perfect moral order (the nation, the state) so that, seized by an overwhelming love for it, he wills it and strives to actualise it.

Fichte's education would not only shape the mind and the will, but also teach practical, artisanal skills. The purpose of manual labour was not only to make the school self-sufficient, a closed commercial state in miniature, so that it could remain sequestered from the depravity of the outside world (just as nations must be quarantined from one another), but also to instil in its charges a sense of honour and self-reliance, as well as bring home to them the value of mutual respect through their duties to the whole. Even the prospective scholar would not be trained in splendid isolation: no dry-as-dust pedant he. The few pupils selected for this career would follow broadly the same curriculum, though the time others later devoted to work and craftsmanship they would spend in solitary cogitation.

This project would be a 'national' education in two separate but linked senses. In the first place it would actively foster a sense of collective identity. If pedagogy had so far been solely concerned with cultivating the individual self, Fichte's scheme would fashion a 'universal and national self' and mould 'the Germans into a totality' animated by a common interest.[24] Secondly, this instruction would be extended to all who were German, regardless of their rank and status, and hence sup- plant Pestalozzi's merely 'popular' education, which, as a charitable enterprise, sought merely to improve the opportunities of the poor and disadvantaged and hence did nothing to heal the divisions in society or abolish entrenched privilege. Fichte wanted to do away with class

---

[24] See below, pp. 17, 19.

distinctions entirely, and only by taking education out of the hands of private persons, by placing it in the care of the state and making it compulsory, could this goal be achieved. Prince and pauper would both receive the same schooling. As such, the provision of education is the most important office that Fichte envisages for the state. The classroom will realise what is now only an imagined community, release the creative potential of the past and future *Urvolk* and be a crucible of German nationhood.

The impact of the *Addresses*

It would be impossible to measure the extent of Fichte's actual influence during the period leading up to Napoleon's decisive defeat at Leipzig in 1813, when the stricken Prussian state introduced the necessary political, educational and military reforms that allowed it to recover.[25] To judge from the letters and later reminiscences of his contemporaries, however, many were moved by his appeal, including Karl vom und zum Stein, Wilhelm von Humboldt, Carl von Clausewitz and even the crown prince of Württemberg. To some degree, then, Fichte did succeed in creating a constituency in which political disagreements were subordinated to the national ideal. Goethe, however, sounded a warning note. Although he praised the *Addresses*, 'particularly their fine style', he presciently remarked of the Germans: 'Their firewood has been stoked up nicely, but a decent oven that will hold together is wanting.'[26]

Fichte may have roused his contemporaries with his oratorical flights, but his real effect on the insurgency against Napoleon was at best negligible. After all, no German state put his ideas into practice – although the Prussian education ministry did send a handful of teachers to Switzerland to train in Pestalozzi's school. Reformers in both Prussia and Austria insisted that patriotism was an essential element in the kind of wars being fought in the revolutionary age, but peace did not result in German unification: the princes were naturally opposed to such a

---

[25] Fichte's son and biographer, Immanuel Hermann (who bears the names of two great German heroes, Kant and Arminius), is keen to suggest that Scharnhorst's reorganisation of the army was 'wholly in tune with Fichte's way of thinking', but this claim is rather far-fetched (*Johann Gottfried Fichte's Leben und literarischer Briefwechsel*, Leipzig: Brockhaus, 1862, p. 418).
[26] Erich Fuchs, Reinhard Lauth and Walter Schieche (eds.), *Fichte im Gespräch* (Stuttgart/ Bad Cannstatt: Frommann-Holzboog, 1978), vol. 4, p. 214.

development since it would destroy their sovereignty and power, and struggled to put the genie back in the bottle. Hence, when reaction set in after the Vienna Congress, German governments cracked down on any subversive 'demagoguery' that would upset the post-war restoration. The *Addresses* were not celebrated as a brave rallying cry to the German nation in its darkest hour, but seen rather, by the Central Commission of Investigation in Mainz, as the *fons et origo* of liberalism and republicanism, corrupting German youth and striving to unite them 'in a community independent of the individual governments'.[27] A second edition of the *Addresses* was accordingly banned in Prussia in 1824, the same state whose censors had given Fichte so much trouble in 1808, and had to be printed in Saxony.

Fichte's influence was also felt by conservative nationalists, who were impressed by his equation of language and identity. Friedrich de la Motte Fouqué, better known as a writer of romantic tales, drew on the conjectures in the Fourth Address in *Etwas über den deutschen Adel* (1819) and *Der Mensch des Südens und der Mensch des Nordens* (1829), but gave them a narrower, more exclusivist sense. For Fouqué the Germans are a race possessed of a Fichtean original language which confers on them a distinctive attitude of mind: their seriousness, moral fortitude, sensitivity and religiosity set them apart from the degeneracy of the 'romanised Teutons' [*verwelschte Germanen*] west of the Rhine. But Fouqué adds his own aristocratic slant: the common *Volk* must be guided by a noble Junker class if it is to thrive: republicanism is a regime quite alien to the Germans. This is typical of the way that the ideas contained in the *Addresses* were channelled into the turbid stream of *völkisch* thought. Though he would not have recognised them as his direct intellectual descendants, Fichte bequeathed to future generations of German nationalists a view of the world that stressed the inherently intuitive, vital and creative quality of Germanness as opposed to the petrified, intellectual and imitative nature of the 'foreign'. Precisely those characteristics which Fichte ascribes to the Latin peoples later anti-Semitic agitators would associate with the Jews.

It was only in the second half of the nineteenth century that Fichte's status as a nationalist hero was confirmed. After his death in 1814, his theoretical edifice was overshadowed by that of Hegel, whose system dominated academic philosophy in Germany until the 1860s. But the

[27] Ibid., p. 89.

centenary of Fichte's birth in 1862, the same year as Bismarck became Prussian prime minister, witnessed a remarkable explosion of popular and scholarly interest in the man and his work – the best and most consequential example of which was Heinrich von Treitschke's essay 'Fichte and the National Idea'. If every nation needs a foundation myth, then perhaps so too does nationalism itself: and for this reason Fichte's supposed political efficacy was greatly exaggerated and the *Addresses* themselves were admitted into the German literary canon. As Wilhelm Windelband observed in 1890, these celebrations honoured the patriot Fichte and not the philosopher.[28]

This development peaked in 1914, which marked not only the hundredth anniversary of Fichte's death, but also a new moment of national extremity. In a clear echo of the rhetoric of the Napoleonic period, German intellectuals presented the First World War as a fight for survival, a struggle pitting a superior German *Kultur* against the shallow civilisation of the Triple Entente. For many, the euphoria and spontaneous outpouring of patriotism that greeted the declaration of war was a sign that Germany had become truly united in spirit as in law; when the internal economic, regional, social schisms remaining after 1871 were healed. In the ensuing propaganda battle Fichte was repeatedly invoked not only by established philosophers like the Nobel laureate Rudolf Eucken, but also by lesser figures. For Hermann Reincke-Bloch, for instance, the *Addresses* had only now revealed 'their most secret meaning'. The superiority of the Germans over other Europeans had been proven once and for all, since 'the spirit that our people has shown throughout every class in August 1914 – that is the spirit which Fichte claims as the peculiar property of the Germans.' During the nineteenth century Germans had refused to countenance their uniqueness, and thus ignored their destiny: 'Today the hour has come when the chasm . . . has opened up before our eyes and when the future of the world . . . truly is connected to the fate of the Germans.'[29]

[28] Windelband, *Fichtes Idee des deutschen Staates* (Freiburg: Mohr, 1890), p. 5.
[29] Hermann Reincke-Bloch, *Fichte und der deutsche Geist von 1914* (Rostock: Warkentien, 1915), pp. 8, 14–15. Other appeals to Fichte included: Ottmar Dittrich, *Neue Reden an die deutsche Nation* (Leipzig: Quelle und Meyer, 1916); Hermann Schwarz, *Fichte und Wir* (Osterwieck/Harz: Zickfeldt, 1917). Allied intellectuals were also only too ready blame Fichte for German expansionism: see Emile Hovelaque, *The Deeper Causes of the War* (London: Allen and Unwin, 1916) and George Santayana, *Egotism in German Philosophy* (London: Dent, 1916).

When Fichtean themes were reprised in this way, they were invariably transformed. Fichte had delivered his *Addresses* when Germany did not yet exist. A century later the German Empire was an industrial and military power, and willing to use Fichte's reputation to promote its own expansionist goals. In 1807 Fichte had spoken on his own, beholden to no authority. These professors were loyal servants of the state. Fichte faced a continental war in which France was the aggressor. Now it was Germany. In short, when German philosophers parroted Fichte in 1914, his words had a more ominous force. Uttered at a different historical moment, they served a different purpose and were tied inextricably to the fantasies of those who dreamt of a place in the sun.

A sense of political and existential crisis lingered for the next thirty years. In the immediate, chaotic aftermath of the war, as the Weimar Republic lurched from one emergency to another, yet more editions of the *Addresses* and pamphlets and newspaper articles on Fichte continued to be published, demanding that his proposals be put into practice at last, so that a moral and national rebirth might take place.[30] Even Friedrich Ebert, the first president of the fledgling democracy, appealed to Fichte's name in the coda of his speech on the occasion of the opening of the National Assembly on 6 February 1919. Ebert claimed that the task facing the delegates as they prepared the new state's constitution was to put *Machtpolitik* behind them and realise 'that which Fichte gave to the German nation as its vocation. We desire to establish a realm of justice and truthfulness, founded on the equality of all who wear a human face.'[31] Inevitably, the National Socialists, too, saw in Fichte a figure who could be utilised in their incessant attempts to lend a semblance of legitimacy to the Party's ideology and to justify their own pathological sense of mission. Fichte, along with Nietzsche, was elevated to the higher ranks of the Nazi pantheon of philosophers – most spectacularly in Heidegger's notorious rectorial address in 1933, which, in its picture of a looming spiritual catastrophe, triggered this time by the overweening nihilism of the USA and the Soviet Union and redeemable only by Germany's spiritual leadership, was implicitly modelled on the *Addresses*.

---

[30] See e.g. Anon, *Fichte und Deutschlands Not. Zeitgemäße Randbemerkungen zu Fichtes Reden an die Deutsche Nation* (Berlin Warneck, 1919).

[31] www.unser-parlament.de/download/SHOW/reden_und_dokumente/1848_1933/ebert_1919.

Given Fichte's association with the destructive course of German nationalism, the *Addresses* were once again largely ignored after the Second World War, even as interest in Fichte's wider philosophy, and his place in the post-Kantian tradition, was being rekindled. Now perhaps it is time to rediscover the *Addresses* too. They deserve our attention not only because they so strikingly express the various elements from which German national consciousness was forged; in an age when questions of identity – national, cultural, religious – have acquired a new urgency, the *Addresses* also stand out as an early and impressive attempt to grapple with these ever-current issues. Though we must liberate Fichte from the one-eyed readings of the past, we should take care that we do not smooth out his rough edges and resolve the very ambiguity and contradictoriness that give his work its vitality and continued resonance. For the *Addresses* are at once hard-headed and utopian, sublime and ridiculous, brilliant and obscure, nationalist and cosmopolitan.

Chronology

1793   21 January: Louis XVI executed; 17 March–22 July: Republic of Mainz founded by German Jacobins in French-controlled Rhineland; 6 April: Committee of Public Safety established; 24 June: Jacobin constitution passed; 27 July: Robespierre assumes leadership of Committee of Public Safety; summer: *Reclamation of the Freedom of Thought*; 5 September: Terror begins; 22 October: Fichte marries Johanna Rahn in Switzerland; *Contribution to the Rectification of the Public's Judgement of the French Revolution.*

1794   18 May: Fichte arrives in Jena after being called to the chair of philosophy and begins work on the *Foundation of the Entire Wissenschaftslehre*, parts I and II of which appear later in the year; 27–8 July: Robespierre arrested and executed, fall of the Jacobins and end of Terror, Thermidorian reaction.

1795   *Foundation of the Entire Wissenschaftslehre*, part III; 5 March: following the Peace of Basel, Prussia adopts a policy of neutrality until 1806; 5 October: troops under General Napoleon Bonaparte put down a royalist uprising in Paris; 26 October: Directory begins.

1796   *Foundations of Natural Right* (Part I).

1797   *Foundations of Natural Right* (Part II); 17 October: Treaty of Campo Formio between France and Austria; France annexes Belgium, creation of the Cisalpine Republic; 16 November: death of King Friedrich Wilhelm II, who is succeeded by Friedrich Wilhelm III.

1798   *System of Ethics*; charges of atheism brought against Fichte.

1799   April: the authorities of Saxe-Weimar accept Fichte's resignation of his professorship; July: Fichte moves to Berlin; 9 November (18 Brumaire): Bonaparte stages a coup against the Directory and is named First Consul.

1800   *The Vocation of Man.*

1801   9 February: Peace of Lunéville, cessation of hostilities between France and Austria until 1805.

1802   2 August: Bonaparte made Life Consul.

1804   12 February: Kant dies; 21 March: promulgation of Code Napoléon; 18 May: Bonaparte proclaimed Emperor of the French; 11 August: Holy Roman Emperor Franz II crowned Emperor of Austria.

1805 May: Fichte appointed professor of philosophy at University of Erlangen; 2 December: France defeats Austria and Russia at Battle of Austerlitz.

1806 *Characteristics of the Present Age* and *Way Towards the Blessed Life*; 12 July: creation of the Confederation of the Rhine; 6 August: Franz II dissolves Holy Roman Empire; 14 October: Prussian forces routed at battles of Jena and Auerstedt; 18 October: Fichte flees to Königsberg.

1807 9 July: Treaty of Tilsit exacts a humiliating peace from Prussia, creating Kingdom of Westphalia from its western territories, with Jerome Bonaparte on the throne, and the Duchy of Warsaw, ruled by French ally King Friedrich Augustus I of Saxony.

1807 13 December–20 March 1808: Fichte delivers the *Addresses to the German Nation*; July: Scharnhorst begins process of reforming the Prussian military; 9 October: Stein's Edict of Emancipation abolishes serfdom in Prussia.

1808 Reforms to Prussian central and local government.

1809 Humboldt begins school and university reforms.

1810 Fichte elected first Rector of newly established University of Berlin; October: Hardenberg pushes through a series of economic reforms, including the introduction of free trade.

1812 11 March: Jews granted equal rights in Prussia; 12 June: Napoleon invades Russia.

1813 Conscription introduced in Prussia; 16–19 October: French forces withdraw across Rhine after defeat in 'Battle of Nations' at Leipzig.

1814 Fichte dies on 29 January of typhoid fever at age of 51.

1815 9 June: conclusion of the Congress of Vienna, under the terms of which the German Confederation is established; 18 June: final defeat of Napoleon at Waterloo.

1871 Foundation of the German Empire, the first unified German nation state.

Note on the text and translation

This is the first full translation into English of the *Addresses to the German Nation* since that of R. F. Jones and G. H. Turnbull in 1922, and only the second ever.

The text is based on the first edition of the *Reden an die deutsche Nation* published in 1808 by Reimer in Berlin and has been cross-referenced with the text that appears in vol. 1/10 of the *Gesamtausgabe der Bayerischen Akademie der Wissenschaften* (Stuttgart/Bad Cannstatt: Frommann-Holzboog, 2005). In compiling my notes, I have drawn in part on the commentary included in the latter.

Fichte intended each address to be rushed into print immediately after its delivery. This meant that the manuscripts had to be submitted to the office of the Prussian censor for individual approval. The First Address proved immediately problematic, as Fichte's original version made it quite clear that he was singling out the Prussian state for criticism. Publication was withheld until, through the intervention of Freiherr vom und zum Stein, an exasperated Fichte was persuaded to make a number of minor amendments. The First Address was eventually cleared on 1 April 1808, by which time Fichte had already concluded his course of lectures (on 20 March). The remaining addresses were passed without delay, although there were reservations about the disparaging comments in the Fifth concerning the 'dead' language and culture of the foreign countries, and some more serious misgivings about passages in the Eighth. Only with the final address did the censor again wield his red pencil, and Fichte was once more obliged to make a few small changes.

Because the other addresses had already been printed by the time the First went to press and too many sheets had been set aside for it, Fichte decided to fill the resulting blank pages with extracts from his essay *On Machiavelli as Writer* (published in June 1807 in the first issue of the journal *Vesta. Für Freunde der Wissenschaft und Kunst*, pp. 17–81) and his *Dialogues on Patriotism and its Opposite* (1806–7), which remained unpublished during his lifetime.

The text of the Thirteenth Address is not the same as that delivered by Fichte on 13 March 1808. Although it had been cleared for publication, the manuscript went missing before it could be returned to him. In spite of a number of searches conducted at the behest of Fichte, who was understandably upset, and his publisher, Reimer, who stood to lose money, the text was never found. In the end, Fichte was compelled to rewrite the address from scratch, and this time he added a footnote explaining what had happened. He successfully petitioned for a different censorial office to scrutinise the resubmitted work, even though the original agency strenuously denied any responsibility or ulterior motive for allowing the manuscript to be lost. He was asked to tone down his frustrated criticism of the censor, which he duly did, and the text was finally published.

Given Fichte's views on language, translating the *Addresses* must seem a more than usually quixotic enterprise. Fichte exploits to the full the syntactic elasticity of German; since this is such a dominant feature of his style here, I have tried, as far as English will allow, to reproduce his sinuous periods and not to carve up his sentences into separate units, which would inevitably give the whole a more halting and less fluid feel than the original.

A word of explanation about some of the renderings of Fichte's vocabulary.

Fichte uses two sets of terms to describe his project for reform of German society: *bilden/Bildung* and *erziehen/Erziehung*. The latter two can be given quite unproblematically as 'educate'/'education'. *Bildung* corresponds to the English 'culture', 'cultivation', which can refer to the development of mental, moral and physical faculties in the individual human being as well as to the totality of beliefs, practices and products of a given social group. Fichte uses the word in both senses.

If *bilden* sometimes means 'to cultivate', it also designates one of the basic aims and techniques of his proposed method of education: from their unmediated sensory experience or 'intuitions' (*Anschauungen*) pupils are expected to generate a *Bild* or mental image of the world (so *bilden* in this sense is translated as 'to form an image'). This image, furthermore, is not a mere 'copy' (*Nachbild* – literally 'afterimage') of the world as it is, but a 'pre-figuration' (*Vorbild* or 'fore-image') of how it ought to be. The German play on (perfectly ordinary) words here is impossible to replicate fully ('afterimage' having an entirely different sense in English, for example). This activity is sometimes described as *entwerfen*, which is equivalent to 'to project' (both words signifying 'to devise, design or conceive in the mind' and 'to cast forth'). Anything that can be visualised or imaged in this way is therefore said to be *bildlich* (imageable); anything that is not is *unbildlich* (unimageable).

Erscheinung is translated as 'appearance', except in non-technical contexts where 'phenomenon' would be the more natural English term.

Geist and *geistig* never fail to present problems for the translator. As is well known, the German term embraces a range of meanings that the English word 'spirit' no longer possesses, at least in everyday modern usage. I have preferred 'spirit', 'spiritual' in most cases, except where 'mind', 'mental' are more natural. *Gemüt* is also a slippery and quintessentially German word; it has generally been rendered as 'soul', in the older sense that is the same as 'mind', but sometimes also as 'temper', 'feeling' and indeed 'mind'.

Geschlecht is translated as 'race' or 'generation', with no difference in meaning between the two.

Two key terms for Fichte are obviously *Deutsche* and *Germanier*. *Germanier*, from the Latin *germanus*, refers to the ancient Germanic tribes, rather than the modern inhabitants of central Europe, the *Deutschen* (whom English-speakers of course call 'Germans'). In order to preserve Fichte's clear distinction between the two groups, I have used the somewhat antiquated 'Teuton' for *Germanier* (even though *deutsch* or the older *teutsch* are actually etymologically related to the former).

No conveniently simple English equivalent exists for the German *das Ausland*, the catch-all term (literally 'outlands') that Fichte uses to describe those countries (chiefly France) beyond the natural and linguistic borders of Germany (*Deutschland*). I have used 'foreign lands', 'foreign peoples' or 'foreigners' where appropriate.

Suggestions for further reading

Translations of many of Fichte's major works are available in English: *The Science of Knowledge*, translated and edited by Peter Heath and John Lachs (Cambridge University Press, 1982); *Early Philosophical Writings*, translated and edited by Daniel Breazeale (Ithaca, NY: Cornell University Press, 1988); *Foundations of Natural Right*, translated by Michael Baur and edited by Frederick Neuhouser (Cambridge University Press, 2000); *The System of Ethics*, translated and edited by Daniel Breazeale and Günter Zöller (Cambridge University Press, 2005). Fichte's Berlin writings, including *Characteristics of the Present Age*, to which the *Addresses* are intended as a sequel, can be found in William Smith's somewhat dated but still eminently readable two-volume translation of the *Popular Works*, first published in 1848–9 and reprinted in a facsimile edition by Thoemmes Press in 1999.

Useful guides to Fichte's philosophical context include: Karl Ameriks (ed.), *The Cambridge Companion to German Idealism* (Cambridge University Press, 2000); Frederick C. Beiser, *The Fate of Reason. German Philosophy from Kant to Fichte* (Cambridge, MA: Harvard University Press, 1987); Dieter Henrich, *Between Kant and Hegel: Lectures on German Idealism* (Cambridge, MA: Harvard University Press, 2003); Terry Pinkard, *German Philosophy, 1760–1870* (Cambridge University Press, 2002).

For studies of various aspects of Fichte's thought, see: Daniel Breazeale and Tom Rockmore (eds.), *Fichte: Historical Contexts/Contemporary Perspectives* (Atlantic Highlands, NJ: Humanities Press, 1994); Daniel Breazeale and Tom Rockmore (eds.), *Rights, Bodies and Recognition: New Essays on Fichte's Foundations of Natural Right* (London: Ashgate, 2006); Frederick Neuhouser, *Fichte's Theory of Subjectivity* (Cambridge University

Press, 1990); Günter Zöller, *Fichte's Transcendental Philosophy: The Original Duplicity of Intelligence and Will* (Cambridge University Press, 1998). Anthony J. La Vopa's *Fichte: The Self and the Calling of Philosophy, 1762–1799* (Cambridge University Press, 2001) is a comprehensive intellectual biography. Thus far only the first volume has appeared; although it does not cover the period during which the *Addresses* were written, it includes a detailed discussion of Fichte's attitude towards the French Revolution.

No recent general introduction to Fichte's political thought exists in English. In fact, the only really wide-ranging (though not always reliable) treatment is: H. C. Engelbrecht, *Johann Gottlieb Fichte: A Study of his Political Writings with Special Reference to his Nationalism* (New York: Columbia University Press, 1933). There are useful chapters on Fichte in: Etienne Balibar, *Masses, Classes, Ideas* (London: Routledge, 1994); Frederick C. Beiser, *Enlightenment, Revolution and Romanticism: The Genesis of Modern German Political Thought* (Cambridge, MA: Harvard University Press, 1992); George Armstrong Kelly, *Idealism, Politics and History: Sources of Hegelian Thought* (Cambridge University Press, 1969). On the issue of cultural versus ethnic nationalism in Fichte, see: Arash Abizadeh, 'Was Fichte an Ethnic Nationalist? On Cultural Nationalism and its Double', *History of Political Thought*, 26 (2005), 334–59. An excellent essay on the theory of language in the *Addresses* is: David Martyn, 'Borrowed Fatherland: Nationalism and Linguistic Purism in Fichte's *Addresses to the German Nation*', *Germanic Review*, 72 (1997), 303–15.

The literature on nationalism is vast. The classic study is Elie Kedourie's oft-reprinted *Nationalism* (Oxford: Blackwell, 1993 [1960]), which reserves a special, but by no means sympathetic, place for Fichte. Maurizio Viroli's, *For Love of Country* (Oxford University Press, 1997) is also helpful.

For the historical background of Fichte's activity, see: G. P. Gooch, *Germany and the French Revolution* (London: Longmans, 1920), which is still an extremely good overview, particularly with respect to leading literary and intellectual figures (there is a chapter on Fichte); Stefan Berger, *The Search for Normality: National Identity and Historical Consciousness in Germany since 1800* (New York: Berghahn, 1997); Matthew Bernard Levinger, *Enlightened Nationalism: The Transformation of Prussian Political Culture, 1806–1848* (Oxford University Press, 2000).

Abbreviations

The following abbreviations are used in the notes.

CPA   *Characteristics of the Present Age*, in *Popular Works*, trans. William Smith, 4th edn (London: Trüber, 1889), vol. 2.

GA   *J. G. Fichte–Gesamtausgabe der Bayerischen Akademie der Wissenschaften*, ed. Reinhard Lauth, Hans Gliwitzky and Erich Fuchs (Stuttgart/Bad Cannstatt: Frommann-Holzboog, 1964–).

GC   Heinrich Pestalozzi, *How Gertrud Teaches Her Children* (1801), trans. Lucy E. Holland and Francis C. Turner (London: Allen and Unwin, 1938).

Addresses to the German Nation

Foreword

The following addresses were delivered as a series of lectures in Berlin during the winter of 1807–8 and are a continuation of my *Characteristics of the Present Age*, which I presented during the winter of 1804–5 in the same location (and which were printed by this publisher in 1806). What had to be said to the public in and through them is expressed clearly enough in the work itself, and it therefore had no need of a foreword. Since, however, in the meantime a number of blank pages have resulted by the manner in which these addresses were put together, I have filled this space with material that has in part already been passed by the censor and published elsewhere. Of this material I was reminded by the circumstances that led to these blank pages arising in the first place, for it would seem to have general application in this instance also. I refer the reader in particular to the conclusion of the Twelfth Address, which touches on this same subject.

Berlin, April 1808
Fichte

From a Treatise on Machiavelli as writer, with extracts from his works

I. From the conclusion of that treatise

We can think of two species of men against whom we should like to safeguard ourselves if we could. First, those who assume, just because they are unable in their thoughts to get beyond what is printed in the latest newspaper, that no one else can either; that accordingly everything which is said or written has some relation to this newspaper and should serve as a commentary thereon. I ask these men to consider that none may say: 'Look, such and such is meant here!' who has not judged for himself beforehand whether such and such an individual was really and truly thus and so could be meant here; that therefore none can accuse of satire a writer who remains universal, who as a rule embraces all ages and disregards each particular one, without first himself becoming the original and independent author of this satire and thereby betraying in an exceedingly foolish manner his own most intimate thoughts.

Then there are those who have no dread of anything, save of the words for things, and this dread is boundless. You may trample them underfoot and all the world may watch as you do so; in this they see neither outrage nor evil. But should one strike up a conversation about this trampling underfoot, then to them it were an intolerable nuisance and only then would the evil begin – especially as no man of reason and goodwill would strike up such a conversation out of malicious pleasure, but solely to discover the means whereby the episode may be avoided in the future. The same holds true with respect to future evils; they desire to remain undisturbed in their sweet dreams and therefore shut their eyes to what may come. Since thereby others who keep their eyes open are not prevented from seeing what is looming, and might be tempted to say what they see and call it by its name, they think that the surest remedy against this danger is to restrict the saying and naming of those who see; as if now, in inverse order to reality, not seeing something resulted from not saying it and the non-existence of a thing resulted from not seeing it. Thus does the sleepwalker stride along the brink of the abyss: do not call out to him with mercy in your heart, for he is safe while in this state; should he stir, however, he will fall. If only the dreams of such men partook of the gift, the prerogatives and the security of sleepwalking, so that there were a means of saving them without calling out and waking

4

them! Likewise, it is said, does the ostrich shut its eyes before the approaching hunter, as if the now-invisible danger were no longer there at all. He were no enemy of the ostrich who cried out: 'Open your eyes, see the hunter coming! Run that way to escape him!'

II. Extensive freedom of expression and the press in Machiavelli's age

In sequel to the previous section, and because one reader or another is perhaps wondering how what I have just reported could have been said by Machiavelli,[1] it might be worth the trouble, at the beginning of the nineteenth century and from the vantage-point of those countries that boast of the highest freedom of thought, to cast a glance at the freedom of expression and the press that prevailed at the beginning of the sixteenth century in Italy and in the papal seat of Rome. Of the thousands of examples I shall adduce but one. Machiavelli's *Florentine Histories* was written at the instigation of Pope Clement VII and dedicated to him.[2] In it we find already in Book I the following passage: 'Previous to this time no mention is made of the nephews or families of any pontiff, but future history is full of them; nor is there now anything left for them to attempt, except the effort to make the papal throne hereditary.'[3]

For these *Florentine Histories*, together with *The Prince* and the *Discourses*, the same Clement granted a privilege *honesto Antonii* (as the printer was called) *desiderio annuere volens*,[4] which forbade all Christians from reprinting the work on pain of excommunication and subjects of the Papal States, withal, on pain of confiscation of the illegal copies and a fine of twenty-five ducats.

This may of course be explained. The popes and the eminences of the Church themselves regarded their whole being solely as a deception for the lowest rabble and, if possible, for the Ultramontanes; they were

---

[1] The previous section discussed Machiavelli's 'heathenism' and alleged hostility to Christianity.

[2] The work was commissioned by Leo X (Giovanni de Medici) through the intervention of his cousin Giulio de Medici, then a cardinal, who became Clement VII in 1523.

[3] From Book I, chapter V.

[4] 'wishing to accede to the honourable desire of Antonius'; Antonio de Blado (1490–1567), the Pope's own printer, published an edition of the *Florentine Histories* in 1531.

liberal[5] enough to permit every Italian man of culture and refinement to think, speak and write about these things in the same way as they spoke amongst themselves. They had no wish to deceive the cultivated man, and the mob could not read. It is just as easy to explain why other measures later became necessary. The Reformers taught the German people to read, they appealed to such writers as had written under the eyes of the popes; the example of literacy was contagious and spread to other countries; now the writers became a formidable power and for that very reason had to be placed under more stringent supervision.

Even these times are past, and today, particularly in Protestant states, many branches of literature, for example the philosophical establishment of general principles of every kind, are surely only subject to the censor because tradition so dictates. Since the situation is such that those who know nothing to say save what everyone already knows inside out are allowed in every fashion to use as much paper as they desire; but that if something truly new is to be said the censor, who cannot grasp this at once, and thinking it might contain a hidden poison, prefers to suppress it in order to err on the side of caution; so perhaps many a writer in Protestant countries is not to be blamed if, at the beginning of the nineteenth century, he wished for himself a proper and modest share in that freedom of the press which the popes universally and unhesitatingly conceded at the beginning of the sixteenth.

From the preface to several unpublished
Dialogues on Patriotism and its Opposite

Now, within these limitations demanded by justice and propriety, they could, I should think, indeed permit us to say without fear what they themselves do not shrink from actually doing; for obviously the deed itself, which even without our mentioning it will doubtless arouse attention, causes far greater trouble than what we say about it afterwards. And although there is nothing at all to prevent those who have responsibility for the press by reason of their office from belonging as private persons to one of the two main parties of the intellectual world currently in dispute, they can perceive the interest of their party only were they to step forth themselves as writers; but as public persons they have no party whatsoever

---

[5] The word Fichte uses is *liberal*, the same word that he pours scorn on in the First and Fourth Addresses.

and to reason, which at any rate seeks permission to speak far less often than does unreason, they must grant the same, just as they allow the latter daily to go about its business as it pleases. By no means, however, are they authorised to deny some sound or other from being heard because it strikes *their* ears as strange and paradoxical.

Berlin, July 1806

Preliminary remarks and overview

The addresses that I now begin I have announced as a continuation of the lectures which I delivered here, in this same venue, three winters ago and which have been published under the title *Characteristics of the Present Age*. In those lectures I showed that our age lies in the third principal epoch of world history, which epoch has mere sensuous self-interest as the impulse of all its vital stirrings and motions; that this age also understands and comprehends itself completely by recognising this impulse as the only possible one; and that through this clear insight into its nature it is deeply grounded and unshakeably fixed in this its vital essence.

With us, more than with any other age in the history of the world, time is taking giant strides. Within the three years that have passed since my interpretation of the current epoch, it has at some point run its course and come to an end. At some point[6] selfishness has annihilated itself by its complete development, because it has thereby lost its self and the independence of that self; and, since it would not willingly posit any other end but itself, another, alien purpose has been imposed upon it by an external power.[7] Whoever has once undertaken to interpret his age must ensure that his interpretation keep pace with its progress also, should it enjoy such progress. And therefore it is my duty to acknowledge, before the same audience, that what I described as present is now past and has ceased to be the present.

---

[6] *Irgendwo* – changed to this vaguer formulation on the insistence of the censors.
[7] In other words, French hegemony since Napoleon's victories at Ulm, Austerlitz and Jena-Auerstedt.

9

Whatever has lost its self-sufficiency has simultaneously lost its capacity to intervene in the stream of time and freely to determine the content thereof. If it persist in this state, its age, and itself with the age, are dispatched by the alien power that commands its fate; henceforth it no longer has any time of its own, but reckons its years according to the events and epochs of foreign peoples and empires. From this state, in which its former world lies wholly beyond the reach of its self-active intervention and in the present one only the glory of obedience is left, it could raise itself only on the condition that a new world dawn for it, with whose creation would begin, and further development fill, a new epoch of its own. Yet, since it is subject to an alien power, this new world would have to be so constituted that it remained unnoticed by that power and in no way aroused its jealousy; indeed, that this power would be moved by its own interest to put no obstacle in the path of the formation of such a world. Now, if there is to be a world thus constituted as the means of creating a new self and a new age, for a race that has lost its former self, its former age and its former world, then it would fall to a thorough interpretation of such a possible age to account for the world thus constituted.

Now for my part I affirm that there is such a world, and it is the purpose of these addresses to prove to you its existence and its true properties, to bring before your eyes a vivid picture of this world, and to indicate the means of creating it. In this way, therefore, shall these addresses be a continuation of the lectures I previously delivered on what was then the present age, for they shall disclose the new age that can and should immediately follow the destruction of the realm of selfishness by an alien power.

Before I begin this business, however, I must ask you to assume the following points, to keep them always in mind, and to agree with me upon them, wherever and to whatever extent this is necessary.

1. I speak for Germans only, of Germans simply, without acknowledging, indeed leaving aside and rejecting, all the divisive distinctions that unhappy events have wrought for centuries in this one nation. You, worshipful gentlemen, may be to my outward eye the first and immediate representatives who bring home to me the cherished national characteristics and the visible burning point in which the flame of my discourse kindles; but my spirit gathers about itself the educated portion of the entire German nation, from all the lands over which it is spread, considers and heeds the situation and circumstances common to us all,

and wishes that a part of the vital force with which these addresses perhaps seize you remains also in its mute transcript that alone will come before the eyes of those absent here today, infuses it, and everywhere inflames German souls to decision and action. Of Germans only and for Germans simply, I said. We shall show at the proper time that every other term of unity or national bond either never possessed truth and meaning; or, if they did, that these points of agreement were annihilated by our present situation, have been torn from us and can never return; and that it is solely by means of the common trait of Germanness that we can avert the downfall of our nation threatened by its confluence with foreign peoples and once more win back a self that is self-supporting and incapable of any form of dependency. As we gain insight into this last claim, its apparent conflict with other duties and with interests held sacred, which perhaps some at present fear, will at the same time disappear completely.

Therefore, since I only speak of Germans in general, I shall declare that many things concern us that do not apply in the first place to those assembled here, just as I shall also declare as the concern of all Germans other things that in the first place apply only to us. In the spirit whose emanation these addresses are, I behold the concrescent unity in which no member thinks the fate of another foreign to his own, a unity that shall and must arise if we are not to perish altogether – I behold this unity as already existing, perfected and present.

2. I assume such German listeners as who do not, with all their being, give themselves over utterly to the feeling of pain at the loss they have suffered, and take complacence in this pain, and wallow in their inconsolable grief, and through this feeling think to compromise with the call that summons them to action; but such as who have already raised themselves even above this righteous pain to clear reflection and contemplation, or at least are capable of doing so. I know that pain; I have felt it as much as the next man; I respect it. That stupor which is satisfied when it finds meat and drink and suffers no physical pain, and for which honour, freedom, self-sufficiency are empty words, is incapable of feeling it: but even this pain is only there to spur us on to reflection, decision and action; failing in this ultimate aim, it robs us of reflection and all our other remaining powers, and thus completes our misery; while, moreover, as witness to our indolence and cowardice, it furnishes the visible proof that we deserve our misery. But by no means do I intend to lift you from this pain with the empty promise of help

from without and by indicating all manner of possible events and changes that the passage of time might bring: for, if this way of thinking, which prefers to stroll in the precarious world of possibilities instead of fastening on the necessary, and would rather owe its deliverance to blind chance than to its own efforts, did not already testify to the most atrocious frivolity and the deepest self-contempt, as indeed it does, then all consolations and indications of this sort have anyway absolutely no bearing on our predicament. It can be rigorously proved, and we shall do so at the proper time, that no man and no God and none of the events which reside in the realm of the possible can help us; but that we alone must help ourselves, if we are to be helped at all. Rather, I shall seek to lift you from the pain through clear insight into our situation, into our strength that still remains, into the means of our deliverance. Therefore I shall indeed expect a certain degree of reflection, a certain self-activity, and a little sacrifice, and therefore count on listeners of whom this much can be expected. Incidentally, the objects of this expectation are as a whole not onerous and do not presuppose a greater measure of strength than that which, as I believe, one can impute to our age; but as for danger, there is none at all.

3. In meaning to bring forth clear insight into the Germans as such, into their present situation, I assume listeners who are inclined to see with their own eyes things of this nature, but not at all such as find it more comfortable, in considering these subjects, to allow to be foisted upon them an alien and outlandish instrument of vision, which is either intentionally adjusted to deceive or is naturally, owing to its different point of view and lesser degree of sharpness, never suited to a German eye. Further, I assume that, when these listeners observe with their own eyes, they have the courage to look honestly at what is there and to admit honestly what they see; that they have either already defeated or are yet capable of defeating that widespread inclination to deceive oneself about one's own affairs and to withhold a less pleasing image of these than is compatible with the truth. That inclination is a cowardly flight from one's own thoughts, a childish attitude of mind which seems to believe that, if only one does not see one's misery or at least refuses to admit to oneself that one does, this misery is thereby also abolished in reality, just as it is abolished in one's thoughts. By contrast, it is a sign of manly courage to fix one's gaze upon the evil, to require it to hold its ground, to penetrate it calmly, coldly, and freely, and to resolve it into its component parts. Only through clear insight does one also become

master of the evil and in fighting it walk with confident steps, because, surveying the whole in every part, one always knows where one is and, through the clarity that one has once achieved, is sure of one's cause. By contrast the other, without a firm guiding thread and without secure certainty, gropes blindly and dreamily.

Why should we too dread this clarity? The evil will not grow smaller through our ignorance of it, nor greater with knowledge; indeed, only by knowledge can it be remedied. No blame, however, shall be apportioned here at all. Excoriate indolence and selfishness through bitter censure, through biting mockery, through keen contempt, and incite them, if not to something better, than at least to a hatred of and exasperation towards the admonisher himself, for these are powerful impulses also – by all means do this for as long as the necessary consequence, the evil, is not yet complete, and salvation or mitigation can still be expected if things improve. But once this evil is so complete that we are deprived even of the possibility of continuing to sin in this manner, it becomes futile and looks like malicious pleasure to go on inveighing against the sin that can no longer be committed; and the consideration consequently drops out of the realm of morality into that of history, for which freedom is past, and which regards what has happened as the necessary result of what has gone before. For our addresses no other perspective on the present than this latter one remains, and we shall therefore never take another.

This way of thinking, therefore – that one think of oneself as simply German, that one be not shackled even by the pain, that one desire to see the truth and have the courage to look it full in the face – this way of thinking I assume and count on with every word that I shall utter; and should anyone have come to this assembly with another cast of mind, then he has only himself to blame for the disagreeable feelings that might be caused him here. Let this be said once and for all, and the matter be therewith settled. And I now pass to my other business, namely to present to you in a general survey the substance of all my following addresses.

At some point, I said at the beginning of my address, selfishness has annihilated itself by its complete development because it has lost its self and the capacity to posit its ends independently. This annihilation of selfishness, now accomplished, represents the progress of the age that I mentioned and the wholly new event that in my view makes a continuation of my previous portrait of the age both possible and necessary.

This annihilation would hence constitute our actual present, to which our new life in a new world, whose existence I also asserted, would have to be directly linked; it would therefore form the proper point of departure for my addresses; and above all I would have to show how and why such an annihilation of selfishness necessarily results from its highest development.

Selfishness is developed to its highest degree when, after it has captured, with only a few insignificant exceptions, the totality of those ruled, it then takes possession of the rulers also and becomes their sole impulse in life. In such a government there arises, outwards first of all, the neglect of all ties through which its own security is linked to the security of other states, the surrender of the whole of which it is a member solely so that it be not disturbed in its torpid repose, and the sad delusion entertained by selfishness that it enjoys peace so long as its own borders are not attacked;[8] then, inwards, that slackening of the reins of state, for which the foreign words are humanity [*Humanität*], liberality [*Liberalität*] and popularity [*Popularität*], but which in German are more correctly called slackness [*Schlaffheit*] and undignified conduct [*Betragen ohne Würde*].

When selfishness has taken hold of the rulers also, I said. A people can be thoroughly corrupt – that is, selfish, for selfishness is the root of all other corruption – and yet not only endure but even perform outwardly glorious deeds, if only its government be not corrupt also. Indeed, the latter can even act, externally, without loyalty and neglectful of duty and honour, if, internally, it has the courage to hold the reins of power with a firm hand and to win for itself the greater fear. But where everything that I have just named comes together, the commonwealth[9] goes under with the first serious attack launched against it, and, just as it once severed itself treacherously from the body whose limb it was, so its own parts, which do not fear it but are driven by their greater fear of the foreigner, sever themselves with the same treachery and go each their own way. Those who now stand separately are hereupon seized once again by the greater fear, and to the enemy they give abundantly, and with an

---

[8] An oblique reference to Prussia's policy of neutrality between the Peace of Basel in 1795 and 1806.

[9] *Das gemeine Wesen*; here and elsewhere Fichte had originally written *Staat* [state]. This was changed at the behest of the censor.

expression of forced good cheer, what they gave sparingly and extremely unwillingly to the defender of the fatherland; until later even those rulers, betrayed and abandoned on all sides, are compelled to purchase their continued existence at the price of their subjection and obedience to foreign schemes; and so even those who, in the fight for the fatherland, laid down their arms, now learn under foreign banners to wield them bravely against it.[10] And so it comes to pass that selfishness is annihilated through its highest development, and those who willingly chose to posit no other end but themselves have imposed upon them, by an alien power, a different end such as this.

No nation that has sunk into this state of dependency can raise itself by the usual means employed hitherto. If its resistance bore no fruit when it was still in possession of all its powers, then what good can resistance do now, after it has been robbed of the greater part of them? What might have helped before – namely if the government of that nation had held the reins forcefully and tightly – is now no longer practicable when these reins are only seemingly still clasped in its hand, a hand which is itself directed and guided by a foreign hand. Such a nation can no longer count on itself; and just as little can it count on its conqueror. He would have to be just as unthinking [*unbesonnen*], and just as cowardly and despondent, as that nation itself was, if he did not hold fast to the advantages he had won and pursue them every which way. Or if at some point in the course of time he did indeed become so unthinking and cowardly, then he might perish just as we do, though not to our advantage. Rather, he would become the prize claimed by a new conqueror, and we, as a matter of course, the insignificant supplement to this prize. Should such a sunken nation nevertheless be able to save itself, then this would have to occur by a quite novel means never employed before now: the creation of an entirely new order of things. Let us therefore see what, in the former order of things, was the reason why one day it necessarily had to come to an end, so that in the opposite of this reason for its downfall we find the new element that would have to be inserted into the age so that the sunken nation may pick itself up and start a new life.

In inquiring into this reason one will find that in all hitherto existing systems of government the interest [*Teilnahme*] of the individual in the

---

[10] The princes of the Confederation of the Rhine who were allied with Napoleon; perhaps Fichte is thinking in particular of Prince Karl of Isenburg, who in a proclamation issued on 18 November 1806 sought to raise Prussian regiments for French service.

whole was linked to his interest in himself, by virtue of bonds that somewhere were broken so completely that the individual no longer retained any interest in the whole at all – by the bonds of fear and of hope concerning the affairs of the individual in relation to the fate of the whole, both in the present life and in a future one. The enlightenment of the understanding, with its purely sensuous calculations, was the power that dissolved the connection established by religion between a future life and the present one, and at the same time held such supplementary and vicarious agencies of the moral way of thinking as love of glory and national honour to be misleading chimeras. It was the weakness of governments that removed the individual's fear for his affairs in relation to his conduct towards the whole, even in the present life, by frequently allowing his dereliction of duty to go unpunished, and likewise rendered hope ineffectual by satisfying it all too often, without any consideration of the individual's services to the whole, and according to quite different rules and motives. It was bonds of this kind that somewhere were broken completely and through their breakage caused the commonwealth to disintegrate.[11]

Even so, the conqueror may thenceforth do assiduously what only he can do, namely to reconnect and reinforce the last remaining binding ties [*Bindungsmittel*], fear and hope for the present life; but only he profits thereby and we not at all. For, as surely as he understands his advantage he will link to this renewed bond first and foremost only his own affairs and ours only to the extent that their preservation, as the means to his ends, itself becomes his affair. For such a degenerate nation fear and hope are thenceforth completely abolished, because their control is no longer in its hands; and though it must fear and hope for its own existence, there is no one who still fears it or places his hopes in it. The nation has no choice but to find a new binding tie beyond fear and hope, to unite the affairs of the whole with the self-interest of the individual.

Beyond the sensuous motive of fear or hope, and initially contiguous to it, lies the spiritual motive of moral approval or disapproval, and the higher emotion of pleasure or displeasure at our state or that of others. Just as the outward eye accustomed to cleanliness and order is tormented

---

[11] This sentence originally read: 'These were the bonds which, by their breakage, led to the downfall of the state.' The word 'governments' in the preceding sentence was changed from the more explicit 'the government'.

and distressed, as though actually hurt, by a blemish which does not immediately cause the body pain, or by the sight of objects lying jumbled and confused, whereas one who is used to dirt and disorder is entirely comfortable in such circumstances; so too can man's inner eye be habituated and trained in such a way that the mere sight of his own and his tribe's confused and disordered, unworthy and dishonourable existence can cut him to the quick, irrespective of whatever fear or hope for his sensuous well-being it may inspire, that this pain gives the possessor of such an eye, once again quite independently of sensuous fear or hope, no respite until he has brought to an end, insofar as he is able, the disagreeable state and replaced it with one that can please him alone. In the possessor of such an eye the interest [*Angelegenheit*] of the whole to which he belongs is indissolubly bound by the motivating feeling of approval or disapproval to the interest of his own extended self, which is aware of itself only as part of the whole and can only bear itself when the whole is agreeable. To train such an eye would hence be a sure means, and indeed the only means left to a nation that had lost its independence and with it all influence over public fear and hope, to raise itself back to life after the annihilation it has suffered, and safely to entrust its national affairs, which since its downfall neither God nor man has heeded further, to the new and nobler feelings that have come into being. Thus it follows that the means of salvation, which I have promised to disclose, consists in cultivating a completely new self, a self that has hitherto existed perhaps as an exception among individuals, but never as a universal and national self, and in educating the nation, whose former life has been extinguished and become the appendage of a foreign life, to a wholly new life that shall either remain its exclusive property or, should it also be spread by this nation to others, remain intact and undiminished in spite of infinite division. In a word, what I am proposing is the complete reform of the current educational system as the only means of preserving the existence of the German nation.

That children ought to receive a good education has been said often enough even in our age and repeated until we are tired of hearing it; and it would be a trifling thing were this all we too wished to say. Rather, it will be incumbent upon us, inasmuch as we believe we can accomplish something new, to investigate scrupulously and definitely what has been really lacking in education until now and to indicate what completely new element the reformed education must add to the cultivation of humanity [*Menschenbildung*] practised hitherto.

After such an investigation one must concede to the existing education that it does not omit to bring before the eyes of its pupils some image of the religious, moral and lawful way of thinking, of order in all kinds of things, and of good manners; also, that here and there it faithfully exhorts these same pupils to imprint those images upon their lives. But with exceedingly rare exceptions, which were not due to this education (because then they must have occurred among all who underwent this schooling and thus as the rule), but were rather occasioned by other causes – with these exceedingly rare exceptions, I say, the pupils of this education have by and large followed not these moral ideas and exhortations but rather their selfish impulses, which develop in them naturally and without any assistance from the art of education. This is incontrovertible proof that this art of education may well have been able to fill the memory with a few words and phrases and the frigid and indifferent fancy with some dull and pallid images, but has never succeeded in making its picture of a moral world order so vivid that the pupil is seized by ardent love and longing for it, and by the glowing emotion that impels him to represent it in life and before which selfishness falls away like a withered leaf; that consequently this education has been a long way from reaching down to the root of the real stirrings and motions of life and cultivating it. Rather, neglected by the blind and impotent system, that root has everywhere grown wild, as best it could, bearing good fruit in the few who were inspired by God and bad in the great majority. It is also perfectly sufficient for the time being to sketch this education through these its results, and for our purposes we can exempt ourselves from the tedious business of analysing the internal sap and veins of a tree whose fruit is now completely ripe, has fallen, lies before the eyes of the whole world, and expresses very distinctly and comprehensibly the inner nature of its creator. Strictly speaking, according to this view, the old education has not by any means been the art of cultivating humanity, and nor indeed has it prided itself on being such; but all too often it has frankly admitted its impotence by demanding to be given in advance a natural talent or genius as the condition of its success. Rather, such an art must first be invented, and its invention would be the proper task of the new education. This new education would add to the old one by probing to the root of the stirrings and motions of life, something that has been lacking until now, and just as the old education had at most to cultivate a part of man, so the new one would cultivate humanity itself, and make this culture by no means, as has been the case hitherto, a mere possession, but rather an integral component of the pupil.

Furthermore, this culture that was limited in the way I have described was until now provided only to the very small number of those classes which, for this very reason, are called the cultivated classes. But the great majority, whereupon the commonwealth properly rests, the people, were almost completely neglected by the art of education and abandoned to blind chance. Through the new education we desire to form the Germans into a totality that in all its individual parts is driven and animated by the same single interest [*Angelegenheit*]. But if at this point we wanted to separate once again an educated class, animated by the newly developed motive of moral approval, from an uneducated class, then the latter (since hope and fear, which alone could still affect it, no longer work for us but rather against us) would fall away and be lost to us. There is thus nothing we can do save bring the new education to all who are German, without exception, so that it becomes not the education of a particular class but simply of the nation as such, and without exempting a single individual member; in which – namely in the cultivation of an ardent pleasure in what is right – all distinctions of class, which may in the future obtain in other branches of development, are completely abolished and disappear; and that in this way there arises among us not a popular education [*Volks-Erziehung*] but rather a specifically German national education [*National-Erziehung*].

I shall demonstrate to you that an art of education such as we desire has in reality already been invented and is being practised, so that we need do no more than accept what is available, and this, as I promised earlier with respect to the proposed means of salvation, doubtless requires no greater measure of strength than can be justifiably assumed in our age. To this promise I added another; namely, that there is no danger at all connected with our proposal, because the self-interest of the power ruling over us demands that the realisation of our scheme be sooner encouraged than hindered. I think it expedient to express myself clearly on this point at the very outset of this first address of mine.

In ancient as in modern times the arts of seduction and of moral degradation of subject peoples have been used all too frequently, and with success, as a means of mastery: by mendacious fictions and artful confusion of ideas and language the princes have been vilified before the people, and the people before the princes, so that those thus divided may be ruled more easily; every vain and self-seeking impulse has been cunningly roused and nurtured to make the subjugated contemptible, so that with a kind of good conscience they may be trodden underfoot.

But to strike out along this path with us Germans would be a mistake leading surely to ruin. Setting aside the bond of fear and hope, the cohesion of those foreign lands with which we are presently in contact rests on the motives of honour and national glory; but German clarity of mind has long ago seen to the point of unshakeable conviction that these are but empty phantoms, that no wound and no mutilation inflicted on the individual is healed by the glory of the nation as a whole. And we might become, if no higher view of life is brought before us, dangerous preachers of this easily understood teaching with no little appeal. Without therefore bringing new ruin upon ourselves, we are already by nature a fatal prize. Only by carrying out my proposal can we become a salutary one: and thus, as surely as the foreigner understands his advantage, so, motivated by this interest, he would rather we were the latter than the former.

With this proposal my address is now directed in particular at the cultivated classes of Germany, because it hopes to be understood by them first of all, and then invites them to make themselves the authors of this new creation. In doing so they shall partly reconcile the world with their former efficacy and partly earn their continued existence in the future. In the course of these addresses we shall see that to this day all higher development of humanity in the German nation has proceeded from the people, that it was before the people that the great national affairs were always first brought, by the people were they managed and advanced; that therefore this is the first time that the task of guiding the original and onward development of the nation has been offered to the cultivated classes, and that, if they really accept this offer, then this too would also happen for the first time. We shall see that these classes cannot reckon on how much longer it will be in their power to take the lead in this matter, for my scheme is already almost ready and ripe to be delivered to the people, and is being put into practice with a few of their number. After a short time the people will, without any of our assistance, be able to help themselves: which for us simply means that those who are presently cultivated, and their descendants, will become the people, yet from the existing people a different, highly cultivated class will arise.

Finally, it is the general purpose of these addresses to bring courage and hope to the despondent, to proclaim joy amidst deep sorrow, to guide us softly and gently through our hour of greatest need. The age seems to me a shade that stands grieving over its corpse, from which it has just been driven out by a host of diseases, unable to tear its gaze from the once beloved husk, desperately trying every means to enter once more the refuge of contagion. The quickening breezes of the other world, into which the deceased has passed, may already have received it and surrounded it with the warm breath of love; the familiar voices of its sisters may already joyously greet it and bid it welcome; inwardly it may already stir and stretch itself in all directions, so as to unfold the more glorious form that it shall assume; but still it has no feeling for these breezes, nor ear for these voices; or if it did, it has been overwhelmed by the pain of its loss and believes it has lost itself at the same time. What is to be done with it? Even now the dawn of the new world has already broken, gilding the mountain tops and pre-figuring the day to come. I wish, so far as I am able, to take hold of the rays of this dawn and to weave them into a mirror wherein the disconsolate age shall behold itself, so that it may believe that it still exists, and wherein its true essence, and the evolutions and formations thereof, shall appear and pass before it in a prophetic vision. The image of its former life will then doubtless also sink and vanish into this intuition, and the corpse may be borne to its place of rest without excessive lamentation.

On the nature of the new education in general

My proposed means of preserving the German nation, to the clear perception of which these addresses might lead you, and along with you the entire nation, proceeds from the complexion of the age, as well as from the national characteristics of the Germans, and this means must in turn affect the age and the formation of these national characteristics. Consequently, this means will not be rendered perfectly clear and intelligible until it has been compared together with these and these with it, and both presented in complete interpenetration. This business requires a little time, and thus perfect clarity can be expected only at the conclusion of our addresses. Since we must begin with one of these individual elements, however, it will be most expedient to consider first of all that means itself, in isolation from its surroundings in time and space, by itself in its inner nature, and so today's address and the one immediately following shall be devoted to this task.

The means indicated was an entirely new system of German national education, the like of which has never before existed in any other nation. In the foregoing address I described the distinction between this new education and the old thus: until now education at most only exhorted its pupils to good order and morality, but these exhortations bore no fruit in real life, which is constituted on the basis of principles that are quite different and wholly inaccessible to this education. By contrast, the new education must be able to cultivate and determine the real vital stirrings and motions of its pupils, according to rules that are certain and infallible.

And what if here someone had said, just as those who are in charge of the current education do indeed say almost without exception: what more could one expect of an education than to show the pupil what is right and exhort him faithfully to do it? Whether he wishes to follow these exhortations is his own affair; if he does not, then it is his own fault. He has free will, which no education can take from him. To this I would reply thus, so as to delineate my proposed new education more sharply: that precisely in this acknowledgement and in this reckoning on the pupil's free will lies the first error of the existing education, and the clear admission of its impotence and futility. For in admitting that, despite its best efforts, the will is still free – that is, remains wavering between good and bad – this system admits that it neither can nor means nor at all desires to form the will or, since the will is the proper primary root of man himself, to form the human being, and that it holds this to be altogether impossible. By contrast, the new education would consist precisely in this, that, on the soil whose cultivation it takes over, it completely annihilates freedom of will, producing strict necessity in decisions and the impossibility of the opposite in the will, which can now be reckoned and relied on with confidence.

All education strives to bring forth a fixed, definite and permanent being [*Sein*], one that no longer becomes but is and can be nothing else but what it is. If it did not strive for such a being, then it would not be education but some frivolous game; if it had not brought forth such a being, then it would not yet be complete. Whoever must exhort himself and be exhorted to will the good, does not yet have a firm and ever-ready will [*Wollen*], but determines it in each situation that arises. Whoever has such a firm will wills what he wills for all eternity, and in no possible situation can he will differently than how he always wills; for his freedom of will has been annihilated and subsumed by necessity. The previous age has thereby shown that it had neither the right conception of the cultivation of humanity nor the power to realise this notion, that it wished to improve men through hortatory sermons and grew vexed and reproachful when these sermons bore no fruit. But how could they? The direction of the will is already fixed prior to and independently of the exhortation; if it accords with your exhortation, then the exhortation comes too late, and even without it the individual would have done exactly the same as you exhorted him to do; if the exhortation is in conflict with the direction of the will, then at most you may benumb him for a few moments; but when the opportunity comes he forgets himself and your exhortation and follows his natural inclination. If you wish to have influence over him, then you must do more than merely appeal to him; you must fashion him, fashion him such that he cannot will anything save what you want him to will. It is futile to say 'fly!' to one who has no wings, and for all your exhortations he will never lift himself more than two steps above the ground. But develop, if you can, his mental pinions, let him train and strengthen them, and, without any exhortations from you, he will want, or be able, to do nothing but fly.

The new education must bring forth this firm and no longer wavering will according to a sure rule that is valid without exception; it must itself produce with the same necessity the necessity that it intends. Those who have hitherto become good have done so thanks to their natural disposition, which outweighed the influence of their bad surroundings; but on no account thanks to their education, for otherwise all who have received such an education were bound to become good. And just as little did those who sank into corruption do so owing to their education, for otherwise all who received it would have been corrupted; rather, they went bad by themselves and owing to their natural disposition; in this respect the influence of education was naught and not at all pernicious. The real formative agency was spiritual nature. The cultivation of humanity [*Bildung zum Menschen*] shall henceforth be taken out of the hands of this obscure and incalculable power and brought under the sway of a deliberate art that reliably achieves its aim without exception in everything entrusted to it; or, where it does not achieve its aim, at least knows that it was unsuccessful and that therefore the pupil's education is not yet complete. The education that I propose shall be a sure and deliberate art to form a firm and infallibly good will in man, and this is its first attribute.

Further – man can only will what he loves. His love is at once the sole and infallible impulse of his willing and of all his vital stirrings and motions. The statecraft practised hitherto, as the education of man in society, assumed as a certain and universally valid rule that each loves and wills his own sensuous well-being; and to this natural love it artificially linked, by means of hope and fear, the good will that it desired, the interest in the commonwealth. Setting aside the fact that with this method of education he who has become outwardly a harmless or useful citizen remains inwardly a wicked person, for wickedness consists precisely in loving only one's sensuous well-being and being motivated solely by hope and fear for that sensuous well-being, whether in the present or a future life – setting this fact aside, we have already seen that we can no longer apply this measure because hope and fear no longer work for us but against us, and sensuous self-love can in no way be turned to our advantage. Therefore, necessity, too, compels us to will the cultivation of men who are intrinsically and fundamentally good, for only in them can the German nation live on; wicked men, however, will necessarily cause it to merge with foreign peoples. We must therefore replace this self-love, which can no longer be connected with anything that is good for us, with another kind of love, one that aims directly at the good, simply as such and for its own sake, and plant it in the minds of all those whom we wish to reckon among our nation.

Love of the good simply as such, and not for the sake of its usefulness for us, takes, as we have already seen, the form of pleasure in the good: so profound a pleasure that one is driven thereby to represent it in one's life. This profound pleasure, then, is what our new education ought to bring forth in the pupil, as his fixed and unalterable being; the necessary effect of which would be the formation in the pupil of an equally unalterable good will.

A pleasure that drives us to bring about a certain state of affairs that does not yet exist in reality presupposes an image [*Bild*] of this state which, before it comes into being, is present to the mind and elicits the pleasure that drives us to realise it. Consequently, this pleasure presupposes, in the person who will be moved by it, the faculty [*Vermögen*] of self-actively projecting images of this kind, images that are independent of reality and in no way copies [*Nachbilder*] but rather pre-figurations [*Vorbilder*] thereof. I must now speak of this faculty and I ask you not to forget during these deliberations that an image brought forth by this faculty can be pleasing simply as an image, as that in which we feel our formative power, without being taken as the pre-figuration of a reality and without being pleasing to the degree that drives us to realise it. Do not forget that the latter instance is something quite different, indeed it is our real purpose, and we shall not omit to speak of it later. The former constitutes merely the precondition for achieving the true final goal of education.

That faculty of self-actively projecting images that are by no means merely copies but rather potential pre-figurations of reality must be the starting-point for the cultivation of the race by the new education. To project self-actively, I said, such that the pupil produces these images by his own agency and is not merely able passively to apprehend the image imparted to him by education, to understand it adequately, and to reproduce it just as he received it, as if the mere existence of such an image was at issue. The reason for this insistence on the pupil's own self-active formation of images is the following: only under this condition can the projected image elicit his active pleasure. For it is one thing simply to appreciate something and have nothing against it – such passive appreciation can arise at best from passive submission. But it is quite another thing to be so overwhelmed by pleasure that it becomes creative and stimulates all our imaginative power. I am not speaking here of the first kind of pleasure, which was always present in the older system of education too, but rather of the second kind. This second pleasure, however, is kindled only when the pupil's self-activity is excited at the same time and becomes manifest to him in relation to the given object, so that this object is pleasing not only in itself but also as an object of the exercise of mental power, something that is immediately, necessarily and universally pleasurable.

This activity of forming mental images to be unfolded in the pupil is without doubt an activity according to rules, rules which become known to the pupil to the degree that he perceives from his own immediate experience that they alone are possible. Therefore, this activity produces knowledge, namely knowledge of general and universally valid laws. Even in the free and further development of images [*Fortbilden*] which commences from this point on, anything undertaken in conflict with the law is impossible, and no action results until the law is observed. For that reason, even if this free and further development of images initially started from blind experimentation, it would still end with an expanded knowledge of the law. This education is therefore in its final consequence the cultivation of the pupil's faculty of cognition, and on no account an historical schooling in the permanent qualities of things, but the higher and philosophical schooling in the laws according to which such a permanent quality of things becomes necessary. The pupil learns.

Let me add: the pupil learns willingly and with pleasure, and, for as long as this power is exerted, there is nothing he would rather do than learn, for when he learns he is self-active, and this gives him directly the greatest possible pleasure. Here we have found an outward mark of the true education, at once evident and unmistakable. And it is this, that regardless of the variety of natural dispositions, and without a single exception, each pupil who receives this education learns with pleasure and with love, simply for the sake of learning and for no other reason. We have discovered the means of kindling this pure love of learning, of stimulating this, the immediate self-activity of the pupil, and of making it the foundation of all knowledge, such that what he learns is learned through it.

Just to stimulate the pupil's own activity in relation to some point known to us is the first objective of the art of education. Once this has been accomplished, it is henceforth only a matter of giving fresh life to the activity thus stimulated, which is only possible through regular progress and where every error made by education reveals itself on the spot by the failure of what was intended. We have thus also found the indissoluble bond between the intended result and the procedure we have indicated: the eternal and universal fundamental law governing man's spiritual nature, namely that he aims immediately at mental activity.

Should someone, misled by the common experience of our days, even harbour doubts about the existence of such a fundamental law, then for his benefit we shall remark superfluously that man is by nature sensuous and selfish only as long as he is driven by immediate necessity and the sensuous needs of the present moment, that he will not allow himself to be held back from satisfying these by any spiritual need or tender feeling of consideration; that after these merely sensuous needs are satisfied, however, he has little inclination to work up the painful image thereof in his fancy and to keep it present to his mind, but would far rather direct his unshackled thought to the free contemplation of that which arouses the attention of his senses, indeed that he does not at all disdain a poetic excursion to ideal worlds, because he is by nature endowed with a light sense of the temporal, so that his sense of the eternal may have some scope for development. This last point is borne out by the history of all ancient peoples, and the various observations and discoveries of them that have been transmitted to us; it is borne out in our own day by the observation of those peoples who still remain in a state of savagery (as long as the climate does not treat them too much like a stepmother) and of our own children; it is even borne out by the frank admission of our zealots against ideals, who complain that it is a far more vexing business to learn names and dates than to soar up into what seems to them a barren field of ideas, which they themselves would only be too glad to do, it seems, if only they would permit themselves. That this natural freedom from care is replaced by anxiety, where tomorrow's hunger and every possible future state of hunger appears in procession before even him who is sated, as the only thing that fills his soul, and goads and drives him on continuously – in our age this is wrought deliberately, in the boy by disciplining his native carelessness, in the adult by the striving to be regarded as a prudent man, which glory is bestowed only on him who never for one moment loses sight of that point of view. Therefore it is by no means nature on which we must reckon here but a corruption[12] imposed with effort upon a recalcitrant nature, a corruption that falls away as soon as that effort is no longer applied.

We said earlier that the education which directly stimulates the pupil's mental self-activity produces knowledge. This gives us the opportunity to describe in more detail the difference between the new education and the old. The proper and immediate aim of the new education is to stimulate regular and progressive mental activity. Knowledge results, as we saw earlier, only incidentally, but as an inevitable consequence. Now, although we would be right to see in knowledge an integral part of the kind of education that we seek, since only thereby can the pupil, once he has become a man, grasp the image for real life that in the future will stimulate his earnest activity, so we cannot nevertheless say that the new education intends this knowledge directly, but rather that knowledge merely falls to its share. By contrast, knowledge, and a certain degree of knowledge of a given subject, was the express object of education hitherto. Moreover, there is a considerable difference between the kind of knowledge that arises incidentally from the new education and that aimed at by the old. The former gives rise to knowledge of the laws conditioning the possibility of all mental activity. For example, when the pupil, in the free exercise of his imagination, attempts to delimit space by drawing straight lines, this is the primary mental activity that is stimulated in him. If he discovers through his experiments that he can delimit no space with fewer than three straight lines, then this knowledge is the by-product of a second quite different activity of the cognitive faculty, one that restricts the free operation of the first faculty to be stimulated. Thus, at its very commencement this education gives rise to a knowledge that truly surpasses all experience, that is supersensuous, strictly necessary and general, that embraces in advance all subsequently possible experience. By contrast, the previous method of instruction aimed as a rule only at the permanent qualities of things, as they exist without one being able to give a reason for them, and as they had to be believed and observed. Hence it aimed at a merely passive apprehension [*Auffassen*] through the faculty of memory, which is employed only in the service of things; by such means one could have no glimmer at all of the mind as the independent and original principle of the things themselves.[13] Modern

---

[12] *Verderben*; *GA* suggests the alternative reading of *Verhalten* (conduct).

[13] That is to say, previous systems of education have made idealism all but impossible.

pedagogy must not think it can defend itself against this criticism by appealing to its oft-attested revulsion for mechanical rote-learning and to its well-known masterpieces in the Socratic manner; for some time ago its practitioners were advised by another writer that these Socratic arguments are likewise only learned mechanically, that this is an even more dangerous kind of rote-learning since it still gives the pupil who does not think the impression that he can indeed think;[14] that there could have been no other outcome with the material which this pedagogy wanted to use to develop independent thought, that to achieve this purpose one must begin with a quite different material. This character of the old method of instruction sheds light on why the pupil in the past has as a rule learned reluctantly – and hence slowly and inadequately – and why, when learning itself did not provide the stimulus, external incentives had to be brought to bear. It also explains past exceptions to the rule. Memory, when it alone is called upon, without having to serve some other mental purpose, is a passivity rather than an activity of the mind, and it is plain to see that the pupil would be extremely unwilling to assume this passive state. Also, the acquaintance with things quite alien to him and in which he has not the slightest interest, and with the properties of these things, is a poor compensation for that passivity inflicted on him. For that reason his disinclination had to be overcome by the promise that this knowledge would be useful in the future, as the only way to earn a living and a reputation, and even, in the immediate present, by punishing and rewarding him. Accordingly, knowledge was from the start installed as the servant of one's sensuous well-being; and this education, which in respect of its content we established earlier was simply incapable of developing a moral way of thinking, was obliged, in order to make any impression on the pupil at all, actually to implant and cultivate moral corruption in him, and unite its own interest with the interest of this corruption. Further, one will find that the natural talent, who, as an exception to the rule, learned willingly and hence well in the schools based on this system of education, and through this higher love reigning

---

[14] Fichte is here thinking of Pestalozzi's criticisms, in *How Gertrude Teaches Her Children* (1801), of the catechistic or Socratic method of teaching favoured by a number of contemporary German writers on education; see e.g. Friedrich Eberhard von Rochow's *Versuch eines Schulbuchs für Kinder der Landleute* (1772), Karl Friedrich Riemann's *Versuch einer Beschreibung der Reckmanschen Schuleinrichtung* (1781) and C. G. Salzmann's *Ameisenbüchlein, oder Anweisung zu einer vernünftigen Erziehung der Erzieher* (1806).

in him overcame the moral corruption of his surroundings and kept his mind [*Sinn*] pure, gained from those subjects of study a practical interest thanks to his natural inclination; that, guided by happy instinct, he aimed at bringing forth knowledge of this kind rather than merely apprehending it; consequently, that those subjects with which, as exceptions to the rule, this education succeeded most generally and felicitously, are on the whole those that it permitted to be practised actively, such as the one classical language, where the aim was to write and speak it as well as read it, and this was done almost universally to a fairly high standard, whereas the other, in which written and oral exercises were neglected, was as a rule learned very badly and superficially, and forgotten in later years. Finally, previous experience also teaches us that only the development of mental activity through instruction produces pleasure in knowledge, simply as such, and thus also keeps the mind [*Gemüt*] open to moral culture, whereas merely passive reception paralyses and deadens knowledge just as it corrupts the moral sense utterly.

To return to the pupil of the new education: it is clear that, impelled by his love, he learns much; and, since he grasps everything in its inter-connections and puts what he has grasped directly into action, he will learn it correctly and never forget it. Yet this is only incidental. More significant is that through this love his self is exalted and admitted, deliberately and according to a rule, into an entirely new order of things, which only a few, by the grace of God, had stumbled on before. He is impelled by a love that absolutely does not aim at some sensuous enjoy-ment, because such a motive holds no appeal to him, but at mental activity and the law governing this activity for their own sake. Now, although it is not this mental activity in general with which morality is concerned – for that purpose a special direction must be given to the activity – this love is nevertheless the general constitution and form of the moral will. And so this method of mental culture is the immediate preparation for the moral one; the root of immorality, however, it eliminates completely, by never allowing sensuous enjoyment to become the motive. Hitherto this motive was the first to be stimulated and developed, because it was believed that otherwise the pupil could not be fashioned at all and a measure of influence gained over him. Should the moral motive have been subsequently developed, then it arrived too late and found the heart already taken and filled with another kind of love. In the new education, conversely, the formation of a pure will shall take precedence, so that, if at some later time selfishness should indeed stir within, or be stimulated from without, it will arrive too late and find no room in a soul already occupied by something else.

Already essential to this first objective as well as to the second, which I shall indicate shortly, is that from the outset the pupil be brought completely and uninterruptedly under the influence of this education, and that he be entirely separated from the community and kept safe from any contact with it. He need not hear at all that one can bestir oneself in life for the sake of its preservation and welfare, no more than he need know that one may learn for that reason or that learning can be of some help towards these ends. It follows that the spiritual development after the manner we indicated earlier must be the only one imparted to him and that he must concern himself with it ceaselessly; that on no account, however, may this mode of instruction alternate with the one requiring the opposing sensuous motive.

Now, although this spiritual development may prevent selfishness from arising and provide the form of a moral will, it is not yet for that reason the moral will itself. If the new education that we propose went no further than this, it would at most school excellent men of learning, as in the past, of whom only a few are required, and who could contribute no more to our proper, humane and national purpose than such men have done previously: exhort and exhort again, allow themselves to be gaped at and on occasion scorned. But it is clear – as I have already said – that this free activity of the mind has been developed with the intention that the pupil thereby projects the image of a moral order of actually existing life, grasps this image with the love that has likewise already developed within him, and by this love is impelled to realise it in and through his own life. The question arises as to how the new education can prove that it has achieved its proper and final aim with its pupil.

In the first place, it is clear that the pupil's mental activity, which earlier was exercised on other objects, must be stimulated to project an image of the human social order, as it ought to be according to the law of reason. Whether this image projected by the pupil is correct can most easily be judged by an education that is in sole possession of this correct image. Whether it was projected by the pupil's self-activity and on no account apprehended merely passively and parroted credulously in schoolish fashion; whether, furthermore, it was raised to the proper degree of clarity and vividness – this the education will be able to judge in the same way as it earlier passed correct judgements on other objects in the same regard. All this is still a matter of knowledge pure and simple, and remains in its domain, access to which is exceedingly easy in this education. A quite different and higher question, however, is this: whether the pupil is so seized by an ardent love for such an order of things that, released from the tutelage of education and declared independent, it will be simply impossible for him not to will this order and work with all his powers for its advancement. There is no doubt that this question cannot be settled by words, and tests framed in words, but only by visible actions.

I solve the task set by this last observation thus: without doubt the pupils of this new education, though separated from adult society, will nevertheless live in fellowship with one another and thus form an independent and self-sustaining commonwealth possessed of its own constitution; one that is clearly defined, grounded in the nature of things, and absolutely demanded by reason. The very first image of a social order that the pupil is stimulated to project in his mind shall be of the community in which he himself lives, in such a way that he is inwardly compelled to form an image of this order point by point, just as it actually appears before him, and that he understands it in all its parts as utterly necessary in relation to its principles. This is once again the mere work of knowledge. In this social order every individual must now in real life continually abstain, for the sake of the whole, from much that, were he alone, he could do without a second thought; and it will be expedient if, in the legislation and in the teaching of the constitution to be based thereon, to each individual all the others are represented as being actuated by an idealised love of order, which perhaps none really has but all ought to have; and that consequently this legislation maintains a high degree of severity and places a great deal of weight on abstentions from certain acts. This, as something that simply must be, and on which the existence of society rests, is in extremity even to be coerced through fear of immediate punishment; and this penal law must be carried out without clemency or exception. This use of fear as a motive is not at all prejudicial to the morality of the pupil, because here it is not the doing of good that is to be encouraged but only the abstention from what is bad according to the constitution. Furthermore, when teaching the constitution it must be made completely clear that he who still requires the idea of punishment or perhaps even the refreshment of this idea by actually suffering punishment himself, stands on a very lowly level of culture. Yet in spite of all this, it is evident that, since one can never know whether obedience is inspired by love of order or fear of punishment, in this circumstance the pupil cannot outwardly prove his good will nor education appraise it.

Conversely, the circumstance in which such an appraisal is possible is the following. The polity must be so arranged that the individual must not merely abstain for the sake of the whole, but also be able to act and work on its behalf. In this commonwealth of pupils, physical exercise, and the mechanical but here idealised labours of agriculture and of various handicrafts, are practised in addition to the development of the mind through learning. It shall be a basic rule of the constitution that everyone who excels in any one of these departments is expected to help instruct the others therein, and to assume various functions and responsibilities; that everyone who discovers an improvement, or is the first to grasp most clearly an improvement suggested by a tutor, is exempted from carrying it out by his own efforts, without his therefore being relieved of his personal tasks of learning and working, which go without saying; that each satisfies these demands willingly and without coercion, while those who are unwilling are also at liberty to refuse them; that he should not expect any reward because in this constitution all are equal in relation to work and enjoyment, nor even praise, because the prevailing mentality in the community is that each is only doing his share; that instead he merely takes pleasure in his activities and work on behalf of the whole, and in being successful in them, should he meet with success. Accordingly, in this polity the acquisition of greater skill, and the effort expended therein, are followed only by renewed effort and more toil, and it is precisely the more capable pupil who will often have to keep watch while others sleep, and reflect while others play.

Those pupils who, regardless of whether all this is perfectly clear and intelligible to them, nevertheless continue gladly to take on that initial effort and all the subsequent exertions that follow from it, and such that they can be reckoned on with certainty, and remain strong in the feeling of their power and activity and grow yet stronger – those pupils education can by all means release into the world without worry. In them its purpose has been achieved; in them love has been kindled and burns right down to the root of their vital stirrings, and from now on it will continue without exception to embrace everything that reaches this vital stirring. And in the larger commonwealth, which they now enter, these pupils will never be able to be anything but what they were in the smaller commonwealth which they are leaving: steadfast and immutable.

In this way the pupil is ready to meet the next demands that the world will inevitably make on him, demands that arise without exception. What education requires from him in the name of this world has been done. But he is not yet complete in and for himself, and what he himself can require of education has not yet been done. As soon as this demand, too, is fulfilled, he will be capable of satisfying those which, in special circumstances, a higher world might make of him in the name of the present one.

Description of the new education – continued

The specific nature of the proposed new education, insofar as it was described in the previous address, consisted in this, that it was the deliberate and sure art of cultivating the pupil to pure morality. To pure morality, I said. This morality is something primary, independent, self-sufficient, and self-existent; and not at all, like the lawfulness often intended before now, linked to and grafted on to a non-moral drive whose satisfaction it serves. It is the deliberate and sure art of this moral education, I said. It does not wander aimlessly and haphazardly, but proceeds according to a fixed rule well known to it and is certain of its success. Its pupil goes forth at the proper time as a fixed and immutable product of its art, who could not go in any other way save that determined by it, who requires no assistance, but continues of himself and according to his own law.

True, this education also cultivates the mind of the pupil and indeed its work begins with this mental culture. Yet this development of the mind is not its primary and sovereign purpose, but only the means by which it imparts moral culture to the pupil. In the meantime, this mental culture, though acquired but incidentally, remains an ineradicable possession of the pupil's life and the eternally blazing beacon of his moral love. However great or small the sum of the knowledge that he takes with him from education, he has surely been left with a mind that for the rest of his life can grasp every truth whose cognition will become necessary to him, that remains as constantly receptive to instruction by others as it is capable of independent reflection.

Thus far had we come in our description of the new education. At the conclusion of the previous address we remarked that it is not yet brought to completion, but must accomplish another task, one that is distinct from those assigned hitherto. And now we turn to the business of delineating this task.

The pupil who shall receive this education is not only a member of human society here on earth and for the short span of life vouchsafed him; he is also, and undoubtedly acknowledged to be such by education, a link in the eternal chain of the life of the spirit in general and subject to a higher social order. It goes without saying that a culture that has undertaken to embrace his entire being must lead him to insight into this higher order; and, just as it led him to trace out, through his own self-activity, an image of that moral order of the world which never is but forever shall be, so it must guide him to project, with the same self-activity, a mental image of that supersensuous world order in which nothing becomes, nor which has itself ever become, but forever only is, and to do this in such a way that he intimately understands and perceives that it could not be otherwise. With proper guidance, he will bring his attempts at such an image to a successful conclusion and then find that nothing truly exists save life, namely the spiritual life that lives in thought [*Gedanken*]; that nothing else truly exists, but only appears to exist, and he will likewise grasp, even if only in general terms, that the ground of this appearance proceeds from thought. He will further understand that, in the manifold forms it has received, not by accident but by a law grounded in God, the spiritual life that alone truly exists is ultimately one, the divine life itself, which exists and is revealed only in living thought. Thus will he recognise his own life, and every other spiritual life, as an eternal link in the chain of the revelation of divine life and learn to hold it sacred. He will find life and light and blessedness only in the immediate communion with God, in the unmediated outpouring of his life from Him; but death, darkness and misery in the remoteness from such immediacy. In a word: this development will cultivate him to religion; and this religion that consists in living our life in God should indeed prevail and be carefully nurtured in the new age also. By contrast, the religion of the past age, which separated the spiritual life from the divine life, and only by falling away from the latter could obtain for the former that absolute existence intended for it;[15] which used God as a thread to introduce selfishness into

---

[15] A possible allusion to Schelling's *Philosophie und Religion* (1804), in which Schelling describes the 'absolute' as the only reality and the ground of finite entities as lying in a 'falling away' (*Abfall*) from the absolute (p. 35).

other worlds even after the death of the mortal frame and, through hope and fear, to fortify the selfishness that had remained weak for the present world – this religion, plainly a handmaiden of selfishness, shall indeed be laid to rest along with the past age. For in the new age eternity does not dawn only beyond the grave, but comes into the midst of the present; selfishness, however, is dismissed from government as well as from service and departs, taking its servants with it.

Education to true religion is hence the final business of the new education. Whether, in projecting the image of the supersensuous world order required for this purpose, the pupil has proceeded with true self-activity, and whether the projected image is on all sides correct, and thoroughly clear and intelligible, this education will be able to judge with ease, in the same way as it does with other objects of knowledge: for this too remains in the realm of knowledge.

More significant, though, is the question of how our education can assess and guarantee that this religious knowledge will not remain cold and dead, but will express itself in the actual life of the pupil. Before addressing this question we must answer another, namely: how and in what way does religion generally manifest itself in life?

In everyday life, and in a well-ordered society, there is no immediate need at all for religion to mould life; true morality is perfectly sufficient for this purpose. In this regard, therefore, religion is not practical, nor can and should it become practical, but is knowledge pure and simple: it renders man perfectly clear and intelligible to himself, provides an answer to the highest question he can pose, resolves the final contradiction, thus bringing perfect self-unity and clarity to his understanding. It represents his complete deliverance and liberation from all external bonds; and thus it owes him education as something that is his due simply and without ulterior purpose. Religion only acquires a domain where it can operate as an impulse either in a highly immoral and corrupt society or when man's sphere of activity lies not within but beyond the social order and he has constantly to create and preserve this order anew – as with the regent, who often could not discharge his office in good conscience without religion. The latter case is not at issue in an education adapted to all and to the entire nation. As for the former case: if, despite a clear recognition of the incorrigibility of the age, work to improve it nevertheless continues unabated; if the sweat and toil of the sowing of the land is unflinchingly endured even with little prospect of a harvest; if even the ingrate is rewarded and those who curse are blessed with charity and goods in the clear foreknowledge that they will curse again; if after a hundredfold failures one still perseveres with faith and love: then it is not mere morality that impels one here, for morality demands a purpose. It is religion, the submission to a higher law unknown to us, the awestruck silence before God, the fervent love for His life that has broken forth in ours, the life that alone shall be saved for its own sake, where the eye sees nothing left to save.

In this way, the religious insight achieved by the pupils of the new education in the little commonwealth in which they initially grow up cannot become practical knowledge; nor should it even. This commonwealth is well ordered, and whatever is deftly undertaken there always meets with success. Also, in these still tender years man should be maintained in his innocence and serene faith in humanity. Let knowledge of its perfidy be postponed until he is ready to experience it firsthand at a mellowed and more settled age.

Only at this riper age, therefore, when life is lived in earnest, and after education has long since left him to his own resources, may the pupil, if his social relations are to advance from simplicity to a higher level, have need of his religious knowledge as a motive. Now, how shall education, which cannot examine the pupil on this point for as long as he remains in its care, yet be sure that, when the need arises, this motive too will work infallibly? I reply: by the pupil being formed in such a way that no knowledge in his possession will remain cold and dead when there is a possibility that it can receive life; rather, all knowledge shall of necessity intervene directly in life, as and when life needs it. I shall substantiate this claim presently, and in doing so elevate in its entirety the idea elaborated in this address and the foregoing one, and incorporate it into a greater system of knowledge, on which, with the help of this idea, I shall in turn throw a new light and bestow a higher clarity. But only after I have given a definite account of the true nature of the new education, whose general description I have just concluded.

This education now no longer appears, as it did at the beginning of today's address, merely as the art of cultivating the pupil to pure morality. Rather, it is evidently the art of cultivating the whole man thoroughly and completely to humanity. Of relevance here are two main points. First, with regard to form, it is the real, living man who is cultivated, all the way down to his vital root, not just the mere shadow and outline of a man; and second, with regard to content, all essential parts of man are developed fully, uniformly and without exception. These parts are the understanding and the will, and education must have for its object the clarity of the former and the purity of the latter. In connection with the clarity of the understanding, however, two principal questions must be raised. First, what is it that the pure will wills, properly speaking, and by what means is that which is willed to be attained (under which head is included all the other knowledge that is to be imparted to the pupil)? Secondly, what is this pure will itself in ground and essence (under which head is included knowledge of religion)? Both these parts we have mentioned, developed until they intervene in life, education demands absolutely and does not think to exempt a single pupil in the least, for each shall be precisely a human being. As to what someone might become above and beyond that, and what particular form general humanity assumes in him, or receives, this is of no concern to our education and lies outside its sphere. I now proceed to the further reasons I promised for my claim that no knowledge can remain lifeless in the pupil of the new education, and to the system into which I mean to elevate everything I have said so far. This I shall do by means of the following propositions.

1. From what I have said it follows that there are, with respect to their education, two quite distinct and completely opposed classes of men. To begin with, every human being, and therefore both these classes also, is alike in that, underlying the manifold expressions of his life, is a drive which, in the midst of change, persists unaltered and remains identical with itself. Incidentally, it is the self-understanding of this drive, and its translation into concepts, that brings the world into being; and there is no other world save this one that creates itself thus in thought, thought that is by no means free but necessary. Now, this drive that must always be translated into consciousness – wherein once again both classes are alike – can be so translated in two ways, according to the two different kinds of consciousness, and it is in the manner of this translation and self-understanding that the two classes are distinct.

The first kind of consciousness to develop is that of obscure feeling. This feeling most commonly and as a rule comprehends [*erfassen*] the fundamental drive [*Grundtrieb*] as love of the individual for himself, and indeed presents this self at first only as one that desires life and well-being. Hence arises sensuous selfishness as the actual fundamental drive and developing power of such a life engaged in translating its original fundamental drive. For as long as man continues to understand himself thus, he must act selfishly and can do no other; and this selfishness is the one thing that is permanent, identical and predictable in the ceaseless change of his life. As a rare exception to the rule, this obscure feeling can also pass over the personal self entirely and comprehend the fundamental drive as a desire for a different, obscurely felt order of things. Hence springs forth the life we have described in sufficient detail elsewhere;[16] the life which, exalted above selfishness, is driven by ideas obscure indeed, but still ideas, and in which reason governs as instinct. This comprehension of the fundamental drive by obscure feeling only is the characteristic of the first class of men, who are formed not by education but by themselves. This class in turn comprises two further subspecies, who are distinguished by a principle that is incomprehensible and beyond the art of man to discover.

The second kind of consciousness, which as a rule does not develop of itself but must be carefully nurtured in society, is clear knowledge. Were the fundamental drive of humanity to be comprehended in this element, it would yield a second class of men quite distinct from the first. Such knowledge, which comprehends the fundamental love [*Grundliebe*] itself, does not leave us cold and uninterested, as another kind of knowledge can; rather, its object is loved above all other things, since this object is but the interpretation and translation of our original love itself. The other kind of knowledge comprehends something alien, and this something remains alien and leaves us cold; this knowledge comprehends the knower himself and his love, and he loves it. Although it is the same original love, only appearing in a different form, that drives both classes, yet we can say, overlooking that circumstance, that there man is driven by obscure feelings, here by clear knowledge.

For such clear knowledge to become an immediate impulse in life, and capable of being counted on with confidence, depends, as I have said, on this, that it is man's real and true love which is interpreted by this knowledge; also that it becomes immediately clear to him that this is so and, at the same time as the interpretation, the feeling of that love is stimulated in him and felt by him; that knowledge is therefore never developed in him without love being developed at the same time, because otherwise he would remain cold, nor is love ever to be developed without knowledge being developed at the same time, because otherwise his impulse would be an obscure feeling; that therefore with each step of his culture the whole unified man is formed. A man who is always treated

[16] *CPA*, Lecture 1.

by education as an indivisible whole will remain one for evermore, and all knowledge will necessarily become for him an impulse in life.

2. Because clear knowledge is thereby made the original point of departure and the true basis of life instead of obscure feeling, selfishness is passed over completely and cheated of its development. For only obscure feeling presents man's self to him as something that seeks pleasure and avoids pain; but on no account does the clear concept do so. Rather, it shows the self as belonging to a moral order; and there is a love for this order, which is kindled and developed at the same time as the concept develops. This education has nothing to do with selfishness, because through clarity it chokes the very root of selfishness, obscure feeling; it no more challenges selfishness than it develops it; it knows nothing of selfishness at all. Even if there were a possibility that one day selfishness might nevertheless stir, it would find the heart already filled with a higher love that leaves it no room.

3. Now, when this fundamental drive of man is translated into clear knowledge, it does not aim at an already given and existing world that can only be accepted passively, as it is, and in which a love that drives original and creative activity were unable to find its own sphere of efficacy. Rather, raised to knowledge, it aims at a world that shall be, an a priori world, one that exists in the future and remains ever in the future. The divine life underlying all appearance therefore never enters as a permanent and given being, but as something that shall be; and after it has become what it should have been, it will once again and for all eternity enter as something that shall be. That divine life therefore never enters in the death of permanent being, but remains always in the form [*Form*] of onward-flowing life. The immediate appearance and revelation of God is love; the interpretation of this love through knowledge first posits a being, a being that for evermore only shall be, and posits it as the only true world, insofar as a world possesses truth. Conversely, the second world, the given world that we find already in existence, is only the shadow and outline from which knowledge builds a fixed shape [*Gestalt*] and visible body for its interpretation of love; this second world is the means and the condition of intuiting the higher world that in itself is invisible. Even in this higher world God does not appear directly, but is mediated by the one, pure, immutable and formless love; in this love alone does He appear directly. To this love is joined the intuitive knowledge, which brings forth from itself an image wherein it clothes the invisible object of love. Yet each time it is opposed by love, and therefore

impelled onwards to the creation of a new image that is opposed in its turn. Only in this way does love, which purely in itself is one, absolutely incapable of progress, of infinity, of eternity, also become, by fusing with the intuition, likewise eternal and infinite. The aforementioned image, which is produced by knowledge, taken by itself and still without application to the distinctly cognised love, is the permanent and given world, or nature. The delusion that the essence of God is somehow revealed directly in nature, and otherwise than by the interagencies I have indicated, originates in a benighted spirit and an impure will.

4. For obscure feeling, as a dissolvent of love, to be as a rule passed over entirely and clear knowledge set in its place as the usual dissolvent, can, as I have already reminded you, happen only by means of a deliberate art of educating humanity, and this has not yet happened. Since, as we have likewise just seen, this method introduces and posits as the rule a kind of man quite distinct from the kind usual until now, such an education would certainly usher in an entirely new order of things, a new creation. This new form humanity can give itself, if the present generation educates itself as the future generation, in the way that only it can: through knowledge, as that alone which can be shared and freely communicated, the true light and air of this world, uniting the world of spirit. Hitherto humanity became simply what it became and could become. This haphazard evolution is over; for where it has developed the most it has become nothing. If humanity is not to remain in this nothingness, it must henceforth make itself into everything that it is yet to become. The true vocation of the human race on earth, I said in those lectures whose sequel these addresses are, shall be this, that it fashions itself with freedom into that which it really and originally is.[17] This self-fashioning, achieved deliberately and according to a rule, must now begin somewhere and somewhen in space and time, so that a second principal epoch, in which the human race develops freely and deliberately, would follow the first, when the development was not free. We are of the opinion that, with respect to time, this time is now, and that at present the race stands at the true midway point of its life on earth, between its two principal epochs. With respect to space, however, we

---

[17] Cf. *CPA*: 'Thus, the whole progress which, upon this view, Humanity makes here below, is only a retrogression to the point on which it stood at first, and nothing in view save that return to its original condition. But Humanity must make this journey on its own feet; by its own strength it must bring itself back to that state in which it was once before without its own co-operation' (Lecture I, p. 10).

believe that it falls first and foremost to the Germans to inaugurate the new age, as pioneers and exemplars for the rest of humanity.

5. Yet even this wholly new creation will not be an abrupt departure from what has gone before, but is, rather, the true natural continuation and consequence of the preceding age, especially among the Germans. It is evident, and I believe universally acknowledged, that all the stirring and striving of the age was directed towards banishing the obscure feelings and securing mastery for clarity and knowledge alone. This striving has been completely successful insofar as the nothingness of the past has been revealed in its entirety. On no account shall this drive to clarity be eradicated or the apathy that obscure feeling engenders be allowed to prevail again; this drive is to be developed further and introduced into higher spheres, so that when the nothing [*Nichts*] is disclosed the something [*Etwas*], the truth that affirms and really posits something, may likewise become manifest. The world that originated in obscure feeling, the world of given and self-creating being, is submerged and shall remain submerged. Conversely, the world that originated in original clarity, the world of being eternally delivered of the spirit, shall dawn and shine forth in all its radiance.

The prophecy of a new life in such forms might seem strange to our age, and it might scarcely have the courage to appropriate this promise, if it looked only to the tremendous gulf separating the prevailing opinions on the subjects we have just discussed from the principles of the new age as I have expressed them. I do not mean to speak here of that education which, as a privilege not extended to all, was previously and as a rule received only by the higher ranks, an education that kept completely silent about a supersensuous world and strove merely to impart a little slickness in the affairs of the sensuous world; for this was obviously inferior. Rather, I wish to attend only to what was popular education, and in a certain, very limited sense could also be called national education, and which did not observe absolute silence about a supersensuous world. What were the tenets of this education? If we establish, as the very first premise of the new education, that there is at the root of man a pure pleasure in the good, and that this pleasure can be developed to the extent that it becomes impossible for him to refrain from doing what he has recognised as good and instead do what he has recognised as bad; then, conversely, education has until now not only assumed but also taught its pupils from early childhood that, first, there inheres in man a natural aversion to God's commandments, and, secondly, it is simply impossible for him to obey them.[18] What else can be expected of such instruction, if it is taken seriously and believed, save that each individual yields to his unalterable nature, does not even attempt to accomplish what has once been presented to him as impossible, nor desires to be better than he and the rest of humanity can be; indeed, that he even accepts the baseness attributed to him, so that he recognises himself in his radical sinfulness and wickedness, while this baseness before God is presented to him as the only means of coming to terms with Him: and that, should a claim such as ours strike his ears, he cannot but think we mean to play a bad joke on him, because deep down he has the ever-present feeling, and grasps with his own hands, that this is not true, but rather that the opposite alone is true? If we assume a knowledge that is quite independent of all given being and even legislates for this being itself; and if from the outset we immerse every human child in this knowledge and keep that child constantly in its domain; and if, conversely, we consider the qualities of things that can only be learned historically as a trivial matter of secondary importance that follows of itself; then the ripest fruits of the previous education confront us, reminding us that, notoriously, there is no a priori knowledge, and saying they would like to learn how one can know other than through experience. And so that this supersensuous and a priori world does not betray itself even in the place where it seemed unavoidable – in the possibility of a knowledge of God – and so that even in God there should arise no self-activity of the spirit, and passive submission remained all in all, the previous education has discovered, as a safeguard against this danger, the bold solution of making the existence of God a historical fact whose truth is ascertained by the examination of witnesses.

That is how matters stand; yet the age should not despair of itself. For these and all other similar phenomena are not themselves self-sufficient, but merely the flowers and fruits of the wild root of the past. If only the age would submit to the grafting of a new, nobler and stronger root, then the old will choke, and its flowers and fruits, starved of further nourishment, will of themselves wither and drop off. For now the age is not yet able to believe our words, which perforce must seem to it a mere fairy-tale. Nor do we desire this belief; we want only the room to create and to act. Then the age will see, and it will believe what it sees with its own eyes.

---

[18] Particularly the religious education of the Reformed Church. See e.g. the fifth response in the Heidelberg Catechism of 1563: 'I am by nature prone to hate God and my neighbour.'

Thus anyone, for example, who is familiar with the productions of recent times will already have noticed that here we are giving voice once again to the same propositions and views that, ever since its birth, modern German philosophy has preached, and preached again, because it was unable to do anything but preach. That these sermons have echoed and faded away in the empty air to no avail is now clear enough; so too is the reason why they were bound to fade away thus. A living thing acts only on other living things; in the actual life of the age, however, there is no affinity for this philosophy, because it goes about its business in a sphere that is not yet open to the age and demands sense organs that are as yet unequal to it. Philosophy is not at home in this age, but a harbinger of the time to come; it is the vital element [*Lebens-Element*], ready in advance, of a race that in it will first awaken to the light. Philosophy must give up on the present race; but in order that it remain not idle until then, it shall now take on the task of forming the race to which it belongs. Only when its immediate business becomes clear to it will it be able to live in peace and harmony with a race that otherwise does not please it. The education that we have described is at once an education for this philosophy. Again, only it can be, in a certain sense, the schoolmistress of this education; and so it was obliged to rush ahead before it could be understood or accepted. But the time will come when it will be understood and accepted with joy; and for that reason the age should not despair of itself.

Let this age hear the vision of an old prophet that was intended for a no less lamentable situation. Thus speaks the prophet by the river of Chebar, the consoler of those held captive not in their own country but in a foreign land: 'The hand of the Lord was upon me, and carried me out in the spirit of the Lord, and set me down in the midst of the valley which was full of bones, And caused me to pass by them round about: and, behold, there were very many in the open valley; and, lo, they were very dry. And he said unto me, Son of man, can these bones live? And I answered, O Lord God, thou knowest. Again he said unto me, Prophesy upon these bones, and say unto them, O ye dry bones, hear the word of the Lord. Thus saith the Lord God unto these bones; Behold, I will cause breath to enter into you, and ye shall live: And I will lay sinews upon you, and will bring up flesh upon you, and cover you with skin, and put breath in you, and ye shall live; and ye shall know that I am the Lord. So I prophesied as I was commanded: and as I prophesied, there was a noise, and behold a shaking, and the bones came together, bone to his bone. And when I beheld, lo, the sinews and the flesh came up upon them, and the

skin covered them above: but there was no breath in them. Then said he
unto me, Prophesy unto the wind, prophesy, son of man, and say to the
wind, Thus saith the Lord God; Come from the four winds, O breath,
and breathe upon these slain, that they may live. So I prophesied as he
commanded me, and the breath came into them, and they lived, and
stood up upon their feet, an exceeding great army.'[19] Let the parts of our
higher spiritual life be just as dried out, and for this very reason also the
bonds of our national unity be just as broken, and lie scattered round-
about in wild disorder, like the prophet's bones of the slain; let these be
bleached and dried by the storms and rains and searing sunshine of
several centuries; – the quickening breath of the spiritual world has not
yet ceased to blow. It will seize too the dead bones of our nation, and join
them together, so that they stand there gloriously in a new and transfig-
ured life.

[19] Ezekiel 37: 1–10.

The principal difference between the Germans and other peoples of Teutonic descent

We have said that the proposed means of cultivating a new race of men must first be applied by Germans to Germans, and that it is a task that quite properly and immediately pertains to our nation. This proposition, too, is in need of proof and here also we shall begin, just as we have done thus far, with that which is highest and most general. We shall demonstrate what the German in and of himself, independently of the fate that has now befallen him, is and has always been in his essential character, ever since he came into existence. And we shall show that his aptitude for and receptivity to a culture such as we envisage lies already in this essential character and separates him from every other European nation.

The Germans are first and foremost one of the Teutonic tribes. As to the latter it will suffice here to define them as those whose task it was to unite the social order established in ancient Europe with the true religion preserved in ancient Asia, and thus to develop out of themselves a new age in opposition to the antiquity that had perished. Furthermore, it is enough to describe the Germans as such in contrast only with the other Teutonic peoples. While some modern European nations, such as those of Slavic descent, seem not to have developed so clearly from the rest of Europe that a definite portrait of them would be possible, others of the same Teutonic stock, to whom the ground of distinction that I shall presently adduce does not apply, like the Scandinavians, are here taken undoubtedly for Germans and included in all the general conclusions of our meditations.

But first let me preface the meditations we are about to begin with the following remark. I shall indicate as the cause of the differentiation of what was originally one stem [*Grundstamm*] an event which, seen simply as an event, lies clearly and incontestably before the eyes of all; I shall then adduce individual aspects of this differentiation that has taken place, and these it ought to be possible to render equally evident as mere events. But as for the connection of the latter, as consequences, with the former, as their cause, and as for the inference of the consequence from the cause, I cannot in general reckon on the same clarity and persuasive power for all. Admittedly, in this regard also I am not giving voice to entirely novel and hitherto unheard-of propositions, for there are in our midst many individuals who are either very well prepared for such a view of things or already familiar with it. Among the majority, however, there are, concerning the matter whereon we shall touch, ideas in circulation which depart significantly from ours, and to correct these and confute every objection which might be raised on the basis of individual cases by those who have no practised sense for the whole would oblige us to exceed our allotted time and depart from our plan. I must content myself with putting before such men, merely as a subject for their further reflection, what I have to say in this connection, which in the totality of my thought ought not to stand so isolated and without foundation in the depths of knowledge as it seems to here. I could not pass over this entirely, neither on account of the thoroughness demanded by the whole nor, certainly, in view of the important consequences that will follow therefrom in the later course of our addresses and which form an integral part of our immediate design.

The first difference between the fate of the Germans and that of the other tribes produced from the same stock to present itself directly to our notice is this: the former remained in the original homelands of the ancestral race, whereas the latter migrated to other territories; the former retained and developed the original language of the ancestral race, whereas the latter adopted a foreign language and gradually modified it after their own fashion. This earliest difference explains those which came later – for example, in the original fatherland, in conformity with ancient Teutonic custom, there continued to exist a confederation of states under a ruler with limited powers, whereas in foreign lands, more in keeping with the hitherto prevailing Roman system, the form of government passed over into monarchies, and so on.[20] But by no means can the later differences explain the earlier one.

---

[20] An allusion to the federal structure of the Holy Roman Empire as contrasted with the centralised state of France.

Now, of the changes indicated above, the first, the change of native soil, is quite insignificant. Man makes his home without difficulty in every region of the earth, and national character, far from being greatly altered by habitat, instead prevails over and alters the latter after its own image. Also, the natural influences in those climes inhabited by the Teutons are not especially diverse. Nor do we wish to attach much weight to the circumstance that in the lands they conquered those of Teutonic stock mingled with the earlier residents: for the victors, rulers and educators of the new people that emerged from this union were after all Teutons. Furthermore, the same intermixing which, in foreign lands, occurred with Gauls, Cantabrians[21] and so on took place in the motherland with Slavs to perhaps just as great an extent; so that it would be no simple task for any of the peoples who trace their origin back to the Teutons to prove a greater purity of descent than the others.

More significant, however, is the second change, that of language, which, I believe, establishes a complete contrast between the Germans and the other peoples of Teutonic descent. And here the issue – and this I wish to make clear at the outset – is neither the specific constitution of the language retained by the one tribe nor that of the language adopted by the other tribe, but only this: that in the former case something peculiar [*Eigenes*] to them has been retained and in the latter something foreign adopted; nor is the issue the prior ancestry of those who continue to speak an original language, but only the fact that this language continues to be spoken without interruption, for men are formed by language far more than language is by men.

To make clear, as far as it is here possible and needful, the consequences of such a difference in the formation of peoples, as well as the particular nature of the contrast in their national characteristics that necessarily follows from this difference, I must invite you to consider with me the essence of language in general.

Language in general, and particularly the designation of objects through the production of sound in the speech organs, does not by any means depend on arbitrary decrees and conventions; rather, there exists in the first instance a fundamental law according to which each concept is expressed by this sound and no other through the human speech organs. Just as objects are represented in the sense organs of the individual with a particular shape, colour and so on, so they are represented in the organs

---

[21] A tribe of northern Spain.

of social man – that is, in language – with a particular sound. It is not really man who speaks; human nature speaks through him and announces itself to others of his kind. And thus one would have to say: there is but one language and this language is absolutely necessary.

Now it may well be (and this is my second point) that language has never and nowhere broken forth for man in general, for man as such, in this unity; that it was on all sides modified and formed by the effects which the climate and more or less frequent use had on the speech organs, and by the succession of the observed and designated objects on the succession of designations. But even here caprice and chance do not hold sway, but rather rigid law; it is necessary that from a speech organ determined by the aforementioned conditions there burst forth not the one and pure human language, but rather an offshoot thereof and precisely this particular offshoot.

If we call a people those men whose speech organs are subject to the same external influences, who live together and develop their language in continuous communication, then we must say: the language of this people is as it is by necessity, and it is not really the people that express their knowledge, but rather knowledge that expresses itself through the people.

During all the changes that occur in the progress of language as a consequence of the aforementioned circumstances, this lawfulness remains uninterrupted; and for all who remain in uninterrupted communication and wherever the new word formed by one individual is heard by all it is one and the same lawfulness. Even after thousands of years, and after all the modifications that during this time the external appearance of the language of this people has undergone, it remains ever the same one linguistic force of nature that must originally erupt just as it did, that has flowed without break through all the different conditions, that under each condition had to become just as it became, at the end had to be just as it is now, and at some future time must become what it must then become. The purely human language, as expressed by the organ of a people from the day it produced its first sound, together with all the developments that this first sound had to acquire under the given circumstances, yields as its final result the present language of the people. For that reason, the language remains ever the same language. Though after several centuries the descendants may not understand the language of their forebears, because the transitions have been lost to them, yet there is from the beginning a continuous transition without leaps, which, always imperceptible at the time and only made perceptible by the accretion of new transitions, does indeed seem to proceed by leaps and bounds. Never has there been a time when contemporaries might have ceased to understand one another, because their eternal mediator and interpreter was and remained the common force of nature that spoke through them all. Thus do matters stand with language as the designation of objects of immediate sensuous perception, and that is what all human language is at the outset. When the people raises itself from this stage of sensuous perception to grasp the super-sensuous, then, if this supersensuous is to be repeated at will and kept from being confused with the sensuous for the first individual, and if it is to be communicated to others and give them suitable guidance, the only way at first to keep a firm hold of it is to designate a self as an organ of a supersensuous world and scrupulously distinguish it from the self that is an organ of the sensuous world – to oppose a soul, a mind and so on to a physical body. Further, since all the various objects of this supersensuous world appear only in that supersensuous organ and exist only for it, they could be designated in language only by it being said that their particular relation to their organ is like the relation of this or that particular sensuous object to its sense organ; that in this relation a particular supersensuous thing is equated with a particular sensuous thing, and thanks to this equation its place in the supersensuous organ can be indicated through language. Language cannot do more in this sphere; it presents a sensuous image of the supersensuous and merely remarks that it is such an image. Whoever wishes to arrive at the object itself must set in motion his own spiritual organ according to the rule indicated to him by the image. – In general it is clear that this symbolic designation of the supersensuous must in each case conform to the stage of development reached by the faculty of sensuous cognition in a given people; that therefore the beginning and further progress of this symbolic designation will take a very different turn in different languages, according to the difference in the relation that obtained and continues to obtain between the sensuous and spiritual development of the people speaking a language.

Let us illustrate this remark, already clear in itself, with an example. Something that arises, according to the comprehension of the funda-mental drive explained in the foregoing address, not through obscure feeling but directly through clear knowledge, and is always a supersen-suous object, is called, by a Greek word that is often used in German also, an *idea* [*Idee*]. This word furnishes exactly the same symbol as the word *vision* [*Gesicht*], as in the following turns of phrase in Luther's translation of the Bible: 'you will see visions, you will dream dreams'.[22] Idea or vision in its sensuous signification would be something that could be perceived only through the physical eye, but not at all through another sense, such as touch, hearing, and so on – something like a rainbow or the shapes that pass before us in dreams. The same word in its supersensuous signification would mean, first of all, according to the sphere in which the word has currency, something that is grasped not at all by the body but only by the mind; then something that cannot, as some things can, be grasped by the obscure feeling of the mind, but only through the mind's eye – that is to say, by clear knowledge. If one were now inclined to make the further assumption that for the Greeks the basis of this symbolic designation was indeed the rainbow and other phenomena of this kind, then one would have to admit that their sensuous knowledge must already have advanced to the stage where they could discern the difference between things, namely that some reveal themselves to all or several senses, some merely to the eye; and that moreover, if it had become clear to them, they would have had to designate the developed concept not in this way but in another. It would therefore also shed light on why their clarity of spirit was superior to that of another people that was not able to express the difference between the sensuous and the supersensuous by a symbol taken from the reflective waking state, but resorted to dream in order to find an image for another world. At the same time it would be plain as day that this difference is grounded not in the greater or lesser strength of the sense for the supersensuous in the two peoples, for example, but only in the disparity between their sensuous clarity at the time when they wished to designate the supersensuous.

Thus, all designation of the supersensuous conforms to the extent and clarity of the sensuous knowledge of him who designates. For him the symbol is clear and expresses, perfectly intelligibly, the relation between the object conceived and the spiritual organ, because this relation is explained to him by another immediate and living relation between that object and his sense organ. This new designation, together with all the clarity that accrues to sensuous knowledge itself thanks to this expanded use of the sign, is now embedded in language; and potential supersensuous knowledge in the future is now designated according to its relation to the totality of supersensuous and sensuous knowledge embedded in

---

[22] Acts 2: 17.

the language as a whole. So it goes on without cessation; and thus the immediate clarity and intelligibility of the symbols are never interrupted, but remain a steady stream. – Further, since language is not the product of arbitrary arrangement but breaks forth as an immediate force of nature from rational life, a language that has continued to develop without interruption according to this law also has the power to intervene directly in life and to stimulate it. As things immediately present to man move him, so too must the words of such a language move him who understands it, for they also are things and by no means arbitrary contrivances. So much for the sensuous world. But it is no different in the supersensuous realm. For although in relation to the latter the constant progress of the observation of nature is interrupted by free reflection and contemplation, and here, so to speak, the unimageable God enters, linguistic designation at once reintroduces that which is unimageable [*das Unbildliche*] into the constant connection of the imageable [*des Bildlichen*]. And thus in this respect also the constant progress of the language that first broke forth as a force of nature remains uninterrupted, and into the stream of designation no arbitrariness enters. For the same reason, even the supersensuous part of a language constantly developed in this way cannot lose its power of stimulating life in him who sets his spiritual organ in motion. The words of such a language in all its parts are life and create life in turn. – Let us also assume, with respect to the development of the language for the supersensuous, that the people of this language have remained in uninterrupted communication and that what one person thought and uttered soon reached the others: then what I have hitherto said in general holds true for all who speak this language. To all who merely wish to think, the symbol embedded in the language is clear; for all those who actually think, it lives and stimulates their life.

Such is the case, I say, with a language that, from the moment its first sound broke forth in the same people, has developed uninterruptedly out of the actual common life of that people; a language that admitted no element that did not express an intuition actually experienced by this people, an intuition that coheres with all the others in an interlocking system. Let the original people who spoke this language incorporate however many other individuals of another tribe and another language: if these newcomers are not allowed to raise the sphere of their intuitions to the standpoint from which henceforth the language will continue to develop, then they remain without voice in the community and without influence on the language until they themselves have gained entry into the sphere of intuitions of the original race. And so they do not form the language but the language forms them.

But the very opposite of what we have said so far takes place when a people gives up its own language and adopts a foreign one that is already well developed for the purpose of supersensuous designation – and not such that the people submits entirely freely to the influence of this foreign language and is content to remain speechless until it has entered the sphere of intuitions of this foreign language; but such that it imposes its own sphere of intuitions on the new language, within which this language must henceforth move and starting from the point at which they found it. This event is without consequences for the sensuous part of language. Among every people children must anyway learn this part of the language as if the signs were arbitrary, and thus recapitulate the past linguistic development of the nation in its entirety. Every sign in this sensuous sphere, however, can be rendered perfectly clear by immediately seeing or touching the object signified. At most this would mean that the first generation of a people that changed its language was required to return as adults to their childhood years; but for their offspring and for future generations order would be restored. Conversely, this change has the most momentous consequences for the supersensuous part of language. This part was made for the first possessors of the language in the manner I have already described; for the later conquerors of the same, however, the symbol contains an equation with an intuition of the senses that either they have already passed over long ago without the accompanying mental development, or else they have not yet had and probably never can have. The most they can do is to have the symbol and its spiritual meaning explained to them, whereby they receive only the flat and lifeless history of an alien culture but not a culture of their own, and get images which for them are neither immediately clear nor a vital stimulus, but which must seem to them as entirely arbitrary as the sensuous part of language. Owing to this merely historical exposition, such a people now finds the entire symbolic sphere of the language dead and closed off, its onward flow interrupted. And although beyond this sphere they may again develop the language and give it life, in their own way and insofar as this is possible from such a point of departure, nonetheless that component of language remains the dividing wall at which the original emergence of language from life as a force of nature, and the return of the actual language to life, are broken without exception. Although such a language may on the surface be stirred by the breeze of life, and thus give the appearance of vitality, deeper down it is dead and cut off from its living root by the admittance of the new sphere of intuitions and the abruption of the old.

Let us illustrate what I have just said with an example, while remarking in passing (for the sake of the example) that a language at bottom dead and unintelligible also lends itself very easily to perversion and misuse in white-washing human corruption, something that is impossible in a language that has never become extinct. I shall take as my example the three notorious words 'humanity' [*Humanität*], 'popularity' [*Popularität*] and 'liberality' [*Liberalität*]. These words, when they are spoken to the German who has learned no other language, are to his ears a wholly empty noise; he is reminded of nothing with which he is already familiar by any resemblance of sound and is thus wrenched completely from the sphere of his intuition and indeed of all possible intuition. If now the strange sonority and noble euphony of the unknown word arouses his attention and he thinks that such a lofty sound must also signify something lofty, then he must have its meaning explained to him at the very outset, as something quite new to him, and blindly trust in this explanation. In this way he grows quietly accustomed to acknowledged as really existing and valuable something which, left to his own devices, he might perhaps never have thought worthy of mention. Do not think it is so very different with the neo-Latin peoples, who utter those words supposedly as words belonging to their mother tongue. Without a learned study of antiquity and its actual language, they no more understand the roots of these words than does the German. If instead of the word *Humanität* we had used the word *Menschlichkeit*, as the former must literally be translated, then the German would have understood us without need for further historical explanation; but he would have added: to say one is a human being and not a wild animal is to say very little. Thus would a German speak, as a Roman would never have spoken, because humanity [*Menschheit*] in general has remained only a sensuous concept in his language and has never, as it did with the Romans, become the symbol of a supersensuous idea – because our forebears observed the individual human virtues and symbolically designated them in language perhaps long before they thought of bringing them together in a single unifying concept designed to serve as a contrast with animal nature; which does not reflect badly on our ancestors in comparison with the Romans. Whoever nevertheless wished to smuggle this foreign symbol of Roman origin artificially into the language of the Germans would obviously degrade their moral way of thinking, because he would present to them as excellent and praiseworthy something that might indeed be such in the foreign language, but which he, in accordance with the ineradicable nature of his national imagination, only grasps as something familiar and indispensable. A closer examination might perhaps show that those Teutonic tribes which adopted the Roman language encountered at the very outset such degradations of their earlier moral way of thinking through inappropriate and foreign symbols; but here I do not wish to attach the greatest weight to this circumstance.

If, furthermore, instead of the words *Popularität* and *Liberalität* I used the expressions 'currying favour with the mob' and 'the lack of a slavish mind', as we must translate these terms literally, then at first the German would not even get a clear and vivid image, such as the Roman of antiquity assuredly got. Every day the latter witnessed with his own eyes the ambitious candidate's supple courtesy to one and all, as well as the excesses of servility, which those words brought to life for him once more. The change in the form of government and the introduction of Christianity deprived the later Roman, too, of these spectacles; whereupon his own language in large part began to die in his own mouth, thanks in particular to the alien religion of Christianity, which he was able neither to resist nor to assimilate. How could this language, already half-dead in its own native land, have been transmitted in a living form to a foreign people? How could it be transmitted to us Germans now? As for the symbol of a spiritual thing that resides in the two expressions, *Popularität* already implies a vice which, by the depravity of the nation and its system of government, was twisted in its mouth to signify a virtue. The German never consents to this distortion, as long as it is presented to him in his own language. But if *Liberalität* is translated as meaning that a man has not the soul of a slave or, to render it according to modern manners, the mentality of a lackey, then the German once again replies that this too is to have said very little.

At a still later point in the development of the neo-Latin languages there were smuggled into these symbols, which even in their pure form among the Romans arose at a lowly stage of moral culture or positively designated a vice, the idea of a lack of earnestness concerning social relations, the idea of self-abasement, of spiritless laxity. These same concepts were introduced into the German language so as to bring them into vogue among us also, surreptitiously and without anyone really appreciating what was being said, by counting on the esteem in which we hold antiquity and the exotic. This has ever been the aim and result of all interfering in language: first, to deprive the listener of the immediate intelligibility and determinacy that are the mark of every original language and to wrap him in obscurity and unintelligibility; then, with the explanation that has now become necessary, to appeal to his blind trust; finally, in this explanation to stir together vice and virtue so that it is no easy task to separate them again. If therefore one had expressed what those three foreign words must properly mean, if they mean anything at all, in the German's own words and drawn from his own symbolic sphere, as *Menschenfreundlichkeit, Leutseligkeit, Edelmut* – then he would have understood us; the aforementioned vices, however, could never have been insinuated into those designations. In the domain of German speech the recourse to unintelligibility and obscurity arises either from clumsiness or malice; it must be avoided, and the corrective, translation into good and proper German, lies always ready to hand. In the neo-Latin languages, however, this unintelligibility is natural and original. There is no remedy, because those who speak them are not in possession of a living language by which they could scrutinise the dead one and, in the strict sense, they have no mother tongue at all.

This single example, which all too easily might have led us through the entire sphere of language and found application everywhere, serves to demonstrate to you what I have said so far as clearly as it can be at this stage. Here we are directly concerned in the first place with the supersensuous and not the sensuous part of language. In a language that has remained continuously living this supersensuous part is symbolical; it summarises at every step the totality of the sensuous and spiritual life of the nation as it is embedded in language in perfect unity, in order to designate a concept that is likewise not arbitrary but necessarily goes forth from the entire previous life of the nation. From this concept and from its designation a keen eye, moving backwards, ought to be able to reconstruct the entire cultural history of the nation. In a dead language, however, this supersensuous part, which while the language was alive was just the same, becomes, through its extinction, an incoherent collection of arbitrary and utterly inexplicable signs of equally arbitrary concepts; and nothing else can be done with either sign or concept beyond simply learning them.

And so we have solved our immediate task, to find the characteristic that distinguishes the Germans from the other peoples of Teutonic descent. The difference resulted immediately from the original separation of the common stock and consists in this, that the Germans still speak a living language and have done so ever since it first streamed forth from nature, whereas the other Teutonic tribes speak a language that stirs only on the surface yet is dead at the root. In this circumstance alone, in the life of one and in the death of the other, do we posit the difference; but by no means do we wish to address the question of the further intrinsic value of the German language. Between life and death there can be no comparison, and the former is infinitely more valuable than the latter. For that reason all direct comparisons between the German and neo-Latin languages are void, they are compelled to discuss things that are not worth discussing. Should the issue of the intrinsic value of the German language arise, then at least another language of the same rank, an equally original one, such as Greek, would have to enter the lists. Our present purpose, however, is far more modest than such a comparison.

What an immeasurable influence the constitution of its language may have on the entire human development of a people, this language that accompanies the individual into the inmost recesses of his mind as he thinks and wills, and either hinders him or gives him wings; which unites in its domain the mass of men who speak it into a single, common understanding; which is the true point of confluence where the world of sense and the world of spirit meet, and the extremities of both are fused so that one cannot say to which language belongs; how different the consequences of this influence may be depending on whether the relationship is one of life or death – all this may be surmised. What immediately presents itself to us is this: that the German has a means not only of fathoming his living language yet more deeply by comparing it with the Roman language, which is closed off and diverges greatly from his own in the evolution of its symbolism, but also to understand Latin more clearly, which is not possible for the neo-Latin, who at bottom remains imprisoned in the orbit of the same one language; that when the German learns the ancestral language of the Romans, he also acquires at the same time to a certain extent those languages descended from it and, should he learn Latin more thoroughly than the foreigner, which for the reason we have adduced he is very well equipped to do, he at the same time learns to understand the foreigner's own languages better, to master them more completely than the foreigner himself who speaks them; that therefore the German, if he avails himself of all his advantages, can always survey the foreigner and understand him perfectly, even better than he does himself, and translate him according to his fullest extent. Conversely, the foreigner, without making the great effort of learning the German language, can never understand the true German and will undoubtedly leave what is truly German untranslated. In these languages, all that can be learned from the foreigner himself are new fashionable locutions, which are mostly the products of boredom and caprice, and one is being very modest indeed if one consents to such instruction. More often than not one would instead be able to show foreigners how they ought to speak, in accordance with their ancestral language and the law that governs its transformation, and show them that the new fashion is useless and offends traditional good manners. – This wealth of consequences in general, and in particular the last mentioned, follow of themselves, as I have said.

But our intention is to understand these consequences as a whole, according to their common thread and in depth, in order thereby to give a detailed description of the German as contrasted with the other Teutonic tribes. Permit me to furnish you with a preliminary summary of these consequences: (1) With a people who speak a living language spiritual culture intervenes in life; with its opposite spiritual culture and life each go their separate ways. (2) For the same reason a people of the first kind takes all spiritual culture very seriously and actively desires that it intervene in life; conversely, for a people of the second kind spiritual culture is rather an ingenious game and more they do not wish it to be. The second kind have spirit [*Geist*], the first have soul [*Gemüt*] as well as spirit. (3) From the former consequence it follows that a people of the first kind are honestly diligent and serious in all things, and are assiduous, whereas the second kind allow themselves to be guided by their happy nature. (4) From all of the foregoing consequences it follows that in a nation that speaks a living language the great mass of people can be educated, and the educators test their discoveries on the people, and desire to influence them; conversely, in a nation of the second type, the cultivated classes divorce themselves from the people and regard them as nothing more than the blind instrument of their plans. The further discussion of these characteristics that I have indicated I shall reserve for the next hour.

Consequences of the difference that has been advanced

With a view to depicting the particularity of the Germans, we have set forth the fundamental difference between them and the other peoples of Teutonic descent, namely that the former remained in the uninterrupted flow of an original language which has developed continuously out of the actual life of the nation, whereas the latter adopted a foreign language which under their influence has become dead. At the end of the previous hour we mentioned that from this fundamental difference there must of necessity follow other phenomena in connection with these disparate tribes; today we shall elaborate on these phenomena and establish them more firmly on their common ground.

An investigation that endeavours to be thorough can avoid becoming involved in disputes and arousing envy. We shall proceed here as we did before in that investigation of which the present one is the continuation. We shall deduce step by step the consequences that follow from the fundamental difference we have advanced, taking care only that this deduction is correct. Now, whether the variety of phenomena which ought to exist according to this deduction occurs in actual experience or not – that I shall leave solely for you and for every observer to decide. True, I shall show at the proper time that, where the German in particular is concerned, he really has revealed himself as, according to our deduction, he was bound to. Where the foreigner of Teutonic origin is concerned, however, I shall have no objection if one among them really understands what is at issue here, if he succeeds in proving that his countrymen have in fact been just the same as the Germans, and if he is able to declare them completely free of the opposing characteristics. In general our description, even of these opposing characteristics, will by no means aim to paint an unfavourable and exaggerated portrait, which brings an easy victory though not an honourable one, but only indicate what follows of necessity, and to express this with as much honour as is compatible with the truth.

The first consequence of the fundamental difference which I indicated was this: among the people of the living language spiritual culture intervenes in life; among the opposites spiritual culture and life both go their separate ways. It will be useful to begin by elucidating the deeper sense of this proposition. In the first place, when we speak here of life and of the intervention of spiritual culture in the same, we mean original life and its onward flow from the source of all spiritual life, that is, from God; we mean the continued development [*Fortbildung*] of human relations according to their archetype [*Urbild*] and thus the creation of something new that has never before existed; but on no account do we mean here the mere preservation of those relations at the stage they have already reached as a safeguard against their decline, still less the assisting of individual members of the commonwealth who lag behind the general development [*Ausbildung*]. So, when we are speaking of spiritual culture, this should be taken to mean first and foremost philosophy – the foreign name we are obliged to use, since the German name proposed some time ago[23] has not found favour with the Germans – philosophy, I say, is what it should be taken to mean first and foremost. For it is philosophy that grasps scientifically the eternal archetype of all spiritual life. It is now claimed that with the people of the living language philosophy and all science based upon it influence life. Now, in apparent contradiction of this assertion, it has often been said, and said even by some among us, that philosophy, science, fine art and the like are ends in themselves and do not serve life; that to value them according to their usefulness in this regard is to degrade them. This is the place to qualify these assertions and to secure them against any misinterpretation. They are true in the following double but limited sense: first, science or art must not, as some have thought, desire to serve life at a certain lower level – for example, the earthly and sensuous life, or the edification of all; secondly, an individual, owing to his personal detachment from the totality of a spiritual world, can give himself over entirely to these particular branches of the universal divine life without the need for an external motive and can find complete satisfaction in them. But by no means are these

---

[23] Fichte has in mind his own notion of philosophy as *Wissenschaftslehre*.

assertions true in the strict sense, because the existence of more than one end in itself is just as impossible as the existence of more than one absolute. The one end in itself, beyond which there can be no others, is spiritual life. This expresses itself only in part and appears as an eternal stream that flows out of itself as from its own source; that is, as eternal activity. This activity constantly receives its model image [*Musterbild*] from science and the knack of shaping itself according to this image from art – and to this extent it might seem that science and art exist as means to the end of active life. But in this form of activity life itself is never completed, never becomes a closed unity; rather, it goes on to infinity. If life is indeed to exist as such a closed unity, then it must do so in another form. This form is that of pure thought [*Gedanke*], which is furnished by the religious insight I described in my third address; a form which as a closed unity simply diverges from the infinity of action [*Tun*] and can never be entirely expressed in action. Accordingly, both thought and activity are only apparently divergent forms. Beyond the world of appearance, however, they are both the same one absolute life; and we cannot possibly say that thought exists, and exists thus, for the sake of action or that action exists, and exists thus, for the sake of thought; but rather that both should simply exist, because even in appearance life ought to constitute a perfect whole, just as it does beyond the world of appearance. Within this sphere, therefore, and in consequence of these reflections, it is not enough to say that science influences life; rather, science is itself life, self-subsistent life [*in sich selbstbeständiges Leben*]. – Or, to tie this to a familiar phrase: What is the use of all knowledge, we hear people occasionally ask, if one does not act in accordance with it? In this question knowledge is viewed as a means for action [*Handeln*] and action as the true end. Conversely, one might ask: how can one do good without knowledge of the Good? And in this question knowledge is seen as the condition of action. Both questions, however, are one-sided. The truth is that both, knowledge as well as action, are in the same way inseparable components of the rational life.

However, science is only self-subsistent life (as we just expressed ourselves) when thought is the true mind and disposition of him who thinks, so that, without especial effort and even without his being clearly conscious thereof, he views and judges according to that fundamental thought everything else that he thinks, views and judges; and, should the fundamental thought influence his action, he acts according to it with equal necessity. But by no means is thought life and disposition if it is only thought as the thought of a foreign life – no matter how clearly and completely it might be conceived as one such merely possible thought, no matter how lucidly one might think how someone else could perhaps think thus. In this latter case there lies between our idle or speculative thinking [*gedachtes Denken*] and our actual thinking [*wirkliches Denken*] a wide field of chance and freedom. This freedom we are unwilling to consummate; and so that idle or speculative thinking remains apart from us, a merely possible thinking, one that has been set free of us and must always be freely recapitulated. In the former case thought has, by its own agency, immediately taken hold of our self and made it into itself; and through this reality that thought has thereby acquired for us we perceive its necessity. No freedom can forcibly bring about this result, as I have just said; rather, it must produce itself and thought itself must take hold of us and form us after itself.

Now, this living efficacy of thought is very much favoured, indeed even made necessary, if the thinking be only of the proper depth and strength – by thinking and designating in a living language. In a living language the sign itself is immediately alive and sensuous, representing anew the whole of its own life and thus taking hold of the same and intervening in it. To the possessor of such a language the spirit speaks directly, and reveals itself to him as one man to another. By contrast, the sign of a dead language does not immediately stimulate anything; to enter the living stream of the sign one must first recapitulate historical knowledge of an extinct world and transport oneself into a foreign mode of thought. How immeasurably powerful would have to be the drive of our own thinking for it not to grow weary in the vast dominion of history and rest content with more modest researches on its plains! If the thinking of one who possesses a living language does not come alive, then without hesitation we can accuse him of not having thought at all but only of having dreamt. In the same case we cannot immediately level this charge at the possessor of a dead language. He may indeed have thought after his own fashion and carefully evolved the concepts embedded in his language; only he did not do that which, were he to succeed, we should have to hail as a miracle.

Incidentally, it is evident that among a people with a dead language the drive to think will be most vigorous and bring forth its most eminent productions at the beginning, when the language is not yet clear enough on all sides; that as the language becomes clearer and more determinate, however, this drive gradually chokes and dies in the shackles of the same; that ultimately the philosophy of such a people will resign itself to the realisation that it is nothing but a commentary on the dictionary or, as an un-German spirit among us has expressed it in loftier-sounding terms, a metacritique of language;[24] finally, that such a people will recognise a mediocre didactic poem in comedy form on the subject of hypocrisy as their greatest philosophical work.[25]

In this way, I say, spiritual culture, and especially thinking in an original language, does not influence life, but is itself the life of him who thinks thus. Yet of necessity it strives to flow from this life that thinks thus towards another life beyond, to influence the existing general life and to shape it in its own image. For precisely because this thinking is life, its possessor feels a profound pleasure in its vitalising, transfiguring and liberating power. But every one in whom salvation has inwardly dawned necessarily desires that all others experience the same salvation, and he is driven to work towards ensuring that the source from which his well-being rose is spread to others also. It is otherwise with him who has grasped merely a foreign way of thinking as one possibility among others. As its content brings him neither weal nor woe, but only agreeably occupies and diverts him in his spare time, so he cannot believe that it can cause another person weal or woe, and in the end he thinks that it makes no difference on what one exercises one's ingenuity and with what one fills one's hours of leisure.

Of the means for introducing into general life [*das allgemeine Leben*] the thinking begun in the individual life the most excellent is poetry; and so poetry is the second main branch of a people's spiritual culture. When the thinker designates his thought in language (which, as we have said, cannot but happen symbolically) and creates new forms beyond the existing sphere of symbolic expression, he is already a poet; and if he is not, then with the first thought language will fail him and with his second attempt thinking itself. To transfuse the enlargement and completion of the symbolic sphere of language instigated by the thinker throughout the entire domain of symbols, so that each receives its proper share of the new spiritual ennoblement, so that life, right down to its ultimate sensuous foundation, appears bathed in the new radiance, pleases, and in unconscious

---

[24] The reference is to Johann Georg Hamann (1730–88), whose polemics against Kant are based on a rigorous linguistic analysis of his philosophical discourse (a 'metacritique'). Hamann introduced the term in his essay *Metacritique of the Purism of Reason* (1784), and it was later picked up by Johann Gottfried Herder, Friedrich Jacobi and Salomon Maimon, all critics of Kant.

[25] Molière's (1622–73) comedy *Tartuffe* (1669).

illusion is ennobled as if by itself – this is the task of true poetry. Only a living language can possess such poetry, for only in a living language can the symbolic sphere be expanded by creative thought; only in a living language do previous creations remain alive and open to the influx of kindred life. Such a language carries within it the capacity for an infinite poetry, eternally refreshed and renewed; for every stirring of living thought in it opens up a new vein of poetic inspiration. And so for a living language poetry is the best means of transfusing into general life the spiritual development [*Ausbildung*] that has been accomplished. A dead language can have no poetry at all in this higher sense of the word, because none of the advertised conditions for poetry are present in it. Nevertheless, a dead language can have a temporary surrogate for poetry in the following way. The outpourings of the poetic art already present in the ancestral language will stimulate interest. Though the newly formed people cannot follow the poetic path trodden by its forebears, for this is alien to its life, it can introduce its own life and new circumstances into the symbolic and poetic sphere through which preceding generations expressed their life and so, for example, dress its knights as ancient heroes and vice versa, and have the old gods exchange their raiment with the new ones. Precisely by being wrapped in an exotic mantle, the familiar will be endowed with a charm akin to the ideal, giving rise to quite pleasing forms. But both – the symbolic and poetic sphere of the ancestral language and the new circumstances of life – are finite and limited quantities; at some stage or other their interpenetration will be completed. Then this people will celebrate its golden age, and the source of its poetry will run dry. There comes a time when the fit between the closed words and the closed concepts, the closed symbols and the closed conditions of life, necessarily reaches its highpoint. Once this point has been passed, the people can do no more than either repeat its most successful masterpieces in modified form, so as to give them the appearance of novelty when in fact they are merely old and familiar works; or, if its members wish to be utterly new, resort to impropriety and indecency, so that in poetry they mix the ugly with the beautiful, and apply themselves to caricature and humour, in the same measure as in prose they are compelled to confuse concepts and muddle vice and virtue, if they desire to find new modes of expression.

When in a people spiritual culture and life both go their separate ways in the manner that I have described, the inevitable consequence is that the classes without access to the former – and which will not even receive, as happens in a living people, the fruits of this culture – are placed at a disadvantage compared to the cultivated classes, are considered, so to speak, a race apart, originally unequal by virtue of their mental powers and the mere fact of their birth; that the cultivated classes therefore have no true love or sympathy for them, no impulse to give them help from the bottom up, because they believe that, due to this original inequality, they cannot be helped at all; that the educated are rather roused to use them as they are and allow them to be so used. Even this consequence of a language's extinction can, when a new people first emerges, be mitigated by a humane religion and the absence of cunning in the higher ranks; but in the course of time this contempt for the people grows ever more naked and cruel. This general reason for the self-exaltation and grandiosity of the cultivated classes has been joined by a more particular factor, which, since it has had a very widespread influence even on the Germans, must not be overlooked here. The Romans, who at the beginning imitated the Greeks without embarrassment, and in comparison with these called themselves barbarians and their own language barbaric, subsequently passed on the appellation they had once borne and found among the Teutons the same true-heartedness as they themselves had shown to the Greeks. The Teutons believed they could not rid themselves of barbarism save by becoming Romans. Those tribes that had migrated to erstwhile Roman lands became Romans as far as it was in their power to do so. In their imaginations, however, the epithet 'barbarian' acquired all too quickly the secondary meaning of 'base', 'vulgar', 'ill-bred'; and 'Roman' thus became synonymous with 'noble'. This distinction reaches all the way down to the general and particular features of these Teutonic languages – in general since, where arrangements were made for a deliberate and conscious development of the language, these aimed at discarding the Germanic roots and forming words from Roman roots, thereby giving rise to Romance as the courtly and learned language; in particular, however, since almost without exception where two words have the same meaning, the one of Germanic derivation signifies what is ignoble and bad, the one of Roman derivation the more noble and excellent.

This malady, almost as if it were the original taint of the entire Teutonic race, afflicts even the German in the motherland, if he does not guard against it with high seriousness. To our ears also Roman words seem all too easily to have a noble ring, to our eyes also Roman manners appear more distinguished, and what is German vulgar; and since we were not so fortunate as to receive all of this firsthand, we enjoy it at secondhand and through the interagency of the new Romans. As long as we are German we seem to ourselves men like other men; if half or more than half of what we speak is un-German, if our conspicuous manners and clothing seem to have come from all too far away, then we think ourselves elegant; but the height of our triumph is no longer to be taken for Germans, but for Spaniards or Englishmen, depending on which of these is currently most in fashion. And we are right. Naturalness on the German side, arbitrariness and artifice on the foreign side – these constitute the fundamental difference. If we keep to the former, then we are just like our people as a whole; our fellow Germans understand us and see us as one of their own; only when we resort to the latter do they cease to understand us and hold us to be of a different nature. For the foreigner, this unnaturalness enters his life spontaneously, because he has departed originally and in an important respect from nature; we Germans must first actively seek out unnaturalness and accustom ourselves to the belief that something is beautiful, becoming and fitting that does not naturally appear so to us. The principal reason for all this is the German's belief in the greater distinction of the Romanised lands, together with his craving to put on equally distinguished airs, and artificially to establish in Germany, too, that divide between the higher orders and the people which in foreign lands developed naturally. It will suffice to have indicated here the primary source of the Germans' affectation of foreign manners [*Ausländerei*]. We shall show at another time how widespread this affectation has been; that all the evils which have led to our ruin are of foreign origin, yet were bound to bring disaster only when allied with German seriousness and the German capacity to influence life.

Besides these two phenomena resulting from the fundamental difference indicated earlier – that spiritual culture either intervenes in life or does not, that either there is a dividing wall between the cultivated classes and the people or there is not – I also mentioned a third, that the people speaking a living language shows diligence and earnestness and effort in all things, whereas the people speaking a dead language looks upon intellectual activity more as an ingenious game and lets itself be guided by its happy nature. This fact follows automatically from what I said above. Among the people with a living language inquiry proceeds from a vital need that must be satisfied, and thus receives all the necessary impulses that life carries with it. Among the people of the dead language inquiry is nothing more than a way of whiling away time in a manner that is agreeable and appropriate to their sense of the beautiful; and having done so, they have realised the goal of inquiry in full. With foreigners this phenomenon is almost necessary; with the German, where it appears, the harping on genius and happy nature is one facet of his undignified aping of all things foreign, which, like all such foreignisms, arises from the desire to put on airs. True, nothing first rate will ever be produced in any people in the world without an original impulse which, as something supersensuous, is rightly called by the foreign name genius. But by itself this impulse excites only the imagination and there projects forms that float in the air, never perfectly definite. For these to be finished and grounded in real life, so that they are given determinacy and stability, requires diligent, deliberate thought that proceeds according to a fixed rule. Genius provides diligence with the material to work on, and without the former the latter would have either only stuff that had already been fashioned or nothing at all. Diligence, however, introduces this material, which without it would remain an empty game, into life. Hence both genius and diligence are able to achieve something only in combination; separately they are ineffectual. Moreover, in a people with a dead language no truly creative genius can burst forth, because this people lacks an original faculty of designation [*Bezeichnungsvermögen*]. Rather, they can only continue what has already been started and carry it over into the pre-existing and completed designation.

As for the greater effort in particular, it naturally falls to the people with the living language. In comparison with another language a living language can stand at a higher level of development, but in itself it can never achieve the same completion and perfection that a dead language easily does. In the latter the range of words is closed, the possibilities for suitable combinations are also gradually exhausted; hence he who desires to speak this language must speak it as he finds it. But once he has learned it, the language speaks itself in his mouth, and thinks and poeticises for him. In a living language, however, if one really lives in it alone, words and their meanings constantly change and multiply, and this is precisely how new combinations become possible. The language that never is but is perpetually becoming does not speak itself; rather, whoever wishes to avail himself thereof must speak it himself after his own manner and re-create it to serve his own needs. Without doubt the latter requires more diligence and practice than the former. Likewise, as I already said above, the inquiries of the people with a living language probe right down to the point at which the concepts stream forth from spiritual nature itself. By contrast, the inquiries of a dead language seek only to penetrate a foreign concept and make it comprehensible, and hence are only historical and interpretative, whereas the former are truly philosophical. It goes without saying that an inquiry of the latter sort may be concluded sooner and more easily than one of the former.

Accordingly, the foreign genius will scatter flowers upon the beaten paths of antiquity and weave a fine robe to wrap around worldly wisdom; this is what easily counts as philosophy for him. Conversely, the German spirit will open up new shafts, bring daylight to their abyssal depths and mine rocks of thought from which future ages will build their dwelling-places. The foreign genius will be a delightful sylph, flitting gently over the flowers that have sprouted forth spontaneously from his soil, setting itself down without causing them to droop and absorbing their quickening dew; or a bee that busily and artfully gathers honey from these same flowers and deposits it, neatly ordered, in regularly constructed cells. The German spirit will be an eagle that with great power lifts its ponderous body skywards and with strong, much-practised wings beats the air and climbs closer to the sun whose aspect delights it.

Let us summarise everything I have said so far under one main head. Consider the overall cultural history of a race of men which historically has been divided into antiquity and modernity, and in particular the relation of the two principal tribes we have described to the original development of this modern world. That branch of the new nation which has become foreign has retained a far greater affinity to antiquity by virtue of having adopted its language. Initially, it will be much easier for this branch to grasp the language of antiquity even in its primitive and unchanged form, to penetrate the monuments of its culture, and to inject into these about as much fresh life as they need to adapt themselves to the new world. In short, this tribe will be the point of departure for the study of classical antiquity in all of modern Europe. Inspired by the tasks the ancient world has left unsolved, it will continue to work on these, but only as one tackles a task arising not from a vital need, but mere curiosity: taking it lightly, grasping it not with the mind [*Gemüt*] as a whole but only with the imagination, and shaping it into an airy and insubstantial body. With the wealth of material that antiquity has left behind and the ease with which one can work in this fashion, this tribe will introduce an abundance of such images into the horizon of the modern world. These images borrowed from the ancient world, already moulded into their new form and having now found their way to that branch of the aboriginal tribe which remained in the stream of original culture by virtue of retaining its language, will stimulate its attention and self-activity also; these images which, had they endured in the old form, might have passed it by, unheeded and unheard. But this branch of the race will, as surely as it really grasps them and does not just pass them on from hand to hand, grasp them in accordance with its nature, not in the mere knowledge of a foreign life but as an integral part of life; and thus not only derive them from the life of the modern world, but also introduce them once more into that life, incorporating what were previously merely airy figures in bodies that are solid and stable in the real vital element.

In this transformation, which the foreign tribes would never have been able to bring about by themselves, these now get back the productions they began. This channel alone makes possible the progress of the human race in the traces of antiquity, a union of its two main branches, and the steady onward flow of human development. In this new order of things the motherland will not invent anything in the proper sense of the word, but in the smallest as in the largest matter it will always be obliged to confess that it was stimulated by foreign countries, which were stimulated in their turn by the ancients. But what they projected only superficially and fleetingly the motherland will take seriously and integrate into life. This is not the place, as I said earlier, to demonstrate this relation with apposite and far-reaching examples, so we shall save it for the following address.

In this way both branches of the common nation remained as one, and only in this simultaneous separation and unity are they a graft on the trunk of ancient culture, which otherwise would have been interrupted by the new age, thus compelling humanity to begin all over again. Departing from different points of origin, but converging at their goal, each branch must now recognise both its own vocation and that of the other, and they must make use of each other in accordance therewith; but most especially each must set out to sustain the other and leave its particularity intact, if there is to be good progress in the general and complete culture of the whole. As for this knowledge, it would probably have to proceed from the motherland, for she is the first to have been endowed with the sense for profundity. But if foreign countries, in their blindness to such relations and carried away by superficial appearances, should ever aim to rob their motherland of independence, and thus to destroy and absorb her, then, should they succeed in their intention, they would thereby sever the last remaining thread still connecting them with nature and with life, and they would succumb entirely to spiritual death: that death which, with the passage of time, has revealed itself to be ever more visibly their essence. Accordingly, the hitherto constant flow of the culture of our race would indeed come to an end; a state of barbarism would return and, in the absence of salvation, advance until like wild beasts we all dwelt in caves once more and preyed on one another. That this is really so, that this must necessarily follow, only the German can see and he alone will see it. To the foreigner, who, since he knows no other culture, has unlimited scope to admire himself in his own, this must and may ever seem like the absurd blasphemy of ill-taught ignorance.

Foreign lands are the earth from which fruitful vapours detach themselves and rise cloudwards, through which even the old gods banished to Tartarus are still connected with the sphere of life. The motherland is the endless sky that envelops the earth, the sky where wispy vapours condense to form clouds, which, impregnated by the otherworldly bolt of lightning hurled by the Thunderer, fall as fructifying rain; rain that unites heaven and earth, allowing those gifts native to the former to take seed in the latter's womb. Do new Titans desire to storm heaven once more? For them, it will not be heaven, for they are earth-born; even the mere sight and influence of heaven will be removed from them, and only their earth remain behind to them as a cold, dark and infertile abode. But what, says a Roman poet,[26] what could Typhoeus avail and mighty Mimas, what Porphyrion in menacing pose, what Rhoetus, and that bold hurler of trees uptorn, Enceladus, as on they rushed against the ringing shield of Pallas? This selfsame shield will undoubtedly cover us too, if we understand how to place ourselves under its protection.

Note to p. 66

The decision as to the greater or lesser euphony of a language should not, in our opinion, be based on immediate impressions, which depend on so many accidental factors; rather, such a judgement would have to be traceable back to a sound principle. The merit of a language in this regard would undoubtedly consist in this, that in the first place it exhausted and comprehensively represented the capacity of the human speech organs; secondly, that it combined individual sounds in a natural and becoming fluency. From this it already follows that nations which develop their speech organs only halfway and one-sidedly, avoiding certain sounds or combinations of sounds under the pretext of their difficulty or

---

[26] Horace, *Odes*, III, 4, 53–8.

discordance, and which must find obviously melodious only those sounds that they can produce and are used to hearing, have no say in such an investigation.

Judgement on the German language in this regard, taking these higher principles into consideration, may be suspended here. The ancestral language of the Romans is itself pronounced by every modern European nation according to its own way of speaking, and to reconstruct the true pronunciation of Latin would be no easy matter. Accordingly, the only question remaining would be whether, compared to the neo-Latin languages, German sounds as cacophonous, harsh and coarse as some are inclined to believe.

Until this question is settled once and for all, we might at least provisionally explain why, to foreigners and Germans themselves, even if they are without prejudice, partiality or hate, it seems to be so. – An as yet uncultivated people blessed with a very lively imagination, a childlike mind and freedom from national vanity (all qualities the Teutons appear to have possessed) is attracted by what lies far away, and gladly transfers to distant lands and remote islands the objects of its desires and the glories whereof it dreams. There develops in such a people a *romantic* sense (the word is self-explanatory and could not be more aptly formed). Sounds and tones from those regions now strike this sense, rousing its whole world of wonders to life, and that is why they are pleasing.

That is perhaps why our countrymen who emigrated were so quick to renounce their own language for a foreign one and why even now its tones give us, their very distant relatives, such marvellous pleasure.

Exposition of German characteristics in history

In the last address we examined what the principal differences would be between a people that continued to develop in its original language and one that adopted a foreign language. We said on that occasion: as far as foreigners are concerned, we wished to leave it to each observer's judgement to decide whether those phenomena really occurred which, according to our assertions, were bound to occur; but as far as the Germans are concerned, we pledged to demonstrate that they really revealed themselves as, according to our assertions, the people with an original language was bound to reveal itself. Today we shall make good our promise and set forth the proof for our claims by examining, first of all, the last great and, in a certain sense, completed world deed [*Welt-That*] of the German people, the Reformation of the Church.

Christianity, which originated in Asia and by its corruption became more Asiatic than ever, preaching dumb submission and blind faith, was something strange and exotic even to the Romans. They never truly penetrated and appropriated it, and divided its essence into two incongruous halves; whereupon the attachment of the foreign part was accomplished with the aid of the melancholy superstition they had inherited from their ancestors. Among the immigrated Teutons this religion acquired adherents who had no prior intellectual training [*Verstandesbildung*] to hinder its acceptance, but also no hereditary superstition favourable to it. And thus it was presented to them as an essential appurtenance of a Roman, which is what they wanted to be, but without especial influence on their lives. It goes without saying that these Christian educators gave their new converts no more instruction in the old Roman culture – or language, as the vessel of that culture – than was compatible with their intentions; and herein too lies one of the reasons for the corruption and extinction of the Roman language in their mouths. When the true and authentic monuments of ancient culture later fell into the hands of these peoples and the drive to self-active thinking and understanding was thereby awakened in them, then – partly because this impulse was new and fresh to them, partly because no hereditary terror of the gods acted as a counterweight – the contradiction between their blind faith and the weird things which in the course of the ages had become the objects of that faith had to hit them far harder than even the Romans when they first encountered Christianity. When the absolute contradiction in what one has hitherto naively believed becomes apparent, it provokes laughter; those who had solved the riddle laughed and mocked, and the priests themselves who had likewise solved it joined in, safe in the knowledge that access to ancient culture, as a talisman against the enchantment, was open only to the very few. Here I am thinking in particular of Italy, the principal seat of neo-Roman culture at that time, with the other neo-Roman tribes still lagging far behind in every respect.[27]

They laughed at the deception, for there was not seriousness enough in them to be embittered. Through their exclusive possession of esoteric knowledge they became all the more surely a distinguished and cultivated class, and were able to accept the fact that the great multitude, for whom they had no feeling [*Gemüt*], remained in thrall to the deception and hence more tractable for their ends. And so it went on, with the people deceived and the man of distinction exploiting the deception and laughing the people to scorn; and, if there had been none save the neo-Romans in the modern age, things would probably have gone on in this way until the end of days.

Here you see clear proof of what we said earlier about the continuation of ancient culture by the modern and about the share which the neo-Romans can have in it. The new clarity dawned in antiquity, its rays first fell on the centre of neo-Roman culture; but there it was developed only as an insight of the understanding [*Verstandes-Einsicht*], without seizing and reshaping life.

But the prevailing state of affairs could not last much longer once this light fell on a soul whose religion was truly serious and reached down into life, once this soul was surrounded by a people to which it could easily communicate its more serious view of the matter, once this people found

---

[27] An allusion to the Italian humanists of the Renaissance.

leaders who set some store by its decisive need. However low Christianity might sink, it has nevertheless always retained a kernel of truth that is sure to stimulate life, if only that life is real and self-sufficient, namely the question: what must we do to become blessed? When this question fell on barren soil – where either it remained moot whether such a thing as blessedness was even seriously possible or, if this possibility was admitted, there was still no firm and resolute will to become blessed oneself – then on this soil religion had not from the very outset intervened in life and influenced the will; rather, it lingered in the memory and imagination only as a flickering and pale phantom, and thus all further elucidations regarding the state of existing religious concepts were naturally bound likewise to remain without influence on life. When, on the contrary, that question fell on an originally living soil, where there was an earnest belief in blessedness and the firm will to become blessed, and where the means to blessedness prescribed by the existing religion had been employed to that end with ardent faith and honest earnestness; then, once the light illuminating the nature of these means finally fell on this soil, which because of its very earnestness had been closed to that light for longer, a terrible disgust had to arise at the deception over the salvation of the soul. And the disquiet that drove one to achieve this salvation in other ways, and that which now appeared to lead only to eternal perdition, could not be taken in jest. Furthermore, the first individual to be gripped by this view of the matter could in no wise be content to save only his own soul whilst remaining indifferent to the welfare of every other immortal soul, because, according to his deeper religion, he would not thereby have saved even his own; rather, he had to wrestle with the same anxiety that he felt for his own soul in order to open the eyes of all men in the world to the contemptible illusion.

In this way, then, did the insight, which long before him a great many foreigners had had and perhaps in greater intellectual clarity [*Verstandesklarheit*], shine into the soul of that German man, Luther. In classical and elegant learning, in scholarship and in other virtues he was surpassed not only by foreigners but also by many men of his own nation. But he was moved by an almighty impulse – anxiety about eternal salvation – and this impulse became the life of his life, placing it constantly in the balance and giving him the strength and the gifts that posterity so admires. Though others may have had worldly goals in the Reformation, they would never have triumphed had there not stood at their head a leader inspired by the eternal. That he, who always saw that the salvation of every immortal soul was at stake, went fearlessly and in good earnest to do battle with all the demons of hell is natural and certainly no cause for wonder. This, then, is proof of German seriousness and German soul [*Gemüt*].

That in this matter, which was a purely human matter and which each individual had to take care of by himself, Luther turned to all men and in the first instance to the whole of his nation lay, as I have said, in the nature of things. How did his people receive this appeal? Did they remain in torpid repose, chained to the ground by their worldly affairs, and plodding along the familiar path undisturbed, or did the unusual manifestation of powerful inspiration merely provoke their laughter? Not at all: rather, the people were seized, as though by a perpetual flame, with the same concern for the salvation of the soul, and this concern quickly opened their eyes as well to perfect clarity, and they accepted with alacrity what was presented to them. Was this inspiration only a momentary exaltation of the imagination that did not hold its ground in life and against all its grave struggles and dangers? Not at all: the people renounced everything and bore every torment and fought in bloody wars of doubtful outcome, solely so that they would never again fall under the sway of the damnable papacy and instead the light of the Gospel, with its monopoly on salvation, might shine on them and their children also. And all the miracles that primitive Christianity laid before its first confessors were renewed for these men and women of a later age. Every utterance of that time is filled with this universal concern for blessedness. Here you see proof of the particularity of the German people. By inspiration they are easily lifted to all manner of inspiration and clarity, and their inspiration endures for life and reshapes it.

In earlier times and in other places, reformers had inspired masses of the people and gathered and formed them into communities. Yet these communities could find no permanence on the ground of the existing constitution, because the rulers and princes did not take their side. Luther's Reformation, too, seemed at the beginning to be reserved for a no more auspicious fate. The wise Elector, before whose eyes it began, seemed to be wise more in the foreign sense than in the German; he seemed not to have properly grasped the real question at issue, not to have attached much weight to what he saw as a dispute between two monastic orders,[28] and at most to be merely anxious about the good

---

[28] Friedrich III (known as the Wise), Elector of Saxony (1486–1525), founder of the University of Wittenberg, which became the spiritual centre of the Reformation. Luther was a member of the Augustinian order, whose rivals were the Dominicans.

reputation of his recently established university. But his successors,[29] though much less wise than he, were seized by the same earnest concern for blessedness that animated their people and, by means of this identity of conviction, became as one with them, joined in life or death, victory or defeat.

Here you see a proof of the aforementioned characteristic of the Germans as a totality and proof of their constitution as established by nature. The great affairs of the nation and of the world have been hitherto brought before the people by spokesmen who have stepped forward of their own volition. If its princes, out of a passion for things foreign, and out of a craving to affect airs and to sparkle, initially divorced themselves from the nation, abandoning or betraying it, nevertheless they were later easily moved to solidarity with it and took pity on their people. That the former has always been the case we shall demonstrate below by other proofs; that the latter will always remain the case we can but fervently hope.

Although we must now concede that in that age's anxiety about the salvation of souls an obscurity and unclarity remained – because it was not a matter of merely replacing the external intermediary between God and man but of dispensing with an external intermediary altogether and finding the bond of union within oneself – perhaps it was yet necessary that the religious development of humanity as a whole should pass through this middling stage. His honest zeal rewarded Luther with even more than he sought and led him far beyond his doctrinal edifice. After he had overcome the anguish of conscience caused by his bold break with the whole of the old faith, his every utterance is filled with jubilation and triumph at the freedom attained by the children of God,[30] who assuredly no longer sought blessedness outside themselves and beyond the grave, but were themselves an eruption of the immediate feeling of the same. In this he became the model for all future ages and worked on behalf of us all. – Here, too, is a characteristic of the German spirit. When it but seeks, it finds more than it sought; for it plunges into the stream of living life, which flows onwards of itself, and is carried away by its currents.

---

[29] Friedrich III was succeeded as both Elector and champion of the Reformation by his brother Johann the Steadfast (1468–1532), who was in turn followed by his son Friedrich Johann I, known as Johann the Magnanimous (1503–54).

[30] Allusion to the title of Luther's *On the Freedom of a Christian* (1520).

The papacy, taken and judged according to its own point of view, undoubtedly suffered an injustice in the way that it was understood by the Reformation. Its utterances were for the most part picked out at random from the existing language, exaggerated in Asiatic and rhetorical fashion, and intended to have whatever value they could bear; it reckoned that more than the due deduction would be made in any case, but they were never seriously measured, weighed or meant. With German seriousness the Reformation took them according to their full weight; and the Reformation was right to think one should take everything thus, but wrong when it believed that foreigners would do so and wrong when it censured them for things other than their natural shallowness and superficiality. Generally speaking, this is the ever-constant phenomenon in every conflict that pits German seriousness against the foreign, whether this foreignness be found at home or abroad – namely, that the latter simply cannot grasp how one can make a fuss over such apparently indifferent things as words and phrases; that foreigners, hearing it spoken again by a German mouth, claim not to have said what they did indeed say, still say and will always say. They complain of slander, which they call twisting their words [*Konsequenzmacherei*], when one takes their utterances literally, as if they were meant in earnest, and views them as elements of a consistent train of thought that can be followed back to its premises and forwards to its conclusions – but we are perhaps far from imputing to them a clear idea of what they are saying, or any consistency. In the demand that one must take everything as it is intended, but need go no further and call into question the right to have opinions and to express them – in that demand foreignism [*Ausländerei*] always betrays itself, no matter how deeply it may be concealed.

This seriousness with which the old system of religious instruction was taken compelled it in turn to become more serious than it had hitherto been: to undertake a new examination, reinterpretation and consolidation of the old doctrine, as well as to show greater caution in future both in doctrine and life. Let this, as well as what I shall presently say, serve as proof of the way in which Germany has always reacted on the rest of Europe. In general, the old doctrine was hereby rendered as harmless as it could be, if it could not be given up entirely; in particular, it presented to its defenders an opportunity and challenge to think more thoroughly and consequentially than had previously been the case. That the doctrine, which had been reformed in Germany, also spread into the neo-Latin countries and even there brought forth the same loftier inspiration is something we shall here pass over in silence, since it was but a fleeting phenomenon – although it is always worthy of remark that the new doctrine failed to achieve state-recognised permanence in any properly neo-Latin land. For it seems that to find this doctrine compatible with the highest authority, and to make it so, required German thoroughness on the part of the rulers and German good-heartedness on the part of the people.

In another respect, however, and this time not in relation to the people but to the cultivated classes, Germany has had through its reform of the Church a general and lasting influence on foreign countries; and through this influence arranged it so that these countries became once more its precursor and its own stimulus to new creations. Even in the preceding centuries, when the old doctrine held sway, free and self-active thinking – or philosophy – had often been stimulated and practised, but the object was by no means to bring forth truth out of itself, but only to demonstrate that the teaching of the Church was true and in what way. Among the German Protestants, too, philosophy was at first charged with the same task and became the handmaiden of the Gospel, just as among the Scholastics it had been the handmaiden of the Church. In foreign lands, which either had no Gospel or had not grasped it with the unalloyed devotion and profundity of soul characteristic of the Germans, the free thinking, inflamed by its glittering triumph, lifted itself higher and more easily, untrammelled by a belief in the supersensuous; but it remained caught in the sensuous trammels of the belief in a natural understanding that grew up without culture and custom;[31] and far from this free thinking discovering in reason the source of self-sustaining truth, the utterances of this coarse understanding became for it what the Church was for the Scholastics and the Gospel for the first Protestant theologians. Whether these utterances were true was not in doubt; the question at issue was merely how they could assert this truth in the face of competing claims.

Because this thinking did not even enter the domain of reason, whose resistance would have been more significant, it found no opponent save for the existing historical religion. This it easily got the better of by measuring religion against the standard of the sound understanding that it posited and showing clearly the contradiction between the two. And so it came about that, as soon as this was all put to rights, the word

---

[31] Fichte is referring to Jean-Jacques Rousseau.

'philosopher' came in foreign lands to be synonymous with 'irreligious man' and 'atheist' and brought the same honourable distinction.

The attempt to rise superior to all belief in external authority, which was the merit of these foreign endeavours, became a new stimulus for the Germans, with whose reform of the Church this movement had first started. To be sure, mediocre and dependent minds among us did no more than parrot this foreign teaching – better the foreign teaching, it seems, than that of their countrymen, which, though it was just as easy to come by, was thought less distinguished – and these minds sought, as well as they were able, to persuade themselves of it. But whenever a more independent German spirit stirred, the sensuous no longer sufficed. Rather, the task arose to seek in reason itself for the supersensuous, which, of course, was not to be taken on external authority, and thus to create for the first time philosophy proper by making free thinking the source of independent truth, as it ought to be. Towards this goal Leibniz strove in his struggle with foreign philosophy; and it was realised by the real founder of modern German philosophy, not without his confessing to having been roused by a foreigner's utterance, which had meanwhile been taken more seriously than it was intended.[32] Since that time we have solved the task completely and philosophy has been perfected, although we must be content to say: until an age comes that understands it.[33] If we assume this, the German motherland, stimulated by an antiquity passed on by the neo-Roman countries, would once again have created something new that had never before existed.

Before the eyes of our contemporaries foreigners have lightly and with fiery boldness seized on another task of reason and philosophy facing the modern world – the establishment of the perfect state – only shortly thereafter to abandon the same, so that they are compelled by their current situation to condemn the mere thought of the task as a crime and would have to strain every nerve in order, if they could, to expunge those

---

[32] Kant's famous remark in *Prolegomena to Any Future Metaphysics* (1783) that he was awoken from his 'dogmatic slumber' by David Hume.

[33] Cf. Fichte's description of the *Wissenschaftslehre* in a memo submitted to the Prussian cabinet in 1804: 'For a short time a system has been in existence, perfect in its external form, which prides itself on the fact that it is absolutely complete in itself, unchangeable and immediately clear; that it provides every other science with its first principles and guiding threads; that it thereby abolishes forever all strife and misunderstanding from the realm of science and unerringly leads the human spirit, which can be strengthened by it alone, to ever greater clarity in the only field of its infinite progress, empirical reality' (*GA* III/5, p. 222).

endeavours from the annals of their history.[34] The reason for this outcome is as plain as day: the state based on reason cannot be built by artificial measures out of any old material that lies to hand; rather, the nation must first be cultivated and educated for it. Only that nation which has first of all solved the task of educating the perfect human being, through actual practice, will also solve that of the perfect state.

Since our reform of the Church foreigners have more than once set about this last-named task of education, with spirit, though in keeping with their own philosophy, and for the moment their attempts have found among us adherents and exaggerators. We shall report in more detail at the proper time on the stage to which at last the German mind has once more in our days brought this matter.

What I have said has given you a clear overview of the entire cultural history of the modern world and of the ever-unchanging relationship of the various elements of the later age to the former. True religion, in the form of Christianity, was the germ of the modern world and its entire task was this: to transfuse this religion into the prior culture of antiquity and thereby to spiritualise and sanctify it. The first step on this path was to abolish from this form of religion its reliance on freedom-robbing external authority and also to introduce to it the free thinking of antiquity. The foreigner provided the stimulus for this step, but it was the German who took it. The second step, which is really the continuation and consummation of the first, is this: to discover this religion, and with it all wisdom, within ourselves. This step, too, the foreigner prepared and again it was the German who accomplished it. The next progression, which now and for evermore remains the order of the day, is the complete education of the nation to humanity. Without this, the philosophy we have gained will never enjoy widespread intelligibility, still less a general application to life; just as, without philosophy, the art of education will in turn never attain perfect clarity in itself. Both – education and philosophy – are thus interconnected and, if there is one without the other, incomplete and useless. Because the German has brought every step in the development of culture to completion (and for this he has been uniquely spared in the modern world) the same task falls to him with respect to education also. Once education is put to rights, the other affairs of humanity will swiftly follow.

---

[34] A reference to the French Revolution and an expression of Fichte's oft-stated conviction that it had been betrayed by Napoleon.

This, then, is the actual relation in which the German nation has hitherto stood to the ongoing development of the human race in the modern age. We are yet to shed more light on a remark I have already made twice about the natural course that this nation took in doing so, namely that in Germany all culture has proceeded from the people. That the matter of ecclesiastical reform was first brought before the people and met with success only because it became the people's affair – this we have already seen. But we must go further and demonstrate that this particular case has been the rule and not the exception.

The Germans who stayed behind in the motherland had retained all the virtues that were once native to their soil: loyalty, integrity, honour, simplicity; but as for cultivation to a higher life of the spirit, they had received no more than the Christianity of that time, and its teachers, could bring to men scattered far and wide. This did not amount to much, and they lagged a long way behind their emigrated kin in this respect. Though honest and upright, they were yet half-barbarians. Among them, however, there rose up cities built by members of the people. In these cities every branch of the life of culture rapidly put forth the most beautiful blossoms. In these cities there developed, on a small scale, but no less splendidly, civil government and civil institutions, and an image of order and a love of order spread out from them over the rest of the land. Their extensive trade helped to discover the world. Kings feared their alliance.[35] Their architectural monuments still survive and have defied the ravages of centuries; before them posterity stands admiringly and must concede its own impotence.

I shall not compare these burghers of the German imperial cities of the Middle Ages with the other estates of that period, nor inquire what the nobility and the princes were doing in the meantime; but in comparison to the other Teutonic nations, not counting a few strips of Italy, and in the fine arts the Germans did not lag behind even these, yet surpassed them in the applied arts and became their masters, – not counting these, the German burghers were now cultured and the others barbarians. The history of Germany, of German power, of German enterprises and discoveries, of German monuments and German spirit, is in this period exclusively the history of these cities, and everything else – the

---

[35] Fichte is thinking of the Hanseatic League, a powerful alliance of Baltic merchant guilds whose roots stretched back to the founding of the city of Lübeck in the twelfth century, and other medieval town leagues such as those in Swabia, the Rhineland and Saxony.

mortgaging and redemption of lands, and such like – is not worth mentioning. This epoch is also the only one in German history in which this nation stands in all its splendour and glory, holding the rank to which it is entitled as an aboriginal people. As its prosperity is destroyed by princely greed and thirst for power, and its freedom trampled underfoot, so the whole sinks gradually ever lower and approaches to its present state; as Germany declines, however, we see the rest of Europe likewise decline, in its essence and not merely in its outward appearance.

The decisive influence of this class, which was in effect the ruling class, on the development of the German imperial constitution, on Church reform, and on everything that was ever characteristic of the German nation and exported abroad is manifest everywhere one looks, and it can be shown that everything that is still venerable among the Germans arose in its midst.

And with what spirit did this German class bring forth and enjoy its heyday? With the spirit of piety, respectability, modesty, community. For themselves they needed but little, for public enterprises they went to immeasurable expense. Seldom does an individual name stand out and distinguish itself, because they were all of like mind and sacrificed themselves for the common weal. Under the same external conditions as were prevailing in Germany, free cities had emerged in Italy also. But compare the histories of both; weigh the continual unrest, the inner discord, even wars, the constant changing of regimes and rulers in Italy against the peaceful tranquillity and concord in Germany. Could it be any clearer that there must exist an intrinsic difference in the tempers of both nations? The German nation is the only modern European nation that has for centuries shown by the deeds of its burgher class that it is capable of supporting the republican constitution.

Of the individual and particular means of raising the German spirit once more, a very effective one would be the publication of an inspiring history of the Germans during this period, which would become a national book, a book for the people, such as the Bible or a hymn book are, until the day when we in turn accomplished something worthy of being recorded. Only instead of enumerating deeds and events like a chronicle, such a history ought to grip us in the most marvellous fashion and, without our co-operation or clear consciousness, transport us right into the midst of the life of those times, so that we seem to walk, to stand, to deliberate, to act with our forebears, and this is done not by childish and trashy fictions, as with so many historical romances, but by means of truth; and the deeds and events would blossom forth as illustrations of that same life. To be sure, such a work could only be the fruit of extensive knowledge and of researches perhaps never before undertaken; but the author would have to refrain from making a show of this knowledge and research, and present to us only the ripened fruit in the modern vernacular, in a manner that is intelligible to every German without exception. Besides this historical knowledge such a work would also demand a large measure of philosophical spirit, which would flaunt itself just as little; and above all a sincere and loving soul.

That time was the youthful dream of a nation moving in limited circles, a dream of future deeds, struggles and victories: and it was the prophecy foretelling what it would one day be when in full possession of its power. The blandishments of society and the allure of vanity have carried away the rising nation into circles that are not its own and, because it desired to shine there also, it finds itself covered with shame and fighting for its very survival. But has it really grown senile and impotent? Has not the source of original life ever since then and until this day continually gushed forth from it as from no other nation? Can those prophecies of its youth, which are confirmed by the qualities of the other peoples and by the developmental plan [*Bildungsplan*] of the entire human race, – can they remain unfulfilled? No longer. Let us first turn this nation back from the wrong path it has taken; show it in the mirror its childhood dreams, its true inclination, its true vocation, until in the midst of these meditations its power unfolds to embrace mightily its destiny. May this appeal help to bring forth a suitably equipped German man who very soon will solve this preliminary task!

A yet deeper understanding of the originality and Germanness of a people

In the foregoing addresses I have set forth, and demonstrated with reference to history, those characteristics which the Germans possess as an original people, and as one that has the right to call itself the people as such, in contradistinction to other tribes that have separated from it, just as the word 'German' in its proper signification denotes exactly that.[36] It will serve our purpose to dwell for another hour on this theme and engage with the possible objection that, if these are peculiarly German qualities, then one is bound to admit that at present there is little that is truly German left among the Germans themselves. Since even we cannot deny this phenomenon, but rather think to acknowledge it and survey it in its individual parts, we shall begin with an explanation thereof.

The relation of the original people of the modern world to the progress of this world's culture is this, that the former is first stimulated by the incomplete and superficial efforts of foreign lands to undertake more profound creations and develop them from its own midst. Since the process from stimulation to creation undoubtedly takes time, it is clear that such a relation will bring about periods in which the original people must seem almost entirely fused with foreigners and identical to them, because it finds itself in the state of merely being stimulated and the intended creation has not yet burst forth. It is in such a period that Germany currently finds itself with respect to the great majority of its cultivated inhabitants, and thence originate those symptoms of foreignism which course through the entire inner nature and life of this majority.

---

[36] The word 'deutsch' is derived from the Indo-European root *þeudō, via the Germanic *thiod* and Old High German *diutisc*, which translates as 'the people'.

We saw in the last address that philosophy, as free thinking released from the shackles of a belief in external authority, is the means by which foreign lands stimulate their motherland. Where this stimulus has not resulted in new creation (which, since the great majority remains incognisant of it, is the outcome in all except a very few cases), there partly that foreign philosophy which we described earlier itself takes on diverse forms, partly its spirit annexes the other sciences bordering most closely on philosophy and regards them from its own point of view; finally, since the German can never cast off his seriousness and his immediate intervention in life, so this philosophy influences public life and its principles and rules. This we shall demonstrate piece by piece.

First and foremost and above all else: man does not form his scientific view freely and arbitrarily, one way or another. Rather, it is formed for him by his life and it is actually the internal root of his life itself, otherwise unknown to him, manifested as an intuition. That which you really and inwardly are steps before your outward eye, and you are unable ever to see anything else. To see differently, you would first have to become different from what you are. Now, the intrinsic nature of the foreign – that is to say, non-originality – is the belief in something final, fixed, immutably permanent; the belief in a limit, on this side of which free life pursues its sport but which life is unable ever to break through, to dissolve and flow into. At some point, therefore, this impenetrable limit, too, necessarily appears before the foreigner's eyes, and he cannot think or believe save by assuming such a limit, unless his entire essence be transformed and his heart torn from his body. He necessarily believes in death as the first and the last, as the original source of all things – even of life.

We should begin by indicating how this basic belief of the foreigner currently expresses itself among the Germans.

It expresses itself first and foremost in philosophy proper. German philosophy of the present day, insofar as it is worthy of mention here, aspires to thoroughness and scientific form, despite its inability to attain these; it aspires to unity, and that also not without an earlier foreign precedent; it aspires to reality and essence – not mere appearance, but the foundation thereof that itself appears in the world of appearance. And in all these points it is right and far surpasses the leading foreign philosophies practised abroad at this time, because it is more thorough and consistent in its foreignism than these. This foundation that is to underlie mere appearance is, according to the further and yet more erroneous determinations of our philosophers, always a fixed being which is what it is and nothing more, wrapped up in itself and bound to its own essence; and thus death and the estrangement from originality, which reside in the philosophers themselves, also step out before their eyes. Because they are unable by themselves to soar up to life simply as such, but always need a support and a crutch for their ascent, they never get beyond this support in their thinking either, which is the reflection of their life: that which to them is not something is necessarily nothing,[37] because between that congealed being and nothingness their eye sees nothing else, since there is nothing else in their life. Their feeling, which is the sole authority to which they can appeal, seems to them infallible; and if someone does not concede this support, they are far from assuming that he has no need of it and is content with life alone. Rather, they believe that he lacks only the astuteness to observe the support, which doubtless bears him too; that he lacks the ability to soar up to their lofty vistas. For this reason, it is vain and impossible to set them right: one would have to, if one could, remake them and remake them differently. In this respect, German philosophy of the present day is not German, but a foreignism.

Conversely, true philosophy, which is complete in itself and has penetrated beyond appearance to its very core, proceeds from the one, pure, divine life, – from life simply as such, which is what it will remain for all eternity, ever one; but not from this or that particular life. It sees how this life endlessly closes and opens again only in the world of appearance, that only by reason of this law is there a being and a something at all. For this philosophy being arises, whereas the other assumes it as given. And so only this philosophy is properly German, that is, original; and inversely, if someone were a true German, then he would not be able to philosophise in any other way.

That system of thought which, although it prevails among the majority of those who philosophise in the German manner, is nevertheless not properly German encroaches, whether it is consciously established as a specific philosophical theory or whether it only unconsciously underpins the rest of our thinking – it encroaches, I say, on the other scientific views of the age; for it is the principal endeavour of our time, a time stimulated by foreign lands, no longer merely to hold fast to scientific material in the memory, as our forefathers did, but to elaborate it by independent

---

[37] A veiled response to those, such as F. H. Jacobi, who had accused Fichte's *Wissenschaftslehre* of nihilism because beyond the original I there was 'nothingness' (cf. *GA* III/3, p. 223).

thinking and philosophising. As regards the endeavour in general, the age is right; but if, as is to be expected, in carrying out this philosophising, it starts from the foreign philosophy of death, it will be wrong. We wish here to cast a glance only at those sciences which border most closely on our scheme as a whole, and seek out the foreign notions and views that pervade them.

That the establishment and government of states is regarded as a free art with its own fixed rules – in this foreign lands have undoubtedly served as our forerunners and they in turn have followed the example of antiquity. In what will such foreign lands – which already in the element of their thinking and willing, in language, possess a fixed, closed and dead support – and all those who follow them in this respect, hold this state-craft to consist? Without doubt in the art of discovering a likewise fixed and dead order of things, from which deadness the vital activity of society is held to proceed, and proceed in the manner intended; in the art of assembling all life in society into a huge, artificial pressure engine and wheelwork, in which each individual part is always compelled by the whole to serve the whole; in the art of solving an arithmetical problem by advancing from finite and concrete quantities to an ascertainable sum, and so, from the premise that each desires his own good to the conclusion that he must be compelled precisely thereby, against his wish and will, to promote the general good. Foreign lands have expressed this principle in manifold ways and delivered masterpieces of this art of social mechanics; the motherland has taken up this theory and further adapted its applica-tion to the production of social machines – and here too, as always, more comprehensively, profoundly, truly, far surpassing its original model. In the event of the previously smooth operation of society grinding to a halt, such statecraftsmen know no other explanation save that one of the cogs must have worn out and are acquainted with no other remedy than this: to remove the faulty cogs and replace them with new ones. The more someone is rooted in this mechanical view of society, the more he under-stands how to simplify this mechanism, by making all parts of the machine as alike as possible and treating them all as uniform materials, then the greater the statecraftsman he is reckoned to be, and rightly so in our age; – for we are even worse off with one who is indecisive, hesitant and incapable of firm opinion.

This view of statecraft inspires respect by its iron rigour and sem-blance of grandeur. It also renders good service, up to a certain point, particularly where there is a tendency towards monarchical and ever purer forms of monarchical government. Once it has arrived at this point, however, its impotence is plain to see. Let us assume that you had obtained for your machine the intended perfection, and that each of its lower parts is unfailingly and irresistibly compelled by a higher part, which is itself compelled from above to exert compulsion on those below it, and so on, right to the very top. Then what compels your final part, in which all compulsion in the machine originates? Suppose you have overcome, just like that, all resistance which might arise from the friction of the parts against that last mainspring and have imparted to it a force compared with which all other force vanishes to nothing, something that you alone can achieve by mechanical means; suppose you have therefore created the most powerful monarchical constitution; how, then, do you mean to set this mainspring in motion and compel it to see and will what is right without exception? How, then, do you mean to insert into your correctly calculated and calibrated but stationary wheelwork that which is eternally in motion? For example, as you occasionally suggest in your embarrassment, should the whole mechanism react on itself and set off its first mainspring? Either this occurs through a force that itself issues from the activation of the mainspring, or it occurs through a similar force that does not issue therefrom but rather obtains in the whole itself, independent of the mainspring; there is no third possibility. Assume the first alternative, and you end up in a circularity that negates all thought and the entire operation of the mechanism; the whole works can compel the mainspring only insofar as it is itself compelled by the spring to do so – insofar as the mainspring compels itself directly – but if it does not compel itself, the very deficiency we wished to remedy, then no motion at all results. Assume the second, and you confess that all motion in your works originates in a force that does not figure at all in your calculations and plans, a force that is not bound at all by your mechanism, a force that without a doubt, and without your co-operation, acts as it can according to its own laws which are unknown to you. In each case you must confess yourselves to be blunderers and impotent braggarts.

Some have indeed felt this, and so under this system which, with its reliance on compulsion, need not concern itself with the other citizens, they have wanted to educate at least the prince, from whom all motion in society proceeds, by all manner of good teaching and instruction. But how does one mean to ensure that one will alight on a nature at all susceptible of being educated as a prince; or, if one had the happy fortune to come across such a specimen, that he, whom no man can coerce, will be obliging and inclined to submit to discipline? Such a view of statecraft is, regardless of whether we encounter it on foreign or on German soil, always foreignism.[38] For the honour of German blood and temper [*Geblüt und Gemüt*], however, we must here observe that, whatever skill we might have shown in the mere theory of these calculations of force [*Zwangsberechnungen*], when it came to putting them into practice we were nevertheless too hampered by the obscure feeling that it does not have to be like this and in this respect we lagged behind foreign lands. Should we therefore also be required to accept the gift of alien forms and laws intended for us, then at least let us not be unduly ashamed of doing so, as if our wit had been incapable of soaring up to the same heights of legislation. Since, when we merely have the pen in our hand, we are inferior to no nation, so might we have felt that this too is not yet the right thing for life, and thus would rather preserve the old until we achieve perfection, instead of merely exchanging the old fashion for a new and equally feeble one.

It is otherwise with genuinely German statecraft. It too desires stability, security and independence from blind and irresolute nature, and on this count it finds itself in complete agreement with foreign lands. Only it does not demand, like the latter, something fixed and certain as the primary element through which the spirit, as the second, is made certain; rather, it demands from the outset, and as the very first and only part, a fixed and certain spirit. This spirit is for it the mainspring whose life issues from itself and is perpetually in motion, the mainspring that will order the life of society and keep it moving. It understands that one can bring forth this spirit not by castigating one's already degenerate adulthood, but only by educating the still unspoilt years of youth; and with this education it does not, like foreigners, mean to address itself only to the lofty peak – that is, the prince – but also to the broad base, the nation, to which the prince too undoubtedly belongs. Just as the state, in the person of its adult citizens, represents the continued education of the human race, so, according to this statecraft, the future citizen must first be reared to be receptive to this higher education. In this way, the German and most modern model of statecraft becomes once again the oldest; for the Greeks also established citizenship on the basis of education and cultivated such citizens as were never seen again by subsequent ages. Henceforth the German will do what in form is the same, though in

---

[38] An allusion to Machiavelli's *The Prince*.

content it will be imbued with a spirit not narrow-minded and exclusive, but universal and cosmopolitan.

The same foreign spirit prevails among the great majority of our people even in their view of the entire life of a race of men and of history as an image of that life. A nation, the foundation of whose language is closed and extinct, can, as we showed on another occasion,[39] attain in all the arts of speech only a certain stage of development permitted by that foundation. This will be its golden age. Without the greatest modesty and self-denial such a nation cannot reasonably think more highly of the whole race than it does of itself; it must therefore assume that for the race, too, there exists a final, supreme and unsurpassable goal of development. Just as a species of animal such as the beaver or the bee still builds today as it built thousands of years ago, and during this long period of time has made no advances in its art, so, they will say, do matters stand with that species of animal called man in every branch of his development. These branches, drives and abilities can be surveyed exhaustively, indeed perhaps in a few members will present themselves to the eye, and then it will be possible to indicate the highest development of each one of them. Perhaps the human race in this respect will be much worse off than the race of beavers or bees, for the latter, though it learns nothing new, yet never declines in its art, whereas man, when once he has reached the summit, is flung back down again and may toil for hundreds or thousands of years to get back to the point at which he ought rather to have been left. The human race, these nations will say, must undoubtedly already have achieved such pinnacles of cultural development; to trace these golden ages in history, to judge all endeavours of humanity in their light, and to trace them back to these endeavours will be their most zealous study. According to these nations history is long since finished and has already been finished many times; according to them there is nothing new under the sun, for beyond and beneath the sun they have obliterated the source of eternal life, and let only ever-recurring death repeat and assert itself time after time.

It is well known that this philosophy of history has come to us from abroad, although at the present time its echo is fading even there and has become almost exclusively German property. From this deeper kinship it follows that this philosophy of history of ours can so thoroughly understand the efforts of foreign lands (which, even if they no longer

[39] In the Fifth Address; see above, p. 65.

often express this view of history, yet do more by acting in accordance with it and building a new golden age), can even divine and mark out the path that still lies before them and can admire them so sincerely, as one who thinks as a German cannot boast of doing. And how could he? Golden ages are for him in every respect a limitation imposed by deadness. Gold may be the most precious material lying in the lap of dead earth, he thinks, but the stuff of the living spirit lies beyond the sun, beyond all suns, and is their source. For him, history, and with it the human race, does not unfold according to the hidden and strange law of a round dance; in his view the true and authentic man fashions history himself, not merely repeating what has been before but creating something wholly new in the stream of time. Hence he never expects mere repetition; and should it nevertheless occur, word for word, as written in the old book, then at any rate he does not admire it.

In a similar manner the deadening foreign spirit spreads, without our being distinctly conscious thereof, over our other scientific views, to demonstrate which the examples already cited will suffice. This happens because at this very moment we are adapting after our own fashion the stimuli we received earlier from foreign lands, and are passing through such a transitional phase. I have adduced these examples because it was relevant to the matter in hand; but also, incidentally, so that no one may think he can confute the assertions expressed here by inferring conclusions from the principles I have indicated. Far from those principles having remained unknown to us or our being unable to rise to their heights, we in fact know them very well and might, if we had more time, find ourselves capable of working backwards and forwards through their logical consequences; we discard them at the very outset, and thus everything that follows from them, of which more resides in our traditional thinking than the casual observer might easily suspect.

As with our scientific view, this foreign spirit influences our ordinary life and its rules; but so that this be clear and the foregoing yet clearer, it is necessary first of all to examine the essence of original life, or of freedom, with a more penetrating gaze.

Freedom in the sense of undecided wavering between several equally possible alternatives is not life, but only the vestibule and portal of real life. At some time this state of wavering must finally come to an end and a move be made towards decision and action, and only then does life begin.

Now, immediately and at first glance each decision of the will appears as something primary, by no means as something secondary, as the effect of something primary that is its cause – but as simply existing through itself and existing as it is. This is the only possible intelligible meaning of the word 'freedom'. But with respect to the inner content of such a decision of the will, two cases are possible: either only appearance appears in it, separate from essence and without essence entering into its appearance in any way, or essence itself appears in this appearance of a decision of the will. In this connection it must be remarked at once that essence can become appearance only in a decision of the will and in nothing else, although conversely there may be decisions of the will in which essence does not emerge at all – only mere appearance. Let us discuss the latter case first.

Mere appearance, simply as such, is unalterably determined by its separation from and opposition to essence, as well as by the fact that it is capable of appearing and representing itself, and hence it is necessarily just what it is and turns out to be. If therefore, as we are assuming, the content of some given decision of the will is mere appearance, then it is to that extent not free, primary and original, but necessary and secondary, a part proceeding just as it is from something higher and antecedent, from the law of appearance in general. Since, as I have had occasion to remind you more than once, the thinking of man represents him as he really is to himself, and remains ever the true imprint and mirror of his inner being, then such a decision of the will, even though it appears free at first glance precisely because it is a decision of the will, by no means appears as such to repeated and deeper thought; rather, it must be conceived as necessary, just as it is in reality and in fact. For those whose will has not yet soared up to a higher sphere than that in which a will merely appears in them, the belief in freedom is nothing but the delusion and fancy of a fleeting and superficial intuition; in thinking alone, which everywhere shows them only the bonds of strict necessity, do they find truth.

The first and fundamental law of appearance, simply as such (we omit to indicate its ground all the more readily since I have done so in sufficient detail elsewhere),[40] is this, that it resolves into a manifold which in a certain respect is infinite and in a certain other respect a closed whole; in which closed whole of the manifold each individual part is

---

[40] Cf. *CPA*: 'But that view only can be called philosophical which refers back to the multiform phenomena which lie before us in experience to the unity of one common principle, and, on the other hand, from that one principle can deduce and completely explain those phenomena' (Lecture I, p. 2).

determined by every other part, and every other part in turn is determined by this individual part. In the event, therefore, that in the individual's decision of the will nothing erupts into appearance but the possibility of appearance [*Erscheinbarkeit*] and of representation [*Darstellbarkeit*], and visibility [*Sichtbarkeit*] in general, which is in fact the visibility of nothing, then the content of such a decision of the will is determined by the closed whole of every possible decision of the will of this and every other possible individual will; and it contains and can contain nothing more than that which remains to will after subtracting all those possible decisions of the will. Hence there is nothing independent, original and specific in it; on the contrary, it is something secondary, the mere consequence of the general connection of the whole of appearance in its individual parts; and, indeed, it has ever been recognised as such by all who found themselves at this stage of culture, yet were capable of thinking with thoroughness, and who expressed this recognition of theirs with the same words as those of which we just now availed ourselves; but all this because in them not essence but only mere appearance enters into appearance.

Conversely, where essence itself enters into the appearance of a decision of the will directly and, as it were, in person and not by proxy, there everything that was mentioned earlier as following from the appearance as a closed whole is likewise present, for appearance appears here also; but such an appearance is not reducible to this component part nor exhausted by it. Rather, there is in this appearance yet something more [*ein Mehreres*], another component that cannot be explained by that connection, but is left over after what is explicable has been subtracted. That first component obtains here too, I said. That surplus [*Mehr*] becomes visible and, by means of its visibility and not at all by means of its inner essence, it comes under the general law and conditions of manifestness [*Ersichtlichkeit*]; but it is still more than that which results from some law or other and which is therefore necessary and secondary. In respect of this moreness, it is what it is through itself, something truly primary, original and free, and hence it also appears as such to that thinking which is deepest and has been brought to a conclusion. The supreme law of manifestness is, as I have said, this: that what appears divides itself into an infinite manifold. That surplus becomes visible, always as more than that which proceeds at each moment from the connection of appearance, and so on to infinity; and thus this surplus itself appears as something infinite. But it is as plain as day that it partakes of this infinity only because each time it is visible and thinkable and discoverable solely by being opposed to and more than that which goes forth to infinity out of the connection of the appearance. Apart from this need of thinking it, however, the surplus is indeed this more-than-all that is infinite, which has the power to represent itself to infinity; it is so from the beginning, in pure simplicity and immutability, and in all infinity it does not become more than this more, nor does it become less. Only its manifestness as more than the infinite – and in no other way can it become visible in its highest purity – creates the infinite and all that appears to appear in it. Now, where this surplus actually enters as such a manifest [*ersichtlich*] surplus, but can only enter in an act of will, there essence itself, which alone exists and alone can exist, and which exists of and through itself, divine essence, enters into appearance and renders itself immediately visible; and there, for that very reason, is true originality and freedom, and so there is also a belief in them.

And so to the general question of whether man is free or not there is no general answer; for precisely because man is free, in the lower sense, because he begins with indecisive wavering and vacillating, he can be either free or not free, in the higher sense of the word. In reality the way in which someone answers this question is the unclouded mirror of his true inward being. Whoever is indeed nothing more than a link in the chain of appearances may well fancy himself free for a moment, but more rigorous thought does not sustain this fancy. As he finds himself, however, so he necessarily conceives his entire race. Conversely, he whose life is seized by the true life, and whose life has sprung forth directly from God – he is free and believes in freedom both in himself and in others.

He who believes in a fixed, stable and dead being does so only because he is himself dead within; and once he is dead, he cannot but believe thus, as soon as he becomes clear to himself. Both he and all his kind from beginning to end seem to him secondary and a necessary consequence of some antecedent term that he must presuppose. This presupposition constitutes his actual thinking, by no means merely his idle or speculative thinking; it is his true mind, the point at which his thinking itself immediately becomes life; and it is thus the source of all the rest of his thinking and of his judging of his race in its past, which is history, in its future, which is his expectations of it, and in its present, which is the actual life of him and others. We have called this belief in death, as opposed to an original living people, foreignism. This foreignism, when once it is found among the Germans, will reveal itself in their actual life also, as quiet resignation to the now unalterable necessity of our being, as the abandonment of all hope of improving ourselves or others through freedom, as the propensity to use ourselves and all others as they are, and to draw from their being the greatest possible advantage to ourselves; in brief, as the profession of the belief, reflected constantly in all the activities of life, in the universal and uniform sinfulness of all men, a belief that I have described adequately elsewhere.[41] I shall leave it to you to read up on this description, as well as to judge how far it tallies with the present. This way of thinking and acting originates in the inward state of deadness, as I have often reminded you, only by it becoming clear to itself; whereas as long as it remains in obscurity, it retains the belief in freedom, which is true in itself and a delusion only when applied to its present being. Here the disadvantage of clarity with internal wickedness is distinctly evident. As long as this wickedness remains obscure, it is constantly disturbed, pricked and impelled by the perpetual demand for freedom, and offers a point of attack to attempts to improve it. But clarity perfects this wickedness and rounds it off within itself; clarity adds to it cheerful resignation, the peace of a good conscience, self-complacence. What they believe comes to pass; they are henceforth incorrigible and fit for nothing in the world save at most for keeping alive in those who are better the pitiless loathing of evil or submission to the will of God.

And so what we have understood by Germans in our description thus far finally stands out in perfect clarity. The proper ground of distinction lies in whether one believes in something absolutely primary and original in man himself, in freedom, in infinite improvability, in the perpetual progress of our race; or whether one does not and indeed fancies that one distinctly perceives and grasps that the opposite of these things holds true. All who either live creatively, bringing forth the new themselves, or, should this not have fallen to their lot, at least decisively abandon things of vanity and keep watch to see whether somewhere they will be caught by the stream of original life, or, should they not have made it this far, at least have an inkling of freedom and do not hate or fear it, but love it: all these are original men; they are, when viewed as a people, an original people, the people as such: Germans. All who resign themselves to being secondary and derivative, and who distinctly know and understand themselves thus, are indeed secondary and derivative, and become ever more so through this belief of theirs; they are an appendage to life, which stirred before them or beside them out of its own motive force, they are

[41] See *The Way Towards the Blessed Life*, Lecture XI [Fichte's note].

an echo resounding from the cliff-face, an echo of a voice that has already fallen silent; they are, viewed as a people, outside the original people and strangers and foreigners unto it. In the nation that to this day calls itself the people as such, or Germans, originality has in the modern age, at least until now, burst forth into the light of day, and the creative power of the new has shown itself; now, through a philosophy that has become clear to itself, a mirror is held up to this nation, a mirror in which it shall recognise with a clear concept what, without distinct consciousness thereof, it has hitherto become through nature and what destiny she has ordained for it. And to this nation a proposal is made, according to this clear concept and with deliberate and free art, an art complete and whole: to make itself into what it ought to be, to renew the covenant and to close its ranks. The principle according to which it must close its ranks we have laid before the nation. Those who believe in spirituality and in the freedom of this spirituality, who desire the eternal progress of this spirituality through freedom – wherever they were born and whichever language they speak – are of our race, they belong to us and they will join with us. Those who believe in stagnation, retrogression and circularity, or who even set a dead nature at the helm of world government – wherever they were born and whichever language they speak – are un-German and strangers to us,[42] and the sooner they completely sever their ties with us the better.

And so, supported by my above remarks on freedom, what this philosophy that rightly calls itself German philosophy actually wants, and wherein it is opposed with earnest and unrelenting rigour to every foreign philosophy with a belief in death, is finally given voice, and he that hath ears to hear, let him hear.[43] And it is given voice not so that those who are dead shall understand it, which is impossible, but so that it shall become more difficult for them to twist its words and pretend they want roughly the same thing and at bottom are of the same mind. This German philosophy raises itself truly and by the act of its thinking – by no means merely boasting, on the basis of some obscure notion, that it must be so but without being able to effect it, – it raises itself to the immutable 'more than all infinity' and finds true being in this alone. Time and eternity and infinity it sees go forth from that oneness as it appears and becomes visible, that oneness which in itself is invisible and

---

[42] Here and in the passage that follows Fichte is sniping at Schelling and his *Naturphilosophie*.
[43] An allusion to Matthew 11: 15.

grasped, correctly grasped, only in its invisibility. This philosophy holds that even infinity is nothing in itself and has no true being at all: it is solely the means whereby that which alone exists, and exists only in its invisibility, becomes visible, and wherefrom an image, a schema and shadow of itself is constructed in the sphere of imagery [*Umkreis der Bildlichkeit*]. Everything else that may become visible within this infinity of the world of images [*Bilderwelt*] is now wholly a nothing born of nothing, a shadow of a shadow, and solely the means by which that first nothing of infinity and of time becomes itself visible and opens up to thought the ascent to invisible and unimageable being.

Within this single possible image of infinity the invisible now immediately emerges only as free and original life for sight, or as a rational being's decision of the will, and cannot emerge and appear in any other way whatever. All stable existence that does not appear as spiritual life is only an empty shadow cast from the domain of sight, a shadow multiply mediated by nothingness, in opposition to which, and by recognising it as multiply mediated nothingness, sight too should raise itself to the recognition of its own nothingness and the acknowledgement of the invisible as the only thing that is true.

That philosophy of being with its belief in death, which even advances to become a philosophy of nature, the deadest of all philosophies, remains caught in these shadows of shadows, fearing and worshipping its own creation.

This permanence is now the expression of its true life, and of its love, and herein this philosophy is to be believed. But if this philosophy then goes on to say that the being which it presupposes as actually existing is one and the same as – is identical with – the Absolute, then it is not to be believed, no matter how often it might make this assertion and swear under oath that it was true. It does not know this, but is only guessing, parroting another philosophy[44] that it does not dare to dispute on this point. If it did know this, then it would have to proceed not from duality as an incontestable fact, which it decrees abolished yet still leaves intact, but from unity; and from this unity it would be able to derive duality and with it all multiplicity in an intelligible and lucid manner. But that requires thought, reflection that is followed through to its conclusion. Partly, this philosophy has not learned the art of such thinking, is wholly incapable of it and can but daydream; partly, it is hostile to this thinking,

---

[44] That of Spinoza.

and refuses even to attempt it, because to do so would disturb its fond illusion.

This is wherein our philosophy is earnestly opposed to that philosophy, and on this occasion we wished for once to express and bear witness to this fact as clearly as possible.

What a people is in the higher sense of the word and what is love of fatherland

The last four addresses answered the question: what is the German in opposition to other peoples of Teutonic descent? This line of argument in support of our inquiry as a whole will be completed if we further add the examination of the question: what is a people? This latter question is identical with, and at the same time helps to answer, another question, often raised and resolved in very different ways: what is love of fatherland? Or, as one might more accurately express oneself: what is the love of the individual for his nation?

If we have thus far proceeded aright in the course of our inquiry, then it must be evident that only the German – the original man whose spirit has not become dead in some arbitrary organisation – truly has a people and is entitled to reckon on one; that only he is capable of real and rational love for his nation.

The following observation, which at first seems to have no connection with the foregoing, will set us on the way to solving our appointed task.

Religion, as we had cause to remark already in our third address, is quite able to transport us beyond all time, and beyond the present, sensuous life, without the least injury to the justness [*Rechtlichkeit*], morality and sanctity of the life seized by this faith. Even with the certain conviction that all our activity on this earth will not leave behind the slightest trace or bear even the smallest fruit, that the divine can indeed be perverted and used as an instrument of evil and yet deeper moral corruption, we can still continue this activity solely to maintain the divine life that has broken forth in us and in relation to a higher order of things in a world to come, in which nothing that is done in God shall perish. Thus the apostles, for example, and the earliest Christians in general, were even in life transported wholly beyond the earth by their belief in heaven; and they renounced the affairs of the world – state, fatherland and nation – so completely that they no longer even deemed these worthy of their attention. However possible this may be and however easy for faith; however cheerfully we must resign ourselves, if it be the unalterable will of God, to having an earthly fatherland no more and finding ourselves outcasts and slaves here below: this is nevertheless not the natural way of the world, it is not the rule, but a rare exception. It is also a very perverse use of religion (of which Christianity, among others, has frequently been guilty), if it proceeds from the outset and without regard for the circumstances at hand to recommend withdrawal from the affairs of state and nation as a truly religious conviction. In such a situation, if that conviction is sincere and not merely brought about by religious enthusiasm, temporal life forfeits its self-subsistence [*Selbstbeständigkeit*] and becomes merely a forecourt of the true life, a severe trial tolerated solely out of obedience and submission to the will of God – and in this view it becomes true that, as many have imagined, immortal spirits are plunged into earthly bodies, as into prisons, simply as a punishment.[45] In the regular order of things, however, earthly life should itself be true life, a life one can rejoice in and enjoy with gratitude, even in the expectation of a higher one. And although it is true that religion is also the consolation of the unjustly oppressed slave, nevertheless this is above all the meaning of religion: that one resists enslavement and refuses to allow religion to degenerate into the last consolation of the captive. It suits the tyrant to preach religious submission and banish to heaven those to whom he is unwilling to grant a place on earth; the rest of us must not be so hasty to make our own the view of religion that he recommends and, if we can, must prevent the earth being made into hell to arouse a yet greater yearning for heaven.

The natural impulse of man, to be surrendered only in case of true necessity, is to find heaven already on this earth and to infuse his daily labours with everlastingness; to plant and cultivate the imperishable in the temporal itself – not merely in a manner beyond comprehension, connected with the eternal only by a gulf impenetrable to mortal eyes, but in a manner visible even to the mortal eye.

I shall begin with an example that is intelligible to all: what nobly thinking man does not wish and aspire to repeat afresh his own life, but in

---

[45] See e.g. Plato, *Phaedrus* 250c, *Phaedo* 81e, 82e.

better wise, in his children and in his children's children, and to live on even on this earth, ennobled and perfected in their lives, long after he is dead; to wrest from mortality the spirit, the mind and the morals which perhaps in his day put perversity and corruption to flight, confirmed rectitude, roused indolence, lifted despondency, and to deposit them, as his best legacy for posterity, in the souls of those who survive him, so that some day they in turn may deposit them, equally embellished and increased? What nobly thinking man does not desire, by actions or by thought, to sow a seed that will bring the endless, continuous perfection of his race, to cast into time something new that has never before existed, that abides and becomes an inexhaustible source of new creations; to pay for his place on this earth and the short span of time allotted to him with something that will last forever here below, so that he, as an individual, even if his name goes unrecorded by history (for a thirst for posthumous fame is a contemptible vanity), nevertheless leaves behind, in his own consciousness and belief, striking monuments as reminders that he too once moved on this mortal round? What nobly thinking man does not desire this, I ask? But the world is to be considered and arranged only according to the needs of those who think thus, as the rule dictating how all men should be. For their sakes alone does the world exist. They are its heart; and those who think otherwise, being only a part of the transitory world themselves so long as they think in this way, also exist only for the sake of noble thinkers, and must accommodate themselves to the latter until they have become like them.

What could warrant the noble man's challenge and his belief in the eternity and imperishability of his work? Plainly, only an order of things that he could acknowledge as itself eternal and capable of receiving something eternal. Such an order, however, is the special spiritual nature of the human surroundings which, though it cannot be comprehended in any concept, nevertheless truly exists, and from which he himself has gone forth, together with all his thought and action, and with his faith in their eternity: the people from which he is descended and among whom he was formed and grew up to be what he is today. For all that it is indisputably true that his work, if he rightly lays claim to its eternity, is by no means the simple result of the spiritual law of nature of his nation, or goes into this result without remainder, but is something more and to that extent streams forth directly from original and divine life; so it is equally true that this something more, at the very moment that it was first formed into a visible appearance, came under that special spiritual law of nature and found sensuous expression only in accordance with it. For as long as this people continues to exist, all further revelations of the divine in it will also occur and take shape in conformity with the same law of nature. Yet this law is itself further determined by the fact that the man existed and worked as he did, and his activity has become a permanent part of it. All who follow will also be bound to submit to and comply with the law in question. And thus he is made certain that the progress he has achieved endures in his people, for as long as his people endures, and becomes the abiding ground of determination for all its further development.

So, taken in the higher sense of the word, when viewed from the standpoint of a spiritual world, a people is this: the totality of men living together in society and continually producing themselves out of themselves both naturally and spiritually; which collectively stands under a certain special law that governs the development of the divine within it. The universality of this special law is what binds this mass of men into a natural whole, interpenetrated by itself, in the eternal world and, for that very reason, in the temporal world also. This law can be comprehended as a whole even in its content, just as we have comprehended it with respect to the Germans as an original people; by considering the appearances of such a people it can be grasped yet more exactly in some of its further determinations; but it can never be completely conceptualised by one who, unknown to himself, remains constantly under its influence – although, in general, it can be clearly perceived that such a law exists. This law is a surplus of imagery [*Bildlichkeit*] which in appearance immediately coalesces with the surplus of unimageable [*unbildlich*] originality; thus in appearance one cannot be separated from the other. That law thoroughly determines and perfects what has been called the national character of a people; that law of the development of the original and divine. From this it is clear that men who, following our earlier description of foreignism, do not believe at all in something original and in its continued development, but merely in a never-ending cycle of apparent life, and who, through their belief, become what they believe, are not a people in the higher sense; and, since they do not, strictly speaking, actually exist, they are equally incapable of possessing a national character.

The belief of the noble man in the eternal continuance of his activity even on this earth is accordingly based on the hope for the eternal continuance of the people from which he has sprung and on the particularity of that same people as given by the hidden law we have mentioned, without admixture of and corruption by some alien element that does not belong to the totality of this legislation. This particularity is the eternal element to which he entrusts the eternity of his self and his continued activity, the eternal order of things in which he lays his own eternity; he must will this particularity, for it alone is the means of release whereby the brief span of his life here below is extended to an everlasting life on earth. His belief and his striving to plant something imperishable, the concept in which he comprehends his own life as an eternal life – these constitute the bond that connects him most intimately with his nation first of all and then, through his nation, the whole human race; and which brings the nation's every need into his enlarged heart until the end of days. This is his love for his people: at first he respects, trusts, rejoices in it, takes pride in his descent from it. The divine has appeared in the people, and that which is original has deemed it worthy to make this its vesture and direct means of flowing into the world; therefore the divine will further break forth from it. Then he is active, effective, sacrificing himself on behalf of his people. Life, simply as life, as the continuation of changing existence, has never possessed value for him; he desired life only as the source of what is permanent; but this permanence is promised to him only by the independent perpetuation of his nation; to save it he must be willing even to die, so that it may live and he live in it the only life he has ever wanted.

So it is. Love, to be truly love and not merely a fleeting desire, never clings to the transitory, but awakens and kindles and resides only in the eternal. Man cannot even love himself unless he conceives himself as eternal; he is unable even to respect or approve himself. Still less can he love anything outside himself, unless, that is, he embraces it in the eternity of his belief and his soul, and joins it to this eternity. He who does not regard himself first and foremost as eternal has no love at all; nor can he love a fatherland, for nothing of the kind exists for him. He who perhaps regards his invisible life as eternal but not his visible life may well possess a heaven and in this heaven his fatherland; yet here on earth he has no fatherland, for this too is seen only under the image of eternity, of visible eternity rendered perceptible to the senses, and he is unable therefore to love his fatherland either. If such a man has none, he is to be pitied; but he who has inherited one, and into whose heart heaven and earth, the invisible and the visible, interpenetrate and thus for the first time create a true and worthy heaven – he fights to the last drop of his blood to bequeath this precious possession undiminished to posterity.

So has it ever been, although it has never been expressed with this generality and clarity. What inspired the noble spirits among the Romans, whose sentiments and way of thinking still live and breathe all around us in their monuments, to toil and sacrifice, to suffer and endure what they did for their fatherland? They themselves state it often and distinctly.[46] It was their firm belief in the eternal continuance of their Rome and their confident expectation of sharing in this eternity and living eternally in the stream of time. Insofar as this belief had foundation, and they themselves would have grasped it had they been perfectly clear within themselves, it did not deceive them. What was truly eternal in their eternal Rome lives on to this very day, and they with it, in our midst, and will always live on in its legacy until the end of days.

In this sense, as the vehicle and pledge of earthly eternity, and as that which can be eternal here below, people and fatherland far exceed the state, in the ordinary signification of the word – far exceed the social order as understood in its simple, clear concept, as it is established and maintained under the guidance of that same concept. This concept demands certain justice, internal peace, that each through his own industry earns his crust and prolongs his sensuous existence for as long as it is God's will to grant it to him. All this is only a means, a condition, a framework for what love of fatherland really desires: that the eternal and the divine may flourish in the world and never cease to become ever more pure, perfect and excellent. This is the very reason why love of fatherland must govern the state itself, as altogether the supreme, final and independent authority, first of all by restricting the state in the choice of means available for its immediate end, internal peace. To attain this end the natural freedom of the individual must of course be limited in various ways; and if this were the only aim and consideration in regard to these individuals, it would be well to limit their freedom as narrowly as possible, so as to bring all their movements under a uniform rule and keep them under constant supervision. Even assuming this stringency were unnecessary, it would at least not harm the pursuit of this solitary end. Only the higher view of the human race and of peoples expands this limited calculus. Even in the agitations of external life, freedom is the soil in which the higher culture can germinate; a legislation that keeps its eye on the latter will allow the former the widest possible scope, even at the

[46] E.g. Horace, *Odes*, III, 2 ('Dulce et decorum est pro patria mori'); Cicero, *De officiis*, I, 57.

risk that a lesser degree of uniform peace and order may result and government become a little more difficult and arduous.

Let us illustrate this with an example: it is a matter of experience that some nations have been told to their faces that they did not need as much freedom as others do. Such talk may even contain an element of forbearance and mitigation, if one really meant to say that they could not tolerate so much freedom and only great severity could prevent them from destroying one another. If the words are taken as they were spoken, however, then they are true on the assumption that such a nation is quite incapable of original life and of the drive towards it. Should such a nation, in which not even a few noble men made an exception to the general rule, be possible, it would in fact require no freedom whatever, for freedom is only for the higher ends that transcend the state; the state requires merely restraint and training so that individuals may live peaceably side by side and the whole is turned into an efficient means for realising arbitrarily [*willkürlich*] posited ends that lie outside its proper sphere. We can leave unanswered the question as to whether this may truthfully be said of any nation, but this much is clear: that an original people needs freedom, that this freedom is the guarantee of its remaining original, and that, as it goes on, it bears an ever increasing degree of freedom without the least danger. And this is the first respect in which love of fatherland must govern the state itself.

Next, love of fatherland must govern the state by putting before it a higher purpose than the ordinary one of maintaining internal peace, property, personal freedom, life and the well-being of all. For this higher purpose alone, and with no other end in view, does the state assemble an armed force. When the question of the deployment of this force arises, when it is a matter of staking all the aims of the state according to its limited concept – property, personal freedom, life and well-being, indeed the continued existence of the state itself; when we are called upon to decide originally, answerable to God alone, and without a clear notion [*Verstandesbegriff*] that what is intended will be surely achieved, which is never possible in things of this nature; then and only then does a truly original and primal life take the helm of state, and at this point only enter the true sovereign prerogatives of government: to hazard, like God, the lower life for the sake of the higher. In maintaining the traditional constitution, laws and civic welfare there is no truly authentic life at all and no original decision. These are the creation of circumstances and contingencies, of legislators perhaps long dead; subsequent ages

continue faithfully along the road once taken and do not in fact live a
public life of their own, but merely repeat a former one. In such times
there is no need for government proper. But if this orderly progress is
imperiled, and now is the time to decide about new and unprecedented
cases, then a life is required that lives out of itself. What spirit is it that
may in such cases take the helm, that with its own sureness and certainty,
and without uneasy to-ing and fro-ing, is capable of making a decision,
that has an undisputed right to command everyone who may be concerned, whether he wants to or not, and to compel the objector, to
jeopardise everything, even his own life? Not the spirit of calm civic
love for the constitution and laws, but the blazing flame of the higher love
of fatherland that embraces the nation as the vesture of the eternal, for
which the noble man joyfully sacrifices himself and the ignoble, who
exists only for the sake of the former, should likewise sacrifice himself. It
is not civic love for the constitution; for such love is altogether incapable
of all this if it remains on the level of the understanding. However things
may turn out, since government does not go unrewarded, a regent will
always be found. Let the new regent even desire slavery (and what is
slavery other than the disregard and suppression of the particularity of an
original people, the like of which does not exist for that higher sentiment?) – let him desire even slavery – since an advantage can be derived
from the life of the slaves, from their number, even from their welfare;
then, even if he is only a calculator to some extent, slavery will be bearable
under him. Life and sustenance at least they will always find. For what
should they therefore take up arms? After life and sustenance it is peace
they desire above all else. And peace is only disturbed by prolonging
the struggle. They will therefore make every effort to end the struggle
quickly; they will submit, they will yield, and why should they not? They
were never interested in more and never expected more from life than to
continue their habitual existence under tolerable conditions.[47] The promise of a life here below beyond the duration of earthly life – this alone
can inspire men to die for the fatherland.

And so too it has ever been. Wherever there has been real government,
wherever bitter struggles have been overcome, wherever triumphs have

---

[47] Possibly an allusion to the statesmen and generals who after Jena lobbied for peace with
France at any cost, resulting in the punitive Treaty of Tilsit; there are echoes (conscious
or unconscious) here also of the notorious proclamation of the Governor of Berlin, Count
von der Schulenburg, on 17 October 1808: 'The King has lost a battle; the first duty of
our citizens is now to remain calm. That is what I ask of the inhabitants of Berlin.'

been won against mighty resistance, it has been the promise of eternal life which governed, struggled and triumphed. Led by their belief in this promise, the German Protestants, whom we have already mentioned in these addresses, went into battle. Did they perchance not know that peoples might be governed by the old faith also, and held together in lawful order, and that one might make a good living under this faith also? Why, then, did their princes determine upon armed resistance, and why did the people offer it with enthusiasm? It was heaven and eternal blessedness for which they willingly spilt their blood. Yet what earthly power could then have penetrated the inner sanctum of their soul and expunged the faith that had now risen in them, and on which alone they based their hopes of blessedness? So it was not even their own blessedness for which they fought; of that they were already assured: it was the blessedness of their children, of their grandchildren as yet unborn, and of all posterity. Their descendants were to be raised in the same doctrine which alone had appeared to them to bring salvation, they too were to share in the salvation that had dawned for them. It was this hope alone that was threatened by the enemy; for that hope, for an order of things that should blossom above their graves long after they were dead, did they spill their blood with such gladness. Let us admit that they were not entirely clear within themselves, that, in designating what was noblest in them, they erred with their words and with their mouths did injustice to their hearts; let us readily concede that their creed was not the sole and exclusive means of partaking of heaven beyond the grave: yet this, at least, is eternally true, that more heaven on this side of the grave, a more courageous and joyful lifting of the gaze from the earth, and a freer stirring of the spirit have through their sacrifice entered the whole life of succeeding ages; and the descendants of their opponents, just as much as we ourselves, their own descendants, enjoy the fruits of their labours down to this day.

In this belief our oldest common forefathers, the ancestral people of the new culture, called Teutons [*Germanier*] by the Romans, bravely opposed the encroaching world dominion of the Romans. Did they not see before their eyes the greater prosperity of the neighbouring Roman provinces, the finer enjoyments there, as well as laws, tribunals, fasces and axes in superabundance?[48] Were not the Romans willing enough to invite them to share in all these blessings? Did they not experience, in the person of several of their own princes, who had been persuaded that war

---

[48] A probable allusion to the symbolic paraphernalia of the French Revolution.

against such benefactors of humanity was rebellion, proofs of the celebrated Roman clemency, since the Romans decorated the complaisant
with royal titles, with generalships in their armies, and with Roman
fillets, and gave them, if perchance they were driven out by their countrymen, asylum and a means of support in their colonies? Did they have no
sense of the excellencies of Roman culture, as for example the better
organisation of their armies, in which even an Arminius[49] did not disdain
to learn the arts of war? None of these instances of ignorance or neglect is
to be charged to their account. Their descendants even appropriated this
culture, as soon as they could without loss of their freedom, and insofar as
it was possible without loss of their particularity. For what cause, then,
did they fight over several generations in bloody war, ever renewed
with the same violence? A Roman writer has their chieftains speak thus:
'Is anything left for us but to assert our freedom or to die before we
are enslaved?'[50] Freedom meant to them that they remained Germans
[*Deutsche*], that they continued to decide their affairs independently and
originally, in keeping with their own spirit, and, likewise in keeping with
their spirit, that they continued to move forward in their development,
and that they passed on this independence to their posterity. Slavery was
the name they gave to all those blessings that the Romans offered them,
because by accepting these they could not but become something other
than Germans; they would have to become half-Romans. It went without
saying, they assumed, that every man would sooner die than become thus
and that a true German could wish to live only in order to be and remain
forever a German and to bring up his children as Germans also.

They did not all die, they did not see slavery, they bequeathed freedom
to their children. To their stubborn resistance the entire modern world
owes the fact that it is as it is. If the Romans had succeeded in subjugating
them also and, as the Romans did everywhere else, in exterminating
them as a nation, then the entire development of humanity would have
taken a different – and surely not a happier – course. We, the immediate
inheritors of their soil, their language and their convictions, owe it to
them that we are still Germans, that we are still borne along by the stream
of original and independent life; to them we owe everything that we have

---

[49] Arminius (or Hermann), a chieftain of the Cherusci, was a commander in the Roman
military and a Roman citizen before he returned to Germania to organise resistance to
Roman expansion. He won a stunning victory in the Battle of Teutoburg Forest in AD 9.
[50] Tacitus, *Annales*, II, 15.

since been as a nation; and, unless it is now the end for us and the last drop of blood descended from them has dried up in our veins, to them we shall owe everything that we shall yet become. Even the other tribes, now foreign to us, but through them our brothers, owe their existence to them. When they conquered eternal Rome not one of these peoples yet existed; the possibility of their future genesis was also won that day.

These men, and all others of like mind throughout the history of the world, triumphed because they were inspired by the eternal, and so this inspiration always and of necessity triumphs over him who is not inspired. It is not the strong right arm or the keen blade that wins victories, but the power of the soul. Whoever sets himself a limited goal for his sacrifices, and likes not to venture beyond a certain point, gives up his resistance as soon as he runs into danger at this point, no matter if it be absolutely vital and must not be surrendered. Whoever has set himself no goal at all, but hazards everything, even the highest boon that he can forfeit here on earth, his life, never ceases to resist, and doubtless triumphs if his opponent has a more limited goal. A people capable, albeit only in its highest representatives and leaders, of fixing its gaze on independence, that vision of the spiritual world, and of being seized by love for it, as were our distant ancestors, assuredly triumphs over one that is used, like the Roman armies, only as the instrument of a stranger's lust for power and to subjugate independent peoples; for the former have everything to lose, the latter merely something to gain. But even a whim prevails over that way of thinking, according to which war is a game of chance for loss or gain in the temporal world, and which has already decided before the game begins how much it is willing to put on the table. Think for example of a Mahomet – not the real Mahomet of history, about whom I confess I have no opinion, but the Mahomet of a well-known French poet[51] – who has got it into his head that he is one of those uncommon natures who are called to guide the obscure and common folk of this earth, and to whom, in consequence of this first assumption, all his notions, inadequate and narrow as they may in fact be, must necessarily seem, because they are his, great and sublime and enrapturing ideas, and all who oppose them obscure and common folk, enemies of their own welfare, evil-minded and odious. Such a man, in order to justify his conceit to himself as a divine calling and utterly consumed by this thought, must stake everything on it and cannot rest

---

[51] Voltaire, whose tragedy *Mahomet* was published in 1742.

until he has trampled underfoot all who do not think as highly of him as he does himself and until his own belief in his divine mission is reflected back at him in the contemporary world. I should not like to say how he would fare if a spiritual vision, true and clear within itself, actually appeared against him on the field of battle, but he certainly wins from those limited gamblers, for he hazards everything against those who do not; they are not driven by a spirit, but he is, albeit a fanatic spirit – that of his mighty and powerful conceit.

From all this it follows that the state, as the mere regiment of human life proceeding along its usual peaceful course, is not something primary, existing for itself, but is merely the means to a higher end, that of the ever-uniform and continuing development of the purely human in this nation; that it is only the vision and love of this eternal development which is unceasingly to supervise the administration of the state, even in times of peace, and which, when the independence of the people is endangered, alone can save it. With the Germans – among whom, as an original people, love for the fatherland is possible and, as we firmly believe, has actually existed hitherto – this love could until now reckon with great confidence on the security of its most vital interest. As was the case only among the ancient Greeks before them, among the Germans the state and the nation were actually separate from each other, and each was represented by itself, the former in the particular German territories and principalities, the latter visibly in the imperial union and invisibly – valid not in consequence of a written law but one living in the hearts of all and in its results striking the eye at every turn – in a multitude of customs and institutions. As far as the German language extended, everyone who had first seen the light of day within its domain could regard himself as a citizen in a twofold sense: partly of the state of his birth, to whose care he was first commended, and partly of the common fatherland of the German nation as a whole. It was open to all to search the length and breadth of the fatherland for the culture most congenial to their spirit or the sphere of activity best suited to it; and talent did not root itself to one spot like a tree, but was allowed to seek its own place in the world. Whoever was estranged from his nearest and dearest by the direction his culture took, soon found a warm reception elsewhere, found new friends to replace those he had lost; he found the time and tranquillity to explain himself more carefully, perhaps even to win over and reconcile the wrathful themselves and thereby to unite the whole. No German-born prince has ever been able to bring himself to confine the fatherland of his subjects within the mountains or rivers he ruled and to view them as bound to their native soil. A truth that could not be uttered in one territory might be published in another and, conversely, perhaps those truths forbidden here were permitted there. And so there came about, despite many instances of one-sidedness and narrow-mindedness in particular states, in Germany as a whole the greatest freedom of inquiry and expression that ever a people possessed; and the higher culture was and has remained everywhere the result of the interaction of the citizens of all German states. This higher culture then gradually descended in this form to the people at large, which never ceased, broadly speaking, to educate itself. As I have said, no German soul sitting at the helm of government has ever diminished this essential guarantee of the continued existence of the German nation; and even though, in view of other original decisions, what the higher German love of fatherland must desire could not always be done, then at least no one has exactly acted against its interests, no one has sought to undermine that love, to eradicate it and to put a conflicting love in its place.

But what if now the original guidance of that higher culture, as well as of the national power which may be used only on behalf of that culture and its continuance, namely the disposal over German goods and German blood, should pass from the jurisdiction of the German soul to that of another – what must necessarily follow?

Here is the place where there is a dire need for that inclination we laid claim to in our first address, namely to be unwilling to be deceived in our own affairs, and to have the courage to want to behold and admit the truth. Moreover, it is still permitted, so far as I know, to discuss the fatherland with one another, or at any rate to sigh over its fate, in the German language, and we would, I believe, not do well to anticipate such a ban by imposing our own and lay the chains of individual timidity on courage, which no doubt beforehand will have considered the risk of the venture.[52]

So picture to yourselves the new regime, which we are presupposing, as benign and well-meaning as you wish, make it as good as God; will you also be able to attribute to it divine understanding? Even though it may, in all sincerity, desire the greatest happiness and welfare of all, will the greatest well-being that it can comprehend also be the welfare of

---

[52] Presumably a swipe at the anxious Prussian censor, who by 31 January, when this address was delivered, had still not passed the first.

Germany? Thus I hope to have been understood correctly by you with respect to the main point that I have presented to you today; I hope that, in the course of my remarks, many of you have thought and felt that I merely express distinctly and in words what has always lain within your hearts; I hope that it will be the same with the other Germans who will one day read this. Moreover, several Germans before me have said approximately the same things; and that conviction has obscurely underpinned their constantly attested opposition to a merely mechanical arrangement and estimation of the state. And now I challenge all who are acquainted with modern foreign literature to prove to me what sage, poet, law-giver among them has ever betrayed even the flickering of an idea similar to the one that views the human race as eternally progressing and relates all its temporal activity to this progress; whether any of them, even at the time of their boldest flights of political creation, demanded more from the state than the abolition of inequality, the maintenance of peace at home and national glory abroad and, in the extremest case, domestic bliss? If this is their highest good, as we must conclude from all these indications, then they in turn will not impute to us any higher needs or higher demands on life. And, always assuming those benevolent sentiments towards us and the absence of all self-interest and craving to be more than we are, they will believe they have provided admirably for us when we are given everything that they alone recognise as desirable. But that which alone the nobler man among us wishes to live for is then expunged from public life, and the people that has always shown itself receptive to the stimulation of these nobler souls (the majority of which people, it might be hoped, could be raised up to that nobility) is treated as the foreigners wish to be treated: degraded, dishonoured, obliterated from the order of things by its confluence with a people of a baser kind.

He in whom those higher demands on life, together with the sense of their divine rightness, still remain vital and powerful, feels himself with deep displeasure thrust back to the earliest days of Christianity, when it was said: 'Resist not evil, but whomsoever shall smite thee on the right cheek, turn to him the other also; and if any man will take away thy coat, let him have thy cloak also.'[53] And rightly so, for as long as he sees you still wearing a cloak he seeks a quarrel with you, so that he may take this too; only when you are quite naked does he turn his attention elsewhere and leave you in peace. Precisely his higher mind [*höherer Sinn*], which

---

[53] Matthew 5: 39–41.

does him honour, makes the earth a hell and an abomination for him; he wishes that he had never been born, he wishes that his eye would shut itself to the light of day, the sooner the better; inexhaustible sorrow envelops his days until the grave shall claim him; he can think of no better gift for those who are dear to him than a dull and contented mind so that they may live with less pain in prospect of an eternal life beyond the grave.

These addresses put before you the sole remaining means, now that the others have been tried in vain, of preventing this annihilation of every nobler impulse that may arise among us in the future and this debasement of our entire nation. They enjoin you to establish the true and all-powerful love for the fatherland – which consists in understanding our people as one that is eternal, as the warrant for our own eternity – deeply and indelibly in the hearts of all, through education. What kind of education can do this, and in what manner, we shall see in the following addresses.

At what point existing in reality the new national education of the Germans will begin

In our last address we furnished and completed several proofs that we had already promised in the first. The only issue for now, we said, and let this be our first task, is to save and perpetuate the existence of the German as such; all other differences vanished before this higher vantage point and the special obligations under which anyone might consider himself to be would not thereby be prejudiced. It is clear, if only we call to mind the distinction we made between state and nation, that even in earlier times the interests [*Angelegenheiten*] of both could never come into conflict. Besides, higher patriotic love for the whole people of the German nation had to assume the supreme leadership of each particular German state, just as it ought to have done. None of these states could lose sight of this higher interest without forfeiting all that was noble and excellent, thereby hastening its own demise: the more someone was seized and animated by that higher interest, therefore, the better citizen he was in service of the particular German state in which his immediate sphere of activity lay. German states could well clash with other German states over certain traditional franchises. Whoever wished the established situation to continue – and doubtless every reasonable man was bound to want this for the sake of its further consequences – had to hope that the just cause would prevail, no matter who its champion might be. At most, a particular German state might aim to unite the entire German nation under its government and introduce absolute rule in place of the time-honoured republic of peoples (*Völkerrepublik*). If it is true (as I, for example, think it is) that precisely this republican constitution has been until now the pre-eminent source of German culture and the primary means of safeguarding its particularity, then, should this unity of government that we supposed just now have borne not the republican but the monarchical form, under which it would have been possible for the despot to nip some offshoot of original culture in the bud throughout the German lands for the duration of his lifetime – if this is true, I say, then it would indeed have been a grave misfortune for the interests of German love of fatherland had this scheme succeeded and every noble man throughout the country were called upon to offer his resistance. Nevertheless, even in this worst of all cases it would still have been Germans who ruled over Germans and originally directed their affairs, and if the characteristic German spirit had briefly gone astray, there would still have remained the hope that one day it would reawaken, and every stouter soul up and down the land could have been sure of obtaining a hearing and making himself understood; a German nation would still have remained in existence, governing itself, and it would not have sunk into an existence of a lower order. Here the essential thing in our reckoning is always either that the German love of nation [*National-Liebe*] itself sits at the helm of the German state or that its influence can at least reach that far. If, however, following our earlier supposition, this German state – and whether it appears as one or as several is of no consequence, for in reality it is always one – passed in general from German to foreign control, then it is sure (for anything else would be contrary to all nature and simply impossible), it is sure, I say, that a foreign interest and not a German one would henceforth be decisive. Where the whole national interest of the Germans had hitherto had its seat and representation, namely at the helm of state, from there it would be expelled. If it is not to be entirely wiped from the face of the earth, then another place of refuge must be prepared, the only one remaining, among the governed, in the citizens. But were it already sheltering among them, and in the majority, then we would not have ended up in the predicament that is the subject of our present deliberations; therefore it is not among them and must first be introduced to them. In other words, the majority of the citizens must be educated to this patriotic sentiment and, so that we can be assured of the majority, this education must be attempted on all. And thus we have at once furnished, plainly and clearly, the proof we promised at an earlier time that education – and nothing else – is the only possible means of recovering German independence. And it would not be our fault if people had still been unable even now to grasp the proper substance and intent of our addresses, and the sense in which all our utterances are to be taken.

To put it yet more briefly and still according to our earlier supposition: if wards are deprived of their paternal and blood-related guardians, and foreign lords and masters have taken their place; if these wards are not to become slaves, they must leave their tutelage and, to enable them to do so, they must first of all be educated to maturity. German love of fatherland has lost its seat; it shall receive another, one broader and deeper, wherein it shall entrench and steel itself in quiet concealment, in order, at the proper time, to burst forth with youthful vigour and restore even to the state its lost independence. Foreigners, as well as the mean-spirited and narrow-minded wretches among us, need not trouble themselves for now; let us reassure them that not one of them will live to see it, and the age that does will think otherwise than they.

Now, as rigorous as the logic of this argument may be, whether it will seize others and rouse them to action depends first of all on whether such things as German particularity and German love of fatherland really exist as we have portrayed them, and whether these are worth preserving and fighting for or not. That the foreigner – both at home or abroad – will answer this question in the negative goes without saying; but he has not been summoned to our counsel. We ought to remark in passing that this question can on no account be decided on the basis of conceptual demonstration; concepts may clarify the issue but are unable to disclose information about the actual existence or value of these things; rather, existence and value can be verified only by each individual's immediate and personal experience. In such a case millions may say: a thing does not exist; yet this can never mean more than that it does not exist in them, by no means that it has no existence whatsoever, and if one man stands up against these millions and affirms that it does indeed exist, then he is right in spite of them all. Since it is I who am speaking now, there is nothing to prevent me from being the individual in the case just mentioned, who affirms that he knows from immediate experience that there is such a thing as German love of fatherland, that he knows the infinite value of its object, that this love alone has driven him to say, regardless of the danger, what he said and will yet say, because nothing at all now remains to us save speech – and even this is curbed and curtailed in all sorts of ways. Whoever feels this within himself will be convinced; whoever does not feel it cannot be convinced, for on this assumption only does my proof rest. On him my words are lost; but who would not gamble with something as cheap as words?

That particular education on which we set our hopes for the salvation of the German nation was described in general terms in the second and third addresses. We characterised it as amounting to a complete regeneration of the human race, and it will be fitting if we proceed from this characterisation to a renewed survey of the whole.

As a rule the world of the senses has been considered as the proper, real, true and actually existing world; it was presented to the pupil first; starting from it he was led to thought, and usually to thought about and in the service of this world. The new education reverses this order exactly. For it only the world grasped by thought is the true and actually existing world; it aims to introduce the pupil to this world from the outset. To this world alone does it wish to bind all his love, all his pleasures, so that in him there necessarily arises and emerges a life lived only in this world of the spirit. Hitherto only flesh, matter, nature lived in most men; thanks to the new education spirit alone shall live in the majority – indeed soon even in all – and impel them. The firm and certain spirit, which earlier we spoke of as the only possible foundation of a well-ordered state, shall be produced as a rule.

Through such an education we shall undoubtedly attain the first goal which we set ourselves and which formed the point of departure for our addresses. That spirit which is to be produced contains within it, as an integral component, the higher love of fatherland, the understanding of earthly life as eternal and of the fatherland as the vehicle of this eternity – and, should this spirit be raised up among the Germans, specific love of the German fatherland. From this love the intrepid defender of the fatherland and the peaceful and law-abiding citizen follow of themselves. Such an education achieves even more than this immediate purpose, as is always the case when a great goal is willed by radical means: the whole man is perfected in all his parts, inwardly rounded off, outwardly endowed with the aptitude needed to realise his aims in time and eternity. Spiritual nature has forged an indissoluble link between our complete deliverance from all the evils that oppress us and the recovery of our health for nation and fatherland.

With the stunned astonishment that such a world of mere thought is asserted, and even asserted as the only possible world, whereas the world of the senses is cast aside altogether; with the repudiation of either the first world in general or only the possibility that the majority of the common people, too, can be initiated into it – with such things we are no longer concerned here; we have already dismissed them entirely. He who does not yet know that there is a world of thought may for the moment instruct himself elsewhere by the available means, since we have no time for this instruction here. But how the majority of the people at large can be lifted up to that world of thought – this we now wish to demonstrate.

As, in our own considered opinion, the idea of such a new education is on no account to be regarded as an image set up simply to exercise our astuteness or disputatiousness but should be carried into action at this very hour and introduced into life, so it is incumbent on us to indicate, first of all, what already exists in the real world from which we can proceed with the execution of this idea.

To this question we reply: it shall proceed from the course of instruction devised and proposed by Johann Heinrich Pestalozzi, and already successfully put into practice under his supervision. We want to give good reasons for our decision and to determine it more exactly.

In the first place, we have read and revolved in our mind the man's own writings, and formed our concept of his art of instruction and education from these writings themselves; but we have taken no heed of what the learned newspapers have reported and opined on this matter and again opined on their original opinions. We mention this in order to recommend that everyone who likewise desires to entertain a concept of this subject take the same path and generally avoid the opposing one. Just as little have we wanted to see something of his actual practice until now: by no means out of disrespect, but because we wished first to obtain for ourselves a firm and certain concept of the author's true intention, which practice can often fall short of. From our concept of his intention, however, that of the practice and its inevitable result follows of itself, without any need to put it to the test; and, equipped only with this first concept, we can understand the practice truly and judge it correctly. Should, as some believe, this course of instruction have already degenerated here and there into a blind empirical groping, into empty play and the misconstruction of mere show [*Schauauslegerei*], then in my estimation the fundamental concept of its inventor at least is entirely blameless in this regard.

This fundamental concept is guaranteed in the first place by the peculiar nature of the man himself, as it is exhibited in his writings with the most faithful and tender-hearted candour. As an example of the characteristics of the German soul he might have served me just as well as Luther or any other man of the same stamp, if indeed there are more, and furnished the gratifying proof that this soul prevails to this day in all its wonder-working power wherever the German tongue is spoken. Throughout his arduous life, struggling with every possible obstacle – inwardly with his own stubborn incertitude and awkwardness, sparingly equipped as he was himself with even the most common resources of a learned education, outwardly with persistent misunderstanding – he too strove towards a goal of which he had merely an inkling and was even quite unconscious, sustained and driven by an inexhaustible and almighty and German impulse: love for the impoverished and neglected people. This almighty love had made him its instrument, just as it had Luther, only in a different way that was more in keeping with his age, and had become the life of his life. Unbeknownst even to him, it was the firm and unalterable guiding thread of this life of his, leading him through the night that surrounded him and crowning the evening of his days – for such a love could not possibly depart the earth unrewarded – with his truly spiritual creation, the achievements of which far surpassed even his boldest hopes. He wanted merely to help the people; but his discovery, when its full implications are taken into consideration, exalts the people, abolishes all differences between them and the cultivated class, provides, instead of the popular education he envisaged, a national education, and might even have the power to help all the peoples and the whole human race to rise from the depths of their present misery.

This fundamental concept of his shines forth in his writings with perfect clarity and unmistakable determinacy. First of all he demands, with respect to form, not the arbitrariness and blind groping that have been the rule until now, but rather a fixed and carefully considered art of education, such as we also demand and as German thoroughness perforce must demand; and he relates with great frankness how a French remark to the effect that he aims to mechanise education helped to wrench him from his dreams and see his purpose more clearly.[54] With respect to content, the first step in the new education I have described is to stimulate and cultivate the pupil's free mental activity, his thinking, in which the world of his love will later dawn on him; with this first step Pestalozzi's writings are chiefly concerned, and our examination of his

---

[54] Pestalozzi wrote: 'Executive Councillor Glayre, to whom I had tried to explain the essence of my works last summer, said to me, "Vous voulez méchaniser l'éducation." I understood very little French. I thought by these words he meant to say I was seeking means of bringing education and instruction into psychologically ordered sequence; and taking these words in this sense he really hit the nail on the head, and according to my view, put the word in my mouth, which showed me the essentials of my purpose and all the means thereto. Perhaps it would have been long before I had found it out, because I did not examine myself as I went along, but surrendered myself wholly to vague though vivid feelings, that indeed made my course certain, but did not teach me to know it' (*GC*, Letter I, p. 25).

fundamental concept will begin here. In this regard his criticism of the existing method of instruction – namely, that it only immerses the pupil in fog and shadows and never permits him to attain to actual truth and reality[55] – is equivalent to our own, when we said that this instruction has been unable either to intervene in life or to cultivate its root. Pestalozzi's proposed remedy, to introduce the pupil to immediate intuition,[56] again amounts to the same as our own, to stimulate his mental activity to project images and to let him learn what he learns only by this free formation of images: for intuition is only possible when it proceeds from what has been freely projected. That this is what Pestalozzi really means, that he understands by intuition by no means a blindly groping and fumbling perception, is demonstrated by the practice which he goes on to indicate. Again quite correctly, this stimulation of the pupil's intuition by education is made subject to this general and far-reaching law: that it should keep pace with the beginning and progress of the powers to be developed in the child.[57]

However, all the shortcomings of Pestalozzi's plan of education in its expressions and proposals have a single common source: that the inadequate and limited goal at which he initially aimed, namely to lend urgent assistance to the destitute children of the people, is, provided that society as a whole remains unchanged, muddled and conflicts with the means, which lead to a far greater end than the one he envisaged. We would secure ourselves against all error, and obtain a perfectly self-consistent concept, if we dropped the first goal and everything that follows from its

---

55 Pestalozzi: 'our unpsychological schools are essentially only artificial stifling-machines for destroying all the results of the power and experience that nature herself brings to [the children]. [...] And after they have enjoyed this happiness of sensuous life for five whole years, we make all nature round them vanish from before their eyes; tyrannically stop the delightful course of their unrestrained freedom, pen them up like sheep, whole flocks huddled together, in stinking rooms; pitilessly chain them for hours, days, weeks, months, years, to the contemplation of unattractive and monotonous letters (and, contrasted with their former condition), to a maddening course of life' (ibid., p. 28).

56 Pestalozzi: 'The child must be brought to a high degree of knowledge, both of things seen and words, before it is reasonable to teach him to spell or read. I was quite convinced that at their earliest age, children need psychological training in gaining intelligent sense-impressions [*Anschauungen*] of all things' (ibid., p. 26).

57 Pestalozzi: 'All instruction of man is then only the Art of helping Nature to develop in her own way; and this Art rests essentially on the relation and harmony between the impressions received by the child and the exact degree of his developed powers. It is also necessary, in the impressions that are brought to the child by instruction, that there should be a sequence, so that beginning and progress should keep pace with the beginning and progress of the powers to be developed in the child' (ibid., p. 26).

pursuit, and kept solely to the latter and carried it through systematically. Pestalozzi's wish to release those children in abject poverty from school as soon as possible, so that they might earn a crust, and yet also to provide them with a means of catching up their interrupted education, was doubtless the sole reason why his loving heart overestimated reading and writing, setting them up almost as the be-all and end-all of popular education, and inspired his naive faith in the pronouncements of past millennia that these were the best aids to instruction; or else he would have discovered that it is precisely reading and writing which have hitherto been the real instruments of wrapping men in fog and shadow and making them overwise. This is undoubtedly the origin of several of his other proposals that contradict his principle of immediate intuition, and especially his thoroughly erroneous view of language as a means of raising our race from obscure intuition to distinct concepts.[58] For our part, we have not spoken of the education of the people as opposed to that of the higher ranks, because we no longer wish to have a people in this sense of the word at all, namely a base and vulgar rabble, nor can German national interests tolerate this sense any more; we spoke rather of national education. If it is ever to come to this, then the paltry wish that education be completed as soon as possible and the child put back to work must never again cross our lips, but be left at the threshold before we enter into our deliberations on this matter. To my mind this education will not be costly: the institutions will in large measure be able to support themselves and work will suffer no loss; I shall set forth my thoughts hereon in due course. Yet even if it were otherwise, the pupil must, unconditionally and at every risk to himself, remain in education until it can be and is completed. Half an education is no better than none at all: it leaves things where they were. If this is what one wants, then one may as well spare oneself the half-measures and declare from the first that one does not wish humanity to be helped. On this assumption, reading and writing can bring no benefit for the duration of the national education, indeed can prove positively harmful, because they might easily lead the pupil astray from immediate intuition to the mere sign; from a state of attentiveness, which knows that it grasps nothing unless it grasps it here and now, to one of distraction, which consoles itself by scribbling things down on paper and intending some day to learn from these scraps of paper what it

---

[58] Pestalozzi: 'The final end of language is obviously to lead our race from vague sense-impressions [*Anschauungen*] to clear ideas' (*GC*, Letter VII, p. 98).

probably never will learn; and, just as reading and writing have always done, generally seduce him into the daydreams that so often accompany our dealings with the written word. Only at the very end of education, as its parting gift, might these skills be taught and the pupil guided, by analysis of the language that he has long since mastered completely, to discover and use letters; with the level of culture he has already achieved it would be child's play.

Thus do things stand with the general national education simply as such. It is otherwise with the future scholar. One day he will not merely pronounce on matters of universal interest, following the promptings of his heart, but also, in solitary reflection, raise up into the light of language those hidden and characteristic depths of his soul that are unknown even to himself; and he must therefore get his hands on the instrument of this private yet also public thinking – that is to say, writing – and learn to manipulate it; yet even with him there will be less need to rush than has hitherto been the case. This will become clearer in due course, when we distinguish national education as such from learned education.

In accordance with this view everything that our author says about sounds and words as the means of developing the power of the mind stands to be corrected and qualified.[59] The plan of these addresses does not permit me to enter into detail. I shall content myself, therefore, with the following remark, one that goes right to the heart of the matter. The foundation of Pestalozzi's understanding of the acquisition of knowledge can be found in his book for mothers,[60] in which, amongst other things, he sets great store by home instruction. As far as home tutoring is concerned, first of all, we do not by any means wish to argue with him over the hopes he invests in mothers. As far as our higher conception of a national education is concerned, however, we are firmly convinced that it can be neither commenced nor continued nor completed in the home, especially among the labouring classes, and indeed without totally

---

[59] Pestalozzi: 'The great peculiarity and highest characteristic of our nature, *language*, begins in the power of making sounds. It becomes gradually developed by improving *sounds* to *articulate words*; and from *articulate words* to *language*. [. . .] Even the simplest sound, by which man strove to express the impression that an object made on him, was an expression of a sense-impression [*Anschauung*]. The speech of my race was long only a *power of mimicry and of making sounds* that imitated the tones of living and lifeless nature. From *mimicry* and *sound-making* they came to *hieroglyphics* and *separate words*, and for long they gave *special* objects *special* names (*GC*, Letter x, pp. 149–50).

[60] Pestalozzi, *Buch der Mütter, oder Anleitung für Mütter ihre Kinder bemerken und reden zu lehren* (1803).

separating the children from their parents. The stress and worry of earning a living from day to day, the attendant penny-pinching and covetousness, would inevitably infect the children, drag them down and prevent them from freely soaring up into the world of thought. This is also one of the unconditional requirements for the execution of our plan and is absolutely indispensable. We have seen to our satisfaction what happens when humanity as a whole must recapitulate in every ensuing age what it accomplished in preceding centuries. If it is to be totally transformed, then a clean break must be made with its past life. Only after a generation has passed through the new education will we be able to consult over which part of the national education we wish to entrust to the domestic sphere. – Setting this aside, and viewing Pestalozzi's book for mothers only as the first foundation of instruction, still its content, namely what he says respecting the body of the child, also seems to us completely misguided. He proceeds from the perfectly correct proposition that the first object of the child's knowledge must be the child himself; but is the body of the child then the child himself? If it were indeed a matter of a human body, would not his mother's be far closer and more visible to him? And how indeed can the child get an intuitive cognition of his body, without first having learned to use it? Such acquaintance [*Kenntnis*] is not real knowledge [*Erkenntnis*], but a mere rote-learning of arbitrary word-signs brought about by the over-estimation of speech. The true basis of instruction and knowledge would be, to put it in Pestalozzi's terms, an ABC of sensations. As the child begins to hear the sounds of language and to form his own out of necessity, he ought to be guided in making himself perfectly clear as to whether he was hungry or sleepy, whether he sees the sensation present to him and designated by this or that expression or rather hears it, and so on, or whether he is merely imagining it; he must be clear as to how the different impressions designated by particular words affect the same sense in different ways – the colours and sounds of various bodies, for example, and so on – and in what nuances and gradations; and all this in the correct sequence that also allows the sensitive faculty itself to develop regularly. Only by this means does the child first acquire an I, which it separates freely and reflectively in a concept and penetrates with this concept. And as soon as the child awakens into life it is endowed with a spiritual eye that from this moment on never leaves it. By this means the forms of measure and number, empty in and of themselves, acquire for subsequent exercises of the power of intuition their distinctly known inner content;

which, following Pestalozzi's procedure, can only be conferred on them by obscure inclination and compulsion. In this connection there appears in Pestalozzi's writings a strange confession made by one of his teachers who, once initiated into this method, began to see only empty geometric bodies.[61] So it would go for all pupils subjected to this method, if spiritual nature did not guard against it without our noticing. Here, too, where what was actually perceived is distinctly grasped, is the place where not the linguistic sign but speech itself, and the need to express oneself to others, forms man and lifts him out of obscurity and confusion into clarity and determinacy. When the child first awakens to consciousness all impressions of the surrounding world press upon him at the same time, mingling in a dull chaos in which no one thing obtrudes from the general tumult. How shall the child ever escape this dullness? He needs the help of others; and he can summon this help only by expressing his need definitely, by making use of the distinctions of similar needs already embedded in language. Guided by these distinctions, he is compelled to attend, wrapt in himself and concentrating, to what he really feels, to compare and to distinguish it from another sensation that he is acquainted with [*kennt*] but does not presently feel. In this way a reflective and free I begins to separate itself in him. This

---

[61] The teacher in question is one Johann Christoph Buss. Pestalozzi quotes him as follows: 'I certainly threw all my energy into the department in which Pestalozzi wanted my help, but for a long time I could not understand a single one of his opinions on drawing, and at first knew not what he wanted when he said: "Lines, angles and curves are the foundations of the art of drawing." In order to explain himself to me, he said, "Here, too, the human being must be raised from dim sense-impressions to clear ideas." But I could not understand how that could be done by drawing. He said, "This must be obtained by the division of squares and curves into parts, and by analysing their parts to units, that can be seen and compared." I tried to find this analysis and simplification, but I could not find the beginning-point of simplicity, and with all my trouble found myself in a sea of single figures that were certainly simple in themselves, but did not make Pestalozzi's laws of simplicity clear. [. . .] In short, for months I did not understand him, and for months did not know what to make of the lines that he gave me as a pattern, until at last I felt, either I ought to know less than I did, or at least must throw away my knowledge, and stand upon the simple points. [. . .] At last my ripened insight compelled me, seeing how far his children were brought by persevering upon his beginning-point, to go down to these points. Then was my attempt at an ABC of *Anschauung* complete in a couple of days. [. . .] Now every thing that I saw suddenly stood between lines that defined its outlines from the object. Now, in my imagination, they freed themselves from it, and fell into measurable forms, from which every deviation was sharply distinct to me. But at first I saw only *objects*, now I saw only *lines*, and believed those must be used with the children absolutely and to the utmost extent before giving them real objects to imitate, or even examine' (*GC*, Letter III, pp. 67–8).

road, first laid by necessity and nature, must be continued by an education that guides us with deliberate and free art.

In the field of objective knowledge, which aims at external things, familiarity with the word-sign adds nothing to the distinctness and determinacy of the inner knowledge for the knower himself, but merely elevates it into a completely different sphere where it can be communicated to others. The clarity of that knowledge rests entirely on the intuition; and that which one can reproduce at will in the imagination, in all its parts and exactly as it is in reality, one knows completely, whether or not one has a word for it. We are even convinced that completion of the intuition must precede familiarity with the word-sign and that the opposing path leads precisely to that world of fog and shadow, and to the early chatter [*Maulbrauchen*],[62] which are both so rightly hateful to Pestalozzi. Indeed, we are convinced that he who desires to know the word as soon as he can, and who thinks he has increased his knowledge when he does so, inhabits that very same world of fog, and is concerned merely to extend its limits. Taking the author's system of thought as a whole, I believe that it was precisely this ABC of sensation which he was striving towards as the first foundation of spiritual development and as the content of his book for mothers, and which hovered obscurely before him when he made all his remarks about language; only his lack of philosophical studies prevented him from becoming perfectly clear within himself on this point.

Now, assuming this development of the knowing subject through sensation, and laying it as the very first foundation of the national education we envisage, then Pestalozzi's ABC of intuition, the doctrine of the relations of number and measure, is the perfectly appropriate and excellent consequence. To this intuition any part of the sensible world can be linked; it can be introduced into the domain of mathematics until the pupil has achieved a sufficient degree of culture through these preliminary exercises to be led on to the projection of a social order of humankind and to the love of that order – the second and most essential step in his formation [*Bildung*].

There is yet another matter relating to the first part of education which Pestalozzi likewise brings up and must not be passed over: the development

---

[62] Pestalozzi: 'In order to make children reasonable, and put them in the way of a power of independent thought, we must guard, as much as possible, against allowing them to speak at haphazard [*ihr Maul brauchen*], or to pronounce opinions about things that they know only superficially' (*GC*, Letter I, pp. 36–7). For Pestalozzi, *Maulbrauchen* signifies all speech that is not based on clear concepts arrived at by experience.

of the pupil's bodily aptitude, which must necessarily advance hand in hand with the mental. He demands an ABC of skill; that is, of physical ability. His most salient pronouncements on this are the following: 'Striking, carrying, throwing, thrusting, pulling, turning, twisting, swinging, and so on are the simplest exercises of strength. There is a natural and graduated progression in these exercises from their simplest beginning to their highest perfection, that is, to the utmost degree of nervous power, which enables us to perform with sureness and in a hundred different ways the actions of thrusting and parrying, swinging and throwing, and makes hand and foot certain.'[63] Here everything depends on the natural progression, and it is not sufficient to set about things blindly and arbitrarily and introduce any old exercise, just so it might be said of us that, like the Greeks, we too had a physical education. In this regard we still have everything to do, for Pestalozzi has not furnished an ABC of skill. It must first be devised, and for that a man is required who, equally at home in the anatomy of the human body and in scientific mechanics, can combine this knowledge with a large measure of philosophical spirit, so as to be able to form an idea of that thoroughly perfect machine which the human body has the potential to become, and to indicate how this machine can be developed from every healthy human body, gradually, such that each step were taken in the only possible order, preparing and facilitating every successive step, and thereby the health and beauty of the body, and such that the power of the mind is not only not endangered but even strengthened and increased. That this component is indispensable for an education that aspires to form the whole man, and is particularly cut out for a nation that shall restore and henceforth preserve its independence, is evident without need for further comment.

What remains to say with regard to the more exact definition of our concept of German national education we shall keep for the next address.

---

[63] This not entirely accurate quotation is from *GC*, Letter XII, pp. 177–8.

Towards a more exact definition
of the German national education

Leading the pupil to make clear to himself first his sensations then his intuitions, hand in hand with a systematic art of training his body, constitutes the first main part of the new German national education. As far as the cultivation of the intuitions is concerned, Pestalozzi has provided us with a suitable method; we still lack one for the cultivation of the sensitive faculty, but he and his collaborators, who are called to solve this task in the first place, will be able to furnish it without much difficulty. A guide to the systematic development of physical strength is yet wanting: we have indicated what is required to solve this task, and our hope is that, should the nation show appetite for this solution, it will be found. This part of education as a whole is only a means and a preliminary exercise for its second essential part, civic and religious education. Whatever needs to be said in general on this matter we have already conveyed in our second and third addresses, to which we have nothing more to add. To deliver a definite guide to the art of this education is – naturally in conference and consultation with Pestalozzi's own art of education – the affair of that same philosophy which is proposing a German national education in general; and, when the need for such guidance arises after the first part has been put into practice and completed, this philosophy will not neglect to provide it. How will it be possible that each pupil, even those born into the lowest rank (for the rank of birth truly makes no difference to their gifts), will grasp, and grasp easily, the instruction in these subjects, which contains, if you like, the profoundest metaphysics and is the result of the most abstract speculation, and which even scholars and minds given to speculation find impossible to grasp at present? Let no one weary himself for the time being by worrying how this may be so: experience will later teach us, if only we obey with regard to the first steps. For the reason alone that our age in general is imprisoned in the world of empty concepts, and has never entered the world of true reality and intuition, we cannot expect it to begin straightaway with the most exalted and spiritual intuition, and afterwards it is already too clever by half. Philosophy must insist that our age surrender the world it has inhabited until now and find for itself an entirely different one; and it is no wonder if such an exacting demand proves fruitless. The pupil of our education, however, has from the very outset made himself at home in the world of intuition and has never known another; he will not change his world but only enhance it, and this takes place of itself. At the same time, this education is, as we intimated above, the only possible education for philosophy and the only means of making it universal.

Education concludes with this civic and religious instruction, and the pupil is now to be discharged. And thus we would have said enough for now with respect to the content of the proposed education.

That the pupil's cognitive faculty must never be stimulated without love for the object of knowledge being stimulated at the same time, because otherwise knowledge remains dead; that love must never be aroused without it becoming clear to knowledge, because otherwise love remains blind – this is one of the main principles of our proposed education, with which Pestalozzi, too, as a consequence of his theory as a whole, must be in agreement. The stimulation and development of this love are now linked to the systematic course of instruction by the thread of sensation and intuition; this arrives of itself and without our intention or co-operation. The child possesses a natural drive towards clarity and order, which is constantly satisfied in that course of instruction, thus filling him with joy and pleasure. In the midst of this satisfaction, however, the drive is once more stimulated, and thus further satisfied, by the new obscurities that now come to light, and so life is passed in the love and pleasure of learning. This is the love by which each individual is joined to the world of thought; it is the bond between the worlds of sense and of spirit. Through this love our education achieves unerringly and by design what formerly arose by chance only among a few favoured minds; that is to say, the easy development of the cognitive faculty and the successful cultivation of the fields of science.

There is yet another love, the kind that binds men together and unites all individuals in a single community of reason sharing the same convictions.

As that love forms knowledge, so this love forms the active life and impels the pupil to represent what is known [*das Erkannte*] in himself and in others. Since it would scarcely assist our true purpose merely to improve the education of scholars (and the national education we have in view aims first and foremost at cultivating not scholars but human beings), it is clearly the bounden duty of this education to develop the second kind of love as well as the first.

Pestalozzi speaks of this subject with heart-warming enthusiasm.[64] Nevertheless, we must confess that nothing he says seemed to us clear in the slightest, let alone clear enough to serve as a foundation for a systematic development of that love. It is therefore necessary that we communicate our own ideas about such a foundation.

The usual assumption, that man is by nature selfish and this selfishness innate even in the child, that education alone implants in him a moral motive, is based on a very superficial observation and quite false. Since out of nothing nothing can be made, for no matter how far a fundamental drive is developed it can never be turned into its opposite, how should education be able to instil morality [*Sittlichkeit*] in the child if it were not already in him, originally and prior to all education? And so it is, in all children born into the world; our task is simply to discover the purest and most original form in which it appears.

The results of speculation as well as all observation agree that this purest and most original form is the drive for respect, that from this drive the moral [*das Sittliche*] enters into knowledge as the only possible object of respect: the right, the good, veracity, the power of self-control. In the child this drive initially manifests itself as the drive to be respected in turn by the one who commands his own highest respect. As a rule – and surely proving that love does not spring from selfishness – this drive is directed far more forcefully and decisively at the father, who is sterner, often absent and does not immediately appear as a benefactor, than at the mother who in her beneficence is ever present. The child desires to be noticed by his father; he desires his applause; only insofar as his father is satisfied with him is he satisfied with himself: this is the natural love of the child for his father, not for the caretaker of his sensuous well-being, but for the mirror in which his own worth or unworth is reflected back at

---

[64] *Ansichten, Erfahrungen und Mittel zur Beförderung einer der Menschennatur angemessenen Erziehungsweise* (Leipzig: Gräff, 1807). [Fichte's note. The relevant passage can be found on pp. 15–16.]

him; to this love the father himself can now easily join strict obedience and every form of self-denial; to earn the reward of his heartfelt applause the child gladly obeys. Again, it is this love which he craves from his father; that the latter notices his efforts to be good and acknowledges him, that the father shows that it gives him pleasure to approve and is terribly sorry when he must disapprove, that he wants nothing more than always to be satisfied with his conduct, that all his demands are intended only to make his child ever better and worthier of his respect. Again, it is this love whose sight continually animates and fortifies the child's love, and gives him renewed strength for his every subsequent endeavour. However, this love is deadened by neglect or constant and unjust misunderstanding; in particular, even hate is aroused if one allows self-interest to be glimpsed in one's treatment of the child and, for example, treats the loss of something caused by his carelessness as a capital crime. He sees himself regarded as a mere instrument, and this offends his obscure but no less present feeling that he must possess his own self-worth.

Let us demonstrate this with an example. What adds shame to the pain of a child's chastisement? And what is this shame? Obviously it is the feeling of self-contempt, which he must direct at himself when his parents and educators make known their displeasure. For that reason, where punishment is not accompanied by shame, there is an end of education, and the punishment appears as an act of violence that the pupil haughtily disregards and laughs to scorn.

This, then, is the bond which joins men together in unity of mind and whose development is a principal component of the education to humanity – not sensuous love, by any means, but the drive to mutual respect. This drive takes two forms. In the child it begins as unconditional respect for the adults around him and becomes the drive to be respected by them and to use their respect for him as a measure of his own self-respect. This trust in an alien and external standard of self-respect is the distinctive characteristic of childhood and immaturity; on its existence alone rests the possibility of instructing and educating the new generation to complete human beings. The mature man carries the measure of his self-esteem within himself and wishes to be respected by others only insofar as they have first made themselves worthy of his respect; with him this drive assumes the form of a longing to be able to respect others and to bring forth outside himself that which is worthy of respect. If there did not exist such a fundamental drive in humanity, how might we explain the phenomenon that even the merely tolerably good man is pained to find men worse than he thought them and deeply hurt to have to despise them; whereas on the contrary selfishness would delight in being able to rise arrogantly above others? This latter characteristic of maturity the educator should embody, just as the first can be reckoned on in the pupil. The purpose of education in this regard is precisely to produce maturity in the sense we have indicated, and education is really complete and brought to its conclusion only once this goal has been achieved. Until now many men have remained children throughout their lives – those who required for their satisfaction the applause of their fellow men and thought they had not truly accomplished anything unless they found favour with them. Set against them are the few strong and robust characters who were able to rise above the judgement of others and satisfy themselves, and these as a rule have been hated, while the others, though not respected, were nevertheless thought likeable.

The foundation of all moral education is this, that one knows there is such a drive in the child and firmly presupposes it; then recognises its appearance and gradually develops it ever further, by giving it suitable stimulation and providing material to satisfy it. The very first rule is that one should direct this drive at the only object appropriate to it, the moral, but by no means fob it off with a material alien to its nature. Learning, for example, is its own incentive and reward. The application of effort might earn applause at most as an exercise in self-conquest; but this voluntary effort beyond what was demanded will, at least in the general national education, scarcely find a place. That the pupil learns what he ought to learn must be regarded as something that is simply self-evident and meriting no further discussion. Even the swifter and better learning of the more able mind must be viewed as a mere natural phenomenon that warrants no praise or distinction, but at the very least conceals other shortcomings. Only in the moral [*im Sittlichen*] should this drive be assigned its sphere of activity; but the root of all morality is self-control, self-conquest, the subordination of one's selfish impulses to the idea of the whole. Only by these means, and no other, is it possible for the pupil to win the educator's applause, which he is directed by his spiritual nature, and accustomed by education, to need for his own satisfaction. There are, as we have already advertised in our second address, two very different ways of subordinating the personal self to the whole. First there is that which absolutely must exist and from which no one can be exempted in any shape or form: submission to the law of the constitution drafted for the sake of preserving the order of the whole and nothing more. He who does not transgress against this law meets with no disapprobation, that is true, but nor does he receive any applause; likewise he who did transgress against it would be met with real disapprobation and censure, which, since he erred publicly, would have to be expressed publicly, and if censure alone remained fruitless it might even be sharpened by the addition of punishment. Then there is a subordination of the individual to the whole that cannot be demanded but only rendered willingly: to increase and enhance the welfare of the whole through self-sacrifice. In order to inculcate in the pupil from youth onwards the relationship between mere lawfulness and this higher virtue, it will be expedient to permit only him, against whom during a certain time no complaint has been raised in the first regard, to make such voluntary sacrifices, as the reward, so to speak, for his lawfulness, but to refuse permission to him who is not yet quite so assured in regulating and ordering his own person. The objects of such voluntary deeds we have indicated earlier in general terms and they will be treated in greater detail below. This kind of sacrifice will receive active approval and real recognition of its meritoriousness, though by no means publicly, in the form of praise (which might corrupt the soul, open the door to vanity and lead it astray from self-sufficiency), but in private and in the presence of the pupil alone. This recognition must be nothing more than the outward representation of the pupil's own good conscience, the confirmation of his satisfaction with himself and of his self-respect, and the encouragement to continue to have faith in himself. The following arrangement would be an excellent means of promoting the benefits we envisage here. Where there are several educators and educatresses, as we suppose to be the rule, each child should choose, freely, as his trust and feeling dictate, one of them for his special friend and the keeper of his conscience, so to speak. Let the child seek his counsel in all cases where he finds it difficult to do the right thing; let him help the child with friendly words of support; let him be the confidant of the voluntary deeds that the child undertakes and, finally, the one who crowns excellence with his applause. Through the persons of these confessors, then, education would systematically help to raise the individual child, each after his own fashion, to ever greater powers of self-control and self-conquest. In this way resoluteness of character and self-sufficiency will gradually develop; through their production education brings itself to a close and adjourns for the future. The extent of the moral world opens itself up to us most clearly through our own deeds and actions – and on him on whom it has dawned, it has truly dawned. Such a man knows for himself what it contains and no longer needs a stranger's testimonial to his good conduct, but can sit in judgement over himself and, from that moment on, has come of age.

What we have just said has closed a gap remaining in our last address and only now made our proposal truly practicable. Through the new education the pleasure in doing what is right and good for its own sake will take the place of the sensuous hope and fear employed hitherto, and, as the sole existing motive, set all future life in train: this is the essence of our proposal. The first question that arises here is this: but how is this pleasure to be produced? It cannot be produced in the proper sense of the word, for man has no power to create something out of nothing. It must, if our proposal is in any way feasible, exist originally and in all men without exception, and be innate in them. And so it is. Without exception the child desires to do right and be good, and by no means does he seek, like a young animal, merely his own well-being. Love is the essential component of man; it exists just as man exists, whole and complete, and nothing can be added to it: for love lies beyond the continuously growing appearance of sensuous life and is independent thereof. It is only knowledge to which this sensuous life attaches itself and which comes into being and grows with it. This knowledge develops only slowly and gradually, in the course of time. How, then, should that inborn love develop and exercise itself during the years of ignorance, until there arises a coherent set of concepts of the right and the good to which the motive of pleasure can be linked? Wise nature has solved the difficulty without any assistance from us. The consciousness which the child inwardly lacks is outwardly represented and embodied in the judgement of the adult world. Until a rational judge develops in the child himself, he is referred by a natural impulse to this adult world and thus endowed with an external conscience until one is produced within him. This truth, hitherto little known, the new education should acknowledge, and it should guide the love that exists independently of its efforts towards what is right. Until now this ingenuousness and childish belief of the young in the greater perfection of adults has, as a rule, served to bring them to ruin; precisely their innocence and natural faith in us made it possible, before they could distinguish good from bad, to implant in them, instead of the good, which they inwardly desired, our depravity, which they would have abhorred had they been able to recognise it.

This is the greatest transgression that our age can be charged with. It also explains the phenomenon we encounter on a daily basis, that as a rule man becomes more corrupt, more selfish, more dead to all noble impulses, more incapable of any good deed, the more years he has notched up and the further he has travelled from the early days of his innocence, which for the time being still linger softly in one or two glimmerings of the good. This is further proof that the present generation, if it fails to make a break with its past, must perforce leave behind a posterity even more degenerate and the next generation one more degenerate still. Of such men a venerable teacher of the human race says truthfully and strikingly that it were better if now and then a millstone were hanged about their necks and they were drowned in the depth of the sea.[65] It is a vile calumny on human nature to say that man is born a sinner; if this were true, how could he ever acquire a concept of sin, which is only possible in opposition to what is not sin? Through life does he become a sinner; and as a rule human life has hitherto been a steadily progressing evolution of sinfulness.

What I have said shows in a new light the necessity of avoiding delay in our arrangements for a real education. If only the rising generation could grow up without any contact with adults and wholly without education, then one might always conduct an experiment to see what the result would be. But even if we just leave them in our society, their education takes care of itself without any wish or will of ours; they educate themselves to us: our way of being imposes itself on them as their model, they emulate us, even without our demanding that they do so, and they desire nothing more than to become as we are. Now, as a rule we are in the great majority thoroughly depraved – partly without knowing it and, as naive as our children, taking our depravity to be what is right. Or, even if we were aware of it, how could we suddenly cast off, in the company of our children, what has become, in the course of a long life, second nature, and exchange in full our old soul and spirit for a new one? Through their contact with us our children must become corrupt; that is inevitable. If we possess but one spark of love for them, we must remove them from our foul atmosphere and build a more salubrious abode for them. We must introduce them into the society of men, who, no matter how things may otherwise stand with them, have nevertheless acquired through constant practice and habit at least the knack of remembering that children are watching them, the ability to restrain themselves for that long at least, and the knowledge of how to behave in their presence. We

---

[65] Matthew 18: 6.

must not let the children back from this society into our own until, as is right and proper, they have learned to loathe the full extent of our corruption and are thereby rendered completely immune to any contamination.

This much we have thought necessary to convey here about the education to morality in general.

That the children should live together with their teachers and principals in otherwise total isolation from the adult world, I have mentioned several times. It is self-evident, and requires no further comment, that both sexes must receive this education in the same way. A separation of the sexes in special institutions for boys and girls would run counter to our purpose, and negate several of the main features of the education to perfect humanity. The subjects of study are the same for both sexes; the difference in the kind of work they undertake can, even where the rest of their education is shared, be observed without difficulty. The smaller society in which they are formed into human beings must, just like the larger one which they will one day enter as perfect human beings, consist in a union of both sexes. Each must first recognise and learn to love in the other their common humanity, and have friends of either sex, before their attention turns to the differences between the sexes and they become husbands and wives. The relation of the sexes to each other in the wider community, comprising stout-hearted protection on the one side and loving support on the other, must also be represented in the school and cultivated in the pupils.

If it should come to carrying out my proposal, the first task would be to draft a law governing the internal constitution of these schools. If the fundamental concept we established has been duly penetrated, then this is easily accomplished, and there is no need for us to dwell on the matter here.

A principal requirement of this new national education is that in it learning and work are combined; that the school seems, at least to the pupils, to support itself; and that each is kept aware of the fact that he must contribute to this purpose with all his power. This follows directly from the task of education itself, even without regard to its practicability or the need for thriftiness that doubtless will be expected of our proposal. Partly this is because all who pass only through the general national education are destined for the labouring classes and their training as proficient workers undoubtedly forms part of their education; but more especially because an individual's well-founded confidence that he will always be able to make his way in the world through his own resources, and sustain himself without relying on the charity of others, belongs to man's personal self-sufficiency and conditions his moral self-sufficiency far more than people have seemed to realise. This training would supply another component of education, one that as a rule has also been left to blind chance until now. This we might call domestic education, and it must not by any means be viewed in its inadequate and limited aspect, which some mock with the name of economy, but from the higher vantage-point of morality. Our age often establishes as an incontestable principle the notion that the only way to get on in life is to flatter, grovel and be willing to do anything. Our age does not consider that, even if we wanted to spare it the heroic but altogether true objection – namely, that if that is how things stand, it were better to die than to lead such a life – we might still observe that it ought to have learned to live with honour. Inquire more closely after the persons who distinguish themselves by their dishonourable conduct; you will always find that they never learned to work, or are loath to work, and that moreover they are wretched managers of their own affairs. For that reason the pupil of our education must be accustomed to industriousness, so that he is removed from the temptation to do wrong because he cannot be sure of his next meal; and the idea that it is shameful to wish to owe one's livelihood to anything but one's own labour must be impressed deeply into his soul as the very first principle of honour.

Pestalozzi desires that pupils practise all manner of handicrafts at the same time as they learn.[66] Whilst we do not wish to deny that these activities may be combined – on condition, as he allows himself, that the child can already completely master the handicraft – this proposal seems to us nevertheless to stem from the limitations of his primary goal. Instruction must in my opinion be represented as so sacred and venerable that it requires the pupil's complete attention and concentration to the exclusion of any other activity. If, in those seasons when the pupils are compelled to remain indoors anyway, such crafts as knitting, spinning and the like are pursued during the hours set aside for work, then, so that

---

[66] Pestalozzi: 'I had in my experiments of thirty years ago found the most decisive results. I had already at that time brought children to a readiness of reckoning, while spinning, that I myself could not follow without paper. All depends, however, on the psychology of the form of teaching. The child must have the handicraft, which he carries on with his learning, perfectly in his power; and the task which he thus learns with the work must in every case be only an easy addition to that which he can do already' (*GC*, Letter I, pp. 35–6).

the mind remains active, it will be expedient to associate these with collective mental exercises under supervision of their teachers; nevertheless, here work is the important thing, and these exercises are to be regarded not as instruction but merely as a game to liven up their spirits.

All activities of this lesser sort must generally be presented only as a secondary occupation, never as the chief work. This chief work is the cultivation of fields and garden, the raising of cattle, and the practice of such handicrafts as they need in their miniature state. It goes without saying that the share in this expected of each pupil must be balanced against the physical strength possessed by those of his age, and the deficit made up by new machines and tools that must be invented. Our main consideration here is that they understand, as far as possible, the principles of what they are doing, that for their tasks they have already acquired the necessary knowledge relating to horticulture and the production of crops, the characteristics and needs of the animal body, the laws of mechanics. In this way partly their education itself becomes a systematic training in the profession they are to follow in the future, and the thinking and wise farmer is schooled by immediate intuition; partly their mechanical work is already ennobled and spiritualised, and is just as much proof of the ideas they have grasped in free intuition as it is a means of earning their livelihood. Even in the company of beasts and in proximity to the soil, they still remain in the sphere of the spiritual world and do not descend to the beasts' level.

The basic law of this little agrarian state is this: that no article may be used for food, clothing, and so on, nor, as far as this is possible, any tool, that is not produced and manufactured within it. If this economy requires support from outside, then it will be supplied with objects of nature, but only of the kind that it possesses itself – and such that the pupils do not discover that their own harvest has been increased; or, if it is expedient that they are apprised thereof, they receive it only as a loan that must be repaid by a fixed time. Towards this independence and self-sufficiency of the whole each must work with all his might, without demanding recompense or laying claim to some property or other for himself. Each must know that he is entirely indebted to the whole and prospers or starves – if that it is how things shall be – when the whole prospers or starves. The honourable self-sufficiency of the larger state and of the family, which he will one day enter, and the relation of their individual members to them, are thereby presented to him in living intuition, and take ineradicable root in his soul.

Here, at the point where pupils are initiated into mechanical labour, is where learned education, arising out of the general national education and based upon it, separates itself. To this we must now turn. The learned education arises out of the general national education, I said. I shall leave open the question of whether henceforth too every man who thinks he has means enough to allow him to study, or who for some reason counts himself among the hitherto higher ranks, will be free to tread the path of learned education customary until now. Time will tell how, if it should ever come to this national education, the majority of these scholars with their learning bought with gold will compare not just with the scholar educated in the new school, but even with the common man produced thereby. But I do not wish to speak of these matters now, but of the new method of learned education.

According to its principles, the future scholar, too, must have passed through the general national education, and have received, completely and clearly, the first part of this instruction: the development of knowledge through sensation, intuition and everything connected to the latter. Only the boy who shows a superior gift for learning and a conspicuous inclination to the world of ideas can be allowed by the new national education to take up this profession; but it must allow everyone who exhibits these qualities without exception and without regard for supposed differences of birth; for the scholar is by no means a scholar for his own convenience, and every such talent is a valuable asset whereof the nation must not be deprived.

The vocation of the non-scholar is to maintain the human race at the stage of development it has already reached; that of the scholar to take it forward, according to a clear concept and with deliberate art. With his concept the scholar must always be in advance of the present, must comprehend the future and be able to implant it in the present for its later development. This requires a clear overview of the state of the world until now, a free capacity for pure thought independent of appearance, and, so that he can express himself, the mastery of language down to its living and creative root. All this demands mental self-activity without the guidance of others and solitary contemplation in which, from the hour when his profession is decided and forever after, the future scholar must therefore be practised; and this is by no means, as with the non-scholar, merely a thinking under the watchful eye of his ever-present teacher; it requires a multitude of auxiliary knowledge that is entirely useless for the non-scholar in his vocation. The work of the scholar, and the daily task of his life, will be precisely that solitary contemplation; he shall be initiated into this work at once and released from other mechanical labours. Though the education of the future scholar to humanity would therefore proceed by and large with the general national education as before, and he would attend the relevant classes together with all the others, those hours which they spend working he would have to pass in the study of whatever his future profession specifically demanded; and this would be the sole difference. The general knowledge of agriculture, of other mechanical arts, and of their techniques, which even the ordinary man is expected to possess, he will doubtless have learned already as he passed through the first grade; or, should this not be the case, he would have to catch up this knowledge. That he, far less than any other, can be exempted from the physical exercises we have introduced goes without saying. To indicate, however, the particular subjects that would fall within the province of the learned education, as well as the course of study to be observed thereby, lies beyond the scope of these addresses.

On whom the execution of this plan of education will devolve

The plan of the new German national education has been set forth in sufficient detail for our purposes. The next question that arises is this: who should lead the way in executing this plan, whom can we count on to do so, and on whom have we counted in the past?

We have established this education as the highest and, at the present time, single most urgent concern for German love of fatherland, and wish through it to usher into the world the improvement and regeneration of the entire human race. To begin with, however, that love of fatherland should inspire the state in every German territory, preside over it, and be the driving force behind all its decisions. It ought to be the state, therefore, on which we first fix our expectant gaze.

Will the state realise our hopes? What can the foregoing lead us to expect of it – always, it goes without saying, looking not to one particular state but to Germany as a whole?

In modern Europe education did not actually proceed from the state, but from that power from which states for the most part derived their own: from the celestial spiritual realm of the Church. The Church saw itself not so much as a constituent of the earthly commonwealth as a colony of heaven quite alien to it, sent to enlist citizens for this foreign state wherever it could take root; its education aimed at nothing save that men would not be damned in the other world but blessed. Through the Reformation this ecclesiastical power, which continued to regard itself as before, was simply united with the secular authority with which it had previously come into conflict all too often; in that respect, this was the only difference resulting from that event. Hence the old view of education persisted also. Even in the most recent times, and indeed to this day, the cultivation of the propertied classes has been considered as the private affair of the parents, who might arrange it to their liking, and the children were as a rule only taught whatever would make them useful to their parents. The only public education, however, that of the people, consisted solely in preparation for attaining blessedness in heaven; the main thing was a little Christianity, some reading, and writing, if it could be managed – all for the sake of Christianity.[67] All other development of men was left to the haphazard and blind influence of the society in which they grew up and to the experience of real life. Even the institutions of higher education were primarily geared towards the training of the clergy; divinity was the principal faculty to which the others formed only an appendix, and for the most part received only the scraps from its table.

For as long as those who stood at the head of government remained in the dark about its true purpose and were seized even in their own person by that conscientious concern for their own blessedness and that of others, their zeal for this kind of public education and their earnest efforts on its behalf could safely be counted on. But as soon as the purpose of government became clear to them and they grasped that the state's sphere of activity lies within the visible world, they were compelled to recognise that such concern for the eternal blessedness of their subjects could not be their burden and that whoever wanted to be blessed should look to himself to see how he might accomplish it. From this point on they believed they had done enough if they merely left those foundations and institutions established in more pious times to pursue their original vocation. However unsuitable and inadequate these may have been for a quite different age, they did not think themselves obliged to contribute to them by stinting on their other aims, or entitled actively to intervene and replace the antiquated and useless with what was new and fit for purpose. All suggestions of this kind were met with the ever-ready reply: the state has no money for it. If once an exception was made to this rule, then it was to the advantage of the institutions of higher education, which shed lustre far and wide and brought glory to their patrons. The education of that class which is the actual bedrock of the human race, from which

---

[67] A Prussian cabinet order issued on 31 December 1803 decreed: 'The children of the labouring classes ... shall learn to read their catechism, Bible and hymnbook, to read and write in keeping with their humble and limited circumstances, to fear and love God and to act accordingly, to respect authority and to love their neighbour.'

higher education constantly replenishes itself and on which it must always react – that of the people – was neglected and found itself, since the Reformation and until this day, in a state of increasing decline.

If in the future and from this hour forward we are to be able to hope for better things of the state in the matter that concerns us here, then it would have to exchange the fundamental concept of the purpose of education which it seems to have had hitherto for a quite different one; to see that it was quite right to have rejected responsibility for the eternal blessedness of its citizens, because for this blessedness no special cultivation is required, and such a nursery for heaven as the Church, whose power was finally transferred to the state, does not exist, only stands in the way of all good cultivation, and must be relieved of its duties; that, conversely, there is a pressing need for a thorough education for life on earth and that from this the education for heaven follows of itself as a ready supplement thereto. Until now the more enlightened the state thought itself, the more firmly it seems to have believed that it could achieve its true purpose by coercive measures alone, without regard to the religion and morality of its citizens, who might do as they saw fit in these matters. May the state have learned from recent experiences at least this, that it cannot do so and has landed in its present predicament precisely because of a lack of religion and morality!

May the state's doubts as to whether it has the resources to cover the cost of a national education be allayed and may it be persuaded that through this single expenditure it will meet most of its other commitments in the most economical way; that, if the state assumes responsibility for a national education, soon only this principal expenditure will remain! Until now, by far the greatest part of the income of the state has gone towards maintaining standing armies. The result of this investment we have seen; let this suffice, for to delve deeper into its specific reasons by examining the organisation of these armies lies outside our scope. Conversely, the state that universally introduced our proposal for a national education would, from the moment a younger generation had graduated from it, have no need of a special army; rather, it would have in them a host such as no age has ever seen. Each individual is well practised in every possible application of his physical strength and understands on the spot what he has to do, is accustomed to enduring every effort and exertion; his spirit, raised in immediate intuition, is always present and alert, in his soul lives the love of that whole whereof he is a member – the state and the fatherland – and this annihilates every other selfish impulse.

The state can summon them and put them to arms as soon as it wishes, and be sure that no enemy will vanquish them. Another share of the attention and expenditure in wisely governed states was previously given over to the improvement of the political economy, in the widest possible sense of the word, and in all its branches; and, owing to the ineducability and helplessness of the lower orders, much of the care and money lavished on this initiative has been in vain, and it has everywhere made but slight progress. Our education provides the state with labouring classes that from youth are accustomed to reflecting on their trade and already have the ability and inclination to help themselves; if above and beyond this the state is able to lend them a hand in an appropriate manner, they will understand its merest half-word and gratefully receive its instruction. All branches of the economy will, without much effort and in little time, attain a florescence such as no age has ever before witnessed, and the state, if it takes pains to do its sums, and if perchance by then it has also learned the true basic value of things, will recoup a thousandfold interest on its initial outlay. Until now the state has been obliged to do a great deal for the institutions of the judiciary and police, and yet has never been able to do enough; houses of correction and reform were a drain on its finances; finally, the more poor-houses were resorted to, the more spending they required, so that they have seemed until now to be institutions for the manufacture of poor people. In a state that makes the new education universal the former will be much reduced in number, the latter vanish entirely. Strict discipline applied at an early age guards against the need for less reliable discipline and correction in later life; but among a people educated in this way there are no poor at all.

May the state, and all its advisors, have the courage to look its true present situation in the face and admit it to themselves; may they perceive vividly that no other sphere of influence is left in which the state, originally and independently, can operate as a real state and make decisions, save for the education of the coming generations; that this is all it can do if it wishes to avoid doing absolutely nothing; that even this task will be left to it undiminished and unenvied! That we are no longer able to offer active resistance we already assumed earlier, as a fact that is obvious and universally acknowledged. How can we now justify the continuance of our forfeited existence against the accusation of cowardice and of an unworthy love of life? Only if we resolve not to live for ourselves and show this by our actions; if we make ourselves the seed of a more worthy posterity and wish to maintain ourselves for their sake only for as long as it takes to put them in place. Bereft of that primary goal in life, what else could we do? Our constitutions will be made for us, our alliances and the deployment of our armed forces will be dictated to us, our statutes will be borrowed, even the administration of justice and the passing of judgement will now and then be taken out of our hands; for the immediate future we shall be spared such worries as these. Only of education has no one thought; if we are looking for an occupation, then let us seize this! It is to be expected that we will be left undisturbed in it. I hope – perhaps I deceive myself, but because I live only for this hope, I cannot cease to hope – I hope that I shall convince a handful of Germans and grant them the insight that education alone can save us from all the evils that oppress us. In particular I reckon on this, that necessity has made us more inclined to take notice and give ourselves over to more serious reflection. Foreigners have other consolations and other means; we cannot expect, if this idea should ever reach them, that they will give much attention or attach much credence to it. Rather, I hope that it will blossom into a rich source of amusement for the readers of their journals when they learn that someone is promising such great things of education.

May the state and its advisors not let themselves become even slower to take up this task by thinking that the hoped-for outcome lies some way off in the distance! If, from among the manifold and highly tangled reasons that have resulted in our present fate, we wished to separate that which is alone and properly the burden of governments, then it would turn out that these, which are bound before all others to look towards and master the future, have only ever sought, under pressure of the great events of the age, to extricate themselves as best they could from their immediate embarrassment; with respect to the future, however, they have reckoned not on what might be done in the present, but on some stroke of luck that would sever the unbroken thread of cause and effect. But such hopes are deceptive. A motive force, once allowed to enter into time, continues and completes its course, and after the first careless act has been committed, reflection comes too late and cannot stop it. Our fate has taken us beyond the first mistake, that of thinking merely of the present; the present is no longer ours. May we not repeat the second, to place our hopes for a better future in something other than ourselves! Admittedly, the present can offer no consolation for the duty of living to anyone who for life needs something more than food; the hope of a better future is the only element in which we can still breathe. But only the dreamer can base this hope on something other than that which he himself can plant in the present for the development of a future. Let those who rule over us allow us to think just as well of them as we do of ourselves, and as the better man feels. Let them put themselves at the head of this business that to us is quite clear, so that we see arising before our very eyes what one day will wipe from our memory the shame that was done to the German name before our eyes!

If the state accepts the proposed task, then it will make this education universal, across the entire extent of its dominions, for each of its future citizens and without exception. Moreover, it is for this universality alone that we require the state, because for individual beginnings and isolated attempts the wealth of well-meaning private persons would suffice.[68] Now, we cannot by any means expect parents to be universally willing to part from their children and entrust them to this new education, of which it will be difficult to convey any notion to them. Rather, we must assume, following past experience, that everyone who thinks he still has the wherewithal to nurture his children at home will set himself against public education, and especially against a public education that separates parents and children so severely and for so long. In such cases where resistance is likely, we have previously been used to statesmen rebuffing the proposal with the reply: the state has no right to use force for this end. As they now mean to wait until all men possess a good will, and this universal good will cannot be arrived at without education, they are thereby insured against all need for reform and can hope that things will stay as they are until the end of days. Insofar as these men are such as either hold education to be an unnecessary luxury, arrangements for which must be made as thriftily as possible, or see in our proposal only a bold new experiment with humanity, which though it might succeed might just as easily fail, their conscientiousness is to be praised. We cannot expect that such men, who are full of admiration for the current state of public education and delighted at the perfection it has attained under their stewardship, should agree to something of which they are ignorant; there is nothing that they as a group can do to advance our purpose, and it would be lamentable if the decision about this matter should devolve on them. May statesmen be found, and consulted on this matter, who have educated themselves by a deep and thorough study of philosophy and science in general, who take their business seriously, who

---

[68] Fichte was indebted to the charity of a local nobleman for his own education.

possess a firm conception of man and his destiny, who are able to understand the present and to comprehend what humanity urgently needs at this moment in time! If these preconceptions [*Vorbegriffe*] had led them to perceive for themselves that only education can save us from the barbarism and brutalisation that threatens irresistibly to descend on us, if an image appeared before them of the new race of men that would arise through this education, if they were themselves fervently convinced of the infallibility and certainty of the means proposed, then it might also be expected of such men that at the same time they should grasp that the state, as the supreme administrator of human affairs and the guardian of its young charges, answerable only to God and its conscience, has the perfect right to compel them for their own good. Now, where is there a state that doubts whether it has the right to impose military service on its subjects, and to take children from their parents for this purpose, with or without the consent of either the parents or the child? And yet this compulsion to adopt a lasting mode of life against one's own will is far graver and often has the most baneful consequences for the moral condition, health and life of him who is thus compelled; by contrast, that compulsion whereof we speak restores, after completed education, an individual's entire personal freedom and can have none but the most salutary consequences. True, in earlier times military service was voluntary; but when it was found that this was insufficient for the purpose intended, there was no hesitation in backing it up with compulsion, because the matter was important enough for us and necessity dictated compulsion.[69] May our eyes be opened to our necessity in this regard also, and the object become likewise important to us; then our qualms would vanish of themselves. Particularly as compulsion is needed only in the first generation and disappears in the ensuing ones that have passed through this education, the initial compulsion to enter military service will also be abolished, because those educated in this manner will all be equally willing to take up arms for the fatherland. If, to avoid an outcry at the beginning, compulsory public education is limited in the same way as compulsory military service has been in the past, and those classes exempted from the former are released from the latter also, then this will bring no significant disadvantages. The reasonable parents among those exempted will voluntarily commit their children to the care of this

---

[69] National conscription was first introduced throughout Prussia in 1733 by Friedrich Wilhelm I, the Great Elector.

education; those children of the unreasonable parents from these classes – an inconsiderable number compared to the whole – may always grow up as before and survive into the better age to come, useful only as a strange reminder of the old time and as a means of inflaming the new one to a vivid recognition of its greater fortune.

If this education is to be the national education of the Germans as such; if the great majority of all who speak the German language, but by no means the citizenry of this or that particular German state, are to stand forth as a new race of men, then every German state, each for itself and independently of the others, must take up this task. The language in which this matter was first raised, in which the materials are written and will continue to be written, in which the teachers are trained, in which all of this is carried along by a single stream of symbolic meaning, is common to all Germans. I can scarcely imagine how, and with what modifications, this method of instruction as a whole, particularly in the scope that we have given this plan, might be rendered into some foreign language such that it did not appear alien and translated, but as native and issuing from the language's own life. For all Germans this difficulty is removed; for them the matter is settled and they need only take control of it.

How lucky we are in this respect that there are still distinct and separate German states! What so often has been to our detriment can perhaps work to our advantage in this important affair of the nation. Perhaps rivalry among the many and the desire to outdo one another can effect what the quiet self-contentment [*Selbstgenügsamkeit*] of the individual would not have brought forth. For it is clear that the German state which makes a start in this matter will achieve pre-eminence by winning the respect, love and gratitude of all; that it will stand as the supreme benefactor and true founder of the nation. It will encourage the others, give them an instructive example and become their model; it will dispel the doubts in which they remain ensnared; from its lap will the first textbooks and the first teachers go forth and be lent to the others; and the state which follows it will win the second place of honour. As a heartening testimony to the fact that among the Germans a feeling for loftier things has not yet been extinguished, several German tribes and states have previously vied with one another for the glory of higher culture. Some have championed an expanded freedom of the press and a greater freedom from traditional opinion, others better-organised schools and universities; some have trumpeted past glories and merits, others have a different claim to fame; and the contest could never be decided. On the present occasion it will be. That culture alone which strives and ventures to make itself universal, to embrace all men without distinction, is a real component of life and is sure of itself. Everything else is an alien bauble, put on merely for show and not even worn with a clear conscience. Now it will be revealed where it is that the vaunted culture exists only among a few persons of the middle rank, who exhibit it in their writings (men the like of which are to be found in all German states); and where, conversely, the culture has ascended to the upper ranks that advise the state. Then it will also be shown how one should judge the zeal displayed here and there for the erection and flourishing of institutions of higher education; whether underlying it was a pure love for the cultivation of humanity, which would seize with the same zeal every branch thereof and especially its very first foundation, or a mere longing to shine and perhaps petty financial speculations.

The German state which is the first to carry out this proposal will win for itself the greatest glory, I said. And furthermore, this German state will not stand alone for long, for there is no doubt at all that it will quickly attract successors and emulators. The important thing is that a start is made. If nothing else, honour, jealousy, the desire to possess what another has and where possible to have something even better, will drive one state after another to follow the example of the first. Then our earlier reflections concerning the state's own advantage, which at present might strike some as dubious, will seem more plausible once proved true in living intuition.

If right now and from this hour forth all German states made serious preparations to put this plan into practice, then after five and twenty years the better generation that we need would already stand before us, and whoever hoped to live that long could hope to see it with his own eyes.

Should, however – for of course we must reckon on this eventuality also – not one of the presently existing German states have among its highest advisors a man able to perceive what we supposed above and to be seized thereby, a man who at the very least did not have to face the active resistance of the majority of his colleagues, then of course this matter would devolve on well-intentioned private persons, and we would ask them to make a start with the proposed new education. In the first place we are thinking here of the great landowners, who could build such educational institutions on their estates for the children of their tenants. It redounds to Germany's glory and her honour, and distinguishes her before the other nations of modern Europe, that among the aforementioned class there have always been a few who made it their serious business to provide for the instruction and cultivation of the children on their lands and who gladly wished to do the best they could for them.[70] It is to be hoped that even now they will be inclined to apprise themselves of the full extent of the proposal put before them and work towards this greater and far-reaching objective with the same readiness that they previously showed in pursuit of more limited and incomplete ends. Perhaps here and there they might have been motivated by the insight that it was of greater benefit to have educated rather than uneducated subjects. Where the state has taken away this last motive by abolishing the relationship between lord and bondsman[71] – may it reflect all the more earnestly on its indispensable duty not to abolish at the same time the one boon that right-thinking men attached to that relationship; and in this case may it not omit to fulfil what is anyway its obligation after it has relieved those who willingly did so in its stead! With respect to the cities we look to voluntary associations of well-meaning citizens to accomplish this end. Necessity has not yet, as far as I can see, snuffed out the inclination to charity in German souls. Owing to a number of deficiencies in our institutions, which might all be brought together under the head of neglected education, this charity nevertheless seldom alleviates need, but often seems to increase it. May one finally direct that excellent inclination primarily at that charitable act which brings an end to all want and all further charity; that is to say, at education! However, we require and count on a good deed and self-sacrifice of yet another sort, which consists not in giving but in doing and rendering. May young scholars, their circumstances permitting, devote the time between university and their appointment to a public office to learning about the method of instruction employed in these schools and even to teaching in them! Setting aside the fact that they will thereby earn the gratitude of the whole, they can be further assured that the greatest profit will thereby accrue to them. All their knowledge, which they receive so lifelessly from the usual university teaching, will, in the element of general intuition into which they are here transplanted, be endowed with clarity and vitality; they will learn to communicate and apply it with facility, they will acquire for

---

[70] An example would be Friedrich Eberhard von Rochow, who in 1773 established a school for local children on his estate at Reckahn in Brandenburg. In 1776 he published a book entitled *Kinderfreund: Ein Lesebuch zum Gebrauch in Landschulen.*

[71] Serfdom was abolished in Austria in 1781–2, in Baden in 1783, in Prussia in 1807.

themselves, since in the child all the richness of humanity lies pure and manifest, a treasure trove of true knowledge of human nature that alone is worthy of the name; they will be schooled in the great art of life and activity, in which as a rule no university gives instruction.

If the state chooses to ignore the task with which it is charged, then all the more glory is due to the private persons who take it up. Far be it from us to conjecture as to what the future might bring or to strike a note of doubt and hesitation. We have stated clearly what we wish for in the first instance; let us merely observe that, if it should really come to pass that the state and the princes left the matter to private individuals, then this would be entirely in keeping with the previous course of German development and culture, which we earlier noted and demonstrated with examples, and which would therefore remain ever the same until the end. Even in this case the state would eventually follow, at first like an individual who wishes to make the contribution that falls to his share, until it recollects that it is not a part but the whole, that it has the right as well as the duty to provide for everyone. From that hour forward all independent and private endeavours disappear and are subordinated to the state's general scheme.

Should things take this turn, then the improvement of our race that we envisage will of course advance only slowly, without a certain and clear overview of the whole or a possible reckoning of its results. But let that not prevent us from making a start! It lies in the nature of the matter itself that it can never perish but, once set in motion, takes on a life of its own, and spreads outwards, casting its net ever wider. All who have passed through this education will bear witness to it and work zealously for its dissemination; each will pay for the instruction he has received by becoming a teacher himself and attracting as many pupils as he can, who in turn will one day become teachers themselves; and so it must go on until everyone is embraced without exception.

In the event that the state does not address itself to this matter, bringers of private initiatives must fear that all parents of means will refuse to entrust their children to this education. Then in God's name and with total confidence let us turn to the poor orphans, to those who lie about in misery on the streets, to all those whom the adult world has cast out and thrown away! Just as before, particularly in those German states in which the piety of previous generations had greatly increased the number of public schools and richly endowed them, a large number of parents gave their children an education, because at the same time they were afforded a means of subsistence such as they could not expect in any apprenticeship; so, out of sheer necessity, let us do the opposite and give bread to those whom no one else gives it, so that with their bread they receive simultaneously the culture of the spirit. Let us not fear that the misery and ferality of their previous state will be an obstacle to our intentions! Let us tear them away from it, abruptly and completely, and introduce them into an altogether new world; let us leave no reminder of how things used to be, and they will forget themselves and stand there as newly created beings. That only the good is inscribed on this fresh and clean slate is what our course of instruction, and our house regulations, must guarantee. For all of posterity it will be a warning and a testament to our age, if precisely those whom it cast out earn, by dint of their expulsion alone, the privilege of inaugurating a better race; if they bring the blessings of education to the children of those who would not live beside them; and if they become the progenitors of our future heroes, sages, law-givers and redeemers of humanity.

For the first establishment capable teachers and educators are needed before all else. Pestalozzi's school trained the likes of these and is always ready to train more. One of the chief ends in view to begin with will be that every institution of this sort should consider itself simultaneously as a nursery for teachers, and that, as well as the already finished teachers, there gather around these a number of young men who learn and practise teaching at the same time, and through practice learn to do it ever better. This will also, should these schools have to struggle with scarce resources at the outset, greatly facilitate the support of teachers. After all, most of them are there with the intention of learning themselves; therefore, even without further recompense, they may for a time apply what they have learned for the benefit of the school in which they learned it.

Furthermore, such a school requires bricks and mortar, initial equipment, and an adequate plot of land. It seems evident that, as these arrangements progress, there will be found in these institutions a relatively large number of older youths of an age at which, under the existing arrangements, they earn as servants not just their keep but also an annual wage; to these the youths of more tender years will be entrusted; and by industry and wise economy, which are in any case necessary, these schools will be able in large part to sustain themselves. To begin with, as long as the former kind of pupil is not yet at hand the schools may need larger subventions. It is to be hoped that people will be more prepared to make contributions when they can foresee their end. Let parsimony, which undermines our purpose, be far from our thoughts! It is much better that we do nothing than allow ourselves this.

And so I believe that, presupposing only goodwill, the execution of this plan would encounter no difficulty that could not be overcome by the combination of many and by directing all their powers to this one end.

On the means of maintaining ourselves until we achieve our principal purpose

That education which we put before the Germans as their future national education has now been amply described. When once the race formed by this education stands before us, this race driven solely by its taste for the right and good and by nothing else; this race endowed with an understanding that is adequate for its standpoint and recognises the right unerringly on every occasion; this race equipped with every mental and physical power to realise its will – then from the very existence of that race all that we can long for, even in our boldest wishes, will come true and grow out of it naturally. Such an age has so little need of our prescriptions that we would rather have to learn from it.

Since this race is not yet at hand, but must first be raised to maturity; and since, even if our expectations should be surpassed, we shall still have need of a considerable interval of time in order to cross over into that age, there arises the more immediate question: how shall we make it through this interval? Since we can do nothing better, how shall we maintain ourselves, at least as the soil on which the improvement can take place and as the point from which it proceeds? When once the race formed in this way steps forth from its isolation and comes among us, how are we to prevent it from finding in us a reality that has not the slightest kinship with the order of things it has conceived as right; a reality in which no one understands it or harbours the least desire and need for such an order of things, but regards the already existing order of things as wholly natural and the only possible one? Would not those who carry another world in their bosom soon go astray? And so would not the new culture be just as useless for the improvement of actual life as the previous culture, and soon fade away?

If the majority continue in their present heedlessness, thoughtlessness and distraction, then we must expect this to be the necessary consequence. Whoever sets out on his way without attending to himself, and allows himself to be determined by the vagaries of circumstance, is soon accustomed to every possible order of things. However offended his eye may have been when he beheld something for the first time, let it return daily in the same manner and he will get used to it, later find it natural and necessary, finally even grow fond of it, and he would be little served by restoring the original and better state of affairs because to do so would disturb his now familiar routine. In this way we accustom ourselves even to slavery, as long as it does not threaten our sensuous existence, and in time come to like it. And this is precisely what is most dangerous about vassalage: it blunts our feeling for all true honour and then has its very gratifying side for the indolent by relieving them of all care and the need of thinking for themselves.

Let us beware that the sweetness of servitude does not catch us unawares, for this robs even our descendants of the hope of future liberation. If our external activity is clapped in chains, then let us raise our spirit all the more boldly to the thought of freedom, to life in this thought, to the wish and desire for this one thing only. If freedom should vanish for a time from the visible world, let us give it refuge in our innermost thoughts until the new world grows up around us, a world that has the power to represent these thoughts in outward form. With our soul, which in our estimation must undoubtedly remain free, let us make ourselves the pre-figuration, the prophecy, the pledge of what after us shall become reality. Only do not let us be led into captivity, bent and subdued in spirit as in body!

If you ask me how this is to be achieved, then the only comprehensive answer is this: we must become on the spot what we ought to be in any case, Germans. We must not subject our spirit: therefore we must first acquire spirit, a spirit firm and certain; we must in all things become serious and cease our carefree and light-hearted existence; we must formulate sturdy and unshakeable principles to guide us in our thinking and action; life and thought must be of a piece, a single interpenetrating and solid whole; in both we must become more natural and truthful and cast off foreign artifice. In a word, we must acquire character; for to have character and to be German undoubtedly means the same, and in our language the thing has no special name precisely because it ought to go forth, without our knowledge and awareness [*Besinnung*], immediately from our being.

We must first and foremost set our own thoughts in motion and reflect on the great events of our day, their bearing on us and what we can expect from them; we must form a clear and certain view on all these subjects and answer the questions arising here with a firm and decisive yes or no; anyone with even the least claim to culture must do this. In every age man's animal life unfolds according to the same laws, and in this respect all time is identical. Different times exist only for the understanding, and only he who penetrates and brings them under a concept lives in union with them and is present in his own time; any other life is but animal or vegetable life. To let everything that happens pass unremarked before you, to shut your eyes and ears assiduously against its encroachment, even to boast of this thoughtlessness as great wisdom, may befit an unfeeling rock battered by the ocean waves or an insensible tree trunk wrenched this way and that in the storm, but by no means does it befit a thinking being. Even to float in the higher spheres of thought does not release one from this universal obligation to understand one's times. Everything on this loftier plane must desire to intervene in the immediate present after its own fashion, and whoever truly lives in the former must at once live in the latter also; if he did not live in the latter, then this would prove that he did not live but only dreamed in the former. This heedlessness as to what is taking place before our eyes, and the artful diversion of our attention to other objects, is exactly what an enemy of our independence would most wish to encounter. If he is sure that nothing stirs us to think, then he can do what he wants with us as with lifeless instruments; it is precisely thoughtlessness that habituates itself to everything, but where the clear and comprehensive thought, and in that thought the image of what ought to be, remains ever vigilant, there is no habituation.

These addresses have first of all invited you, and they will invite the entire German nation (insofar as it is presently possible to assemble the same by means of the printing press), to come to a firm decision and inwardly agree on the following questions: (1) whether it is true or untrue that there exists a German nation and that its continuance in its particular and independent essence is now in danger; (2) whether or not it is worth the effort to preserve that nation; (3) whether there is some sure and radical way to preserve it and what that way is.

Once it was the established custom among us that when some solemn word was uttered, either in speech or in print, it was taken up by the purveyors of idle gossip and turned into an amusing entertainment to relieve their oppressive boredom. I have not noticed, as I did before, that those around me have made the same use of my present orations; how-ever, I have paid no mind to the current tone of those social gatherings that meet through the press – by which I mean the literary journals and other periodicals – and know not whether to expect jest or earnest from this quarter.[72] However this may be, it at least has not been my intention to joke and set in train once more the well-known wit that our age possesses.

More deeply rooted among us Germans, so that it has almost become second nature and the opposite is virtually unheard of, was the custom of viewing everything that crossed our path as an invitation to anyone who had a mouth promptly and on the spot to have his say, and to inform us whether he was of the same opinion or not; after which poll the matter would be closed and public discussion obliged to hasten on to another subject. In this way all literary intercourse among the Germans was transformed, like Echo in the ancient myth, into a simple and pure sound, without body or physical content. Just as in the notorious evil communications of personal intercourse, so here too all that counted was that the human voice continued to ring out and that each received it without hesitation and passed it on to his neighbour; it did not matter in the least what was being said. If that is not evidence of lack of character and un-Germanness, then what is? It was not my intention to respect this custom and only keep alive the public discussion. Anyway I have, though my purpose was different, long since contributed my personal share in this public entertainment, and it is high time that I were absolved there-from. I do not want to know this minute what this one or that one thinks about the questions I have raised; that is to say, what he has hitherto thought or not thought. He must consider it for himself and think it through until his judgement is ripe and perfectly clear, taking all the time he needs. And if he still lacks the relevant background knowledge and the degree of culture required for a judgement in these matters, then he should take the time to acquire them too. If in this way his judgement is ripe and clear, then we do not exactly demand that he also deliver it publicly; should it coincide with what has been said here, then it has been said

---

[72] A possible allusion to the journal *Der Freimüthige, oder Berlinsches Unterhaltungsblatt für gebildete, unbefangene Leser* (The Plain Speaker, or Berlin Journal for Cultivated and Impartial Readers), which in its issue of 29 January 1808 found fault with some of the sentiments expressed in Fichte's Sixth Address.

already and does not need saying twice. Only he who has something else to say, and something better, is urged to speak; nevertheless, what has been said here must be really lived and pursued by each one in his own way and according to his own circumstances.

Least of all has it been my intention to submit these addresses before our German masters of doctrine and scripture as an exercise in composition, so that they may correct it and give me the opportunity to learn whether my work shows promise or not. In this regard, too, ample good advice and instruction have come my way already, and if improvement were to be expected, I ought already to have shown some.

No, it was first and foremost my intention to lead as many of the educated among us as I could out of the swarm of questions and inquiries, and out of the host of contradictory opinions concerning these, in which they have hitherto been flung back and forth; to lead them to a point where they might stand up for themselves, namely to the one lying closest to us, that of our own common affairs; and on this solitary point to steer them to a firm and immovable opinion, and to a clarity in which they might really find their way. It was my intention to unite them in agreement on this one matter at least, though so much else might still be disputed between them; and finally, in this fashion, to bring out a fixed characteristic of the German, to wit, that he has seen fit to form an opinion about the affairs of Germans, whereas he who has no wish to hear or think anything about this subject may henceforth rightly be regarded as no longer one of us.

The development of such a firm opinion, the coming together and mutual understanding of a number of men on this subject, will, as well as immediately rescuing our character from the dissolution that is unworthy of us, become a powerful means of achieving our principal goal, the introduction of the new national education. Particularly since we ourselves, either individually or collectively, could never make up our minds, and today wanted this and tomorrow that, each of us screaming something else into the confused din, so our governments (which of course listened to us, and often more than was advisable) were led astray, and wavered first one way then another, just like our opinion. If our common affairs are ever to be put on a firm and certain footing, what stops us from beginning with ourselves and setting an example of resolve and fixity of purpose? Let a constant and concordant opinion make itself heard just once, let a decisive need, one that announces itself as universal – a need for a national education, such as we assume – make itself felt; then I believe our governments will listen to us, they will help us if we show a desire to be helped. At least if they did not, then, and only then, would we have the right to complain about them; at the present time, when our governments are more or less as we would wish them to be, complaining ill becomes us.

Whether there is a sure and radical means of preserving the German nation and what this means is – that is the most significant of the questions that I have put before this nation to decide. I have answered this question, and explained my reasons for answering it as I did, not in order to prescribe the final judgement – which would avail nothing, for everyone who lends a hand in this matter must be persuaded in his own mind by his own activity – but only to incite men to their own reflection and judgements. Henceforth I must leave each to his own resources. Only this warning can I give and nothing more: that by shallow and superficial thoughts, which are in circulation even about this subject, you do not allow yourselves to be deceived, to be held back from deeper reflection, and silenced with empty promises.

For example, long before the most recent events, we have had to hear, as a kind of foretoken, what has oft been repeated since, that even if our political independence were lost, we would still retain our language and literature, and through them always remain a nation; and so we could easily console ourselves over everything else.[73]

What grounds are there, first of all, to hope that we shall still retain our language even without political independence? Those who say this surely do not assume that the miraculous power they ascribe to their admonitions and exhortations will be felt even by their children and by their children's children, and by all the generations to come? Those men now living and full-grown who are used to speaking, reading and writing in the German language will doubtless go on doing so; but what of the next generation? And the one after that? What counterweight do we think to place next to these later generations to balance their desire, even through the spoken and written word, to please him who sheds lustre and dispenses patronage? Have we never heard of a language that is the foremost in the world, regardless of the confession that its foremost

---

[73] See e.g. Adam Müller: 'Where shall we seek counsel, help and support save in the sacred flame, to conserve and tend which we Germans are charged? Science and art, or language in image and letter (for both are one), wherein the law, the memory and the spirit of all ages are deposited . . .' (*Vorlesungen über die deutsche Wissenschaft und Literatur* (Dresden, 1806), p. 205).

works have yet to be written? And do we not see before our very eyes that writings have already begun to appear in this language through whose content the authors hope to ingratiate themselves?[74] The example of two other languages is invoked, one ancient and the other modern, which, despite the political downfall of the peoples who spoke them, still continued as living languages.[75] I do not mean to go once more into the whys and wherefores of this continuance, but this much is clear at first glance: that both languages had in them something by which they found favour with their conquerors such as ours can never find. If these consolers had looked around more carefully, they would have come across another example, in our estimation much more fitting: the Wendish language.[76] During the long centuries since its people lost their freedom it has survived in the wretched hovel of the soil-bound serf, so that in it he can bemoan his fate, uncomprehended by his oppressor.

Or let us suppose that our language remains a living language and a language of writers, and so holds on to its literature. What kind of literature can that be, the literature of a people without political independence? What does the discerning writer want? And what can he want? Nothing other than to intervene in general and public life, to shape and recreate it after his own image; and if it is not this that he wants, then all his words are but an empty sound to tickle idle ears. He desires to think originally, proceeding from the root of spiritual life, for those who act just as originally – that is, who govern. Therefore he can only write in such a language as the governors also think in, in a language in which men govern, the language of a people that forms an independent state. What is the final goal of all our labours, even in the most abstract sciences? Let us assume that the immediate aim of these labours is to propagate science from one generation to the next and to preserve it in the world. And why should it be preserved? Obviously only to shape, when the time is right, the general life and the entire human order of things. That is its ultimate aim; accordingly, every scientific endeavour serves the state indirectly, even if only at some point in the distant future. If it abandons this aim, then its dignity and its independence are forfeit also. He who has this aim must write in the language of the ruling people.

[74] E.g. August Wilhelm Schlegel, *Comparaison entre la Phèdre de Racine et celle d'Euripide* (Paris, 1807) or Johannes von Müller, *De la gloire de Frédéric* (Berlin, 1807).
[75] Greek and Italian.
[76] Wendish or Lusatian is the language spoken by the Sorbs, a Slavic minority in eastern Germany.

Just as it is true that, wherever a particular language is found, there exists also a particular nation which has the right to run its own affairs and to govern itself, so, conversely, it can be said that, when a people has ceased to govern itself, it is obliged to surrender its language and merge with its conquerors, thereby ensuring unity and internal peace, and that conditions no longer existing are completely forgotten. Even a halfway intelligent overseer of such a mingling of peoples must make this demand, and we can confidently expect that the demand will be made in our case. Until this fusion is complete, translations of the authorised schoolbooks will be published in the language of the barbarians – that is, of those who are too thick-tongued to learn the language of the ruling people, who thereby exclude themselves from any influence on public affairs and damn themselves to life-long servitude. And they who have condemned themselves to silence about real events will also be permitted to practise their readiness of speech on fictitious disputes of the world, or to imitate old and antiquated literary forms. Proofs of the former case may be found in the ancient language adduced earlier as an example, proofs of the latter in the modern language.[77] Such a literature we may well retain for a while yet, and in such a literature let him who has no better consolation seek solace; but that even those who might be able to pluck up heart to see the truth, to be roused by its sight to decision and action, are kept in a state of indolent slumber by such vain consolation, which would serve well an enemy of our independence – this I should like to prevent if I could.

And so we are promised that a German literature will continue down to future generations. In order to form a better judgement of the hopes we can entertain in this matter, it would be most profitable to look around us to see whether at this moment we still have a German literature in the true sense of the word. The noblest privilege and the most sacred office of the writer is this: to assemble his nation and consult with it on its most important affairs. But in Germany especially this has ever been the exclusive office of the writer, for the nation was divided into a number of separate states and held together as a common whole only by the spoken and written word; most properly and urgently will it be his office in these times, now that the last external bond that united the Germans,

---

[77] Fichte presumably means the works of Hellenistic writers such as Lucian (AD 125 – after 180), whose *A True Story* is a tale about lunar travel, and the literature of the Italian Renaissance, which drew on classical models.

the imperial constitution, has also been torn asunder.[78] Should it now transpire – and here we are not speaking of what we know or fear to be true, but only of a possible case that we must likewise consider in advance – should it transpire, I say, that servants of particular German states were even now so gripped by anxiety, fear and terror that those voices which assumed a nation still existed and addressed themselves thereto were prevented first from being raised and then, by restrictions on the press, from being disseminated;[79] then this would be proof that already we no longer have any writing in German, and we would know what our prospects were for a literature in the future.

What are they afraid of? Perhaps that this man or that man would not gladly hear such voices? Then this would be an ill-chosen moment to show their tender concern, to say the least. They seem unable to prevent abuse and disparagement of all things German and the tasteless hymns of praise to the foreign, so let them not proceed so severely against a patriotic word that rings out in between! It is certainly possible that not everyone hears everything equally gladly; but we cannot worry about that now. We are driven by necessity and must say what it commands us to say. We are fighting for our life; would they have us walk with measured steps, lest some robe of state is besmirched by the swirling dust? We are sinking beneath the rising tide; shall we refrain from crying for help, lest some weak-nerved neighbour take fright?

For who are these men who might not gladly hear it? And under what circumstances might they not gladly hear it? Everywhere it is only unclarity and darkness that causes alarm. Every terrible vision vanishes once we fix our gaze upon it. So, with the same impartiality and frankness with which we have hitherto analysed every subject arising in these discourses, let us face up to this terror also.

Either one assumes that the being[80] to whom has fallen the guidance of a large part of the affairs of the world is a truly great soul or one assumes the opposite; there is no third possibility. As to the first case, whereupon rests all human greatness save on the self-sufficiency and originality of the person? On the fact that he is not an artificial contrivance of his age but has sprouted forth, just as he is, as an outgrowth of the eternal and

---

[78] The Holy Roman Empire of the German Nation was dissolved by Franz II when he surrendered the imperial crown on 6 August 1806.
[79] Fichte was dealing with precisely such nervousness in the office of the Prussian censor.
[80] Napoleon.

independence, we would rather know whether those Germans to whom a kind of guardianship of literature has fallen still permit, even today, the other Germans, who themselves write and read, a literature in the true sense of the word, and whether they believe that at present such a literature is still permitted in Germany or not; but what they really think about this will soon have to be decided.

After all the first thing that we must do, just to maintain ourselves until the complete and thorough regeneration of our tribe, is this: to acquire character and prove it first of all by forming a firm opinion through our own reflection about our true situation and the surest means of improving it. We have shown the vanity of seeking solace in the continuance of our language and literature. There are still other illusions, as yet unmentioned in these addresses, which hinder the formation of such a firm opinion. It answers our purpose to take these into consideration also; but let us reserve that business for the next hour.

Continuation of the reflections already begun

We mentioned at the end of our previous address that there are in circulation among us still more false ideas and delusive theories concerning the affairs of peoples, and that these prevent the Germans from coming to a definite view of their present situation that would be appropriate to their particular character. These phantoms are at this very time being offered around for public veneration with even greater zeal and, since so much else has begun to totter and become uncertain, they might be considered by some solely as a way of filling the vacuum that has arisen; therefore, it seems pertinent to the matter in hand to submit these to a more serious examination than their importance would otherwise merit.

To begin with, and above all else, the first, original and truly natural frontiers of states are undoubtedly their inner frontiers. Those who speak the same language are already, before all human art, joined together by mere nature with a multitude of invisible ties; they understand one another and are able to communicate ever more clearly; they belong together and are naturally one, an indivisible whole. No other nation of a different descent and language can desire to absorb and assimilate such a people without, at least temporarily, becoming confused and profoundly disturbing the steady progress of its own culture. The external limits of territories only follow as a consequence of this inner frontier, drawn by man's spiritual nature itself. And from the natural view of things it is not simply because men dwell within the

---

[*] For the reason why only the contents of this address but not the address itself are given here, see the note at the end of this overview. [Note by Fichte.]

confines of certain mountains and rivers that they are a people; on the contrary, men live together – and, if fortune has so arranged it for them, protected by mountains and rivers – because they were already a people beforehand by a far higher law of nature.

Thus lay the German nation, sufficiently united by a common language and way of thinking, and clearly enough separated from the other peoples, in the middle of Europe, as a wall dividing unrelated tribes. It was numerous and brave enough to protect its frontiers against any foreign incursion, left to its own devices and little inclined by its whole way of thinking to take notice of the neighbouring peoples, to meddle in their affairs or provoke their hostility by harassing them. In process of time its auspicious fate preserved the German nation from an immediate share in the rape of other continents – the event which more than any other has determined the course of recent world history, the destinies of peoples and the greater portion of their ideas and sentiments. Only after this event did Christian Europe become divided into several discrete parts, whereas previously it had been as one, even without being distinctly conscious thereof, and had shown itself to be such in joint endeavours; only after this event was a common source of plunder established, which all desired equally because all could use it equally well, and which each was jealous of seeing in the hands of another; only then did there exist a reason for secret enmity and belligerence pitting all against all. And only then did it profit a people to incorporate another of different descent and language, and to appropriate its resources, either by conquest or, where this was not possible, by alliance. A people that has remained true to nature can, if its territories have become too narrow, desire to enlarge them and gain more space by conquering neighbouring lands, and then it will drive out the former inhabitants; it may wish to exchange a harsh and barren climate for a milder and more fertile one, and again in this case it will drive out the earlier occupants; it may, if it degenerates, set out on marauding raids in which it simply seizes all that it can make use of, without wanting the soil or its inhabitants, and withdraws once more from the emptied lands; it may, finally, treat the former inhabitants of the conquered territory as a likewise useful commodity and share them out among its members as slaves: but there is not the least profit in annexing the alien tribe, just as it is, and making it part of the state, and therefore it will never be tempted to do so. If, however, an attractive, common booty is to be wrested from an equally strong or even stronger rival, then the calculation is quite different. No matter how little the vanquished people might be adapted to us in all other respects, its fists are at least useful in doing battle with the enemy we mean to rob, and every man is welcome as an addition to our armed forces. Suppose now that some sage, desirous of peace and tranquillity, clearly perceived this situation; from what agency could he ever expect peace? Obviously not from the natural limitation of human greed by what is superfluous being of no use to anyone – for there existed a booty that tempts all; and just as little might he have expected it from the will imposing a limit on itself – for in the company of those who grab everything they can for themselves, anyone who shows restraint must necessarily perish. None wishes to share what now he possesses for himself; each desires to rob the other of what he has, if he can. If one of them is quiet, then it is only because he thinks himself not strong enough to start a fight; he will surely start one as soon as he feels he has the requisite strength. Thus, the only means of preserving peace is for no one ever to acquire the power to be able to disturb the same and for each side to know that the other has just as much strength to resist as it does to attack; so that there arises a balance and counterbalance to the total power, by which alone, after every other means has vanished, each is kept in his present possessions and all are kept in peace. Accordingly, that well-known system of the balance of power in Europe presupposes these two things: a robbery to which none has a right but which all equally desire, and, secondly, a universal and actual rapacity that is ever active and stirring. Under these assumptions, this balance would indeed be the only means of preserving peace – if only another means were found of bringing about that balance in the first place and transforming it from an empty idea into reality.

But could in fact those assumptions be made generally and without any exception? Had not the mighty German nation remained in the centre of Europe, unspoiled by this booty, uninfected by the lust for it, and almost incapable of laying claim to it? If only this nation had stayed united as one common will and one common force, then if all the other Europeans had murdered one another on all the seas and all the islands and all the coasts, in the middle of Europe the bulwark of the Germans would have stood firm and prevented them from getting at one another's throats. Here amity would have reigned, and the Germans would have maintained themselves, together with a number of the other European peoples, in peace and prosperity.

That things should remain thus did not suit the self-interest of foreign lands, which in their calculations never saw beyond the next moment's gains. They found German valour useful for waging their wars and German hands useful for wresting the booty from the grasp of their rivals; a means of attaining this end had to be found, and foreign cunning easily triumphed over German simplicity and guilelessness. It was these foreign lands that first exploited the dissension that had arisen in Germany as a result of the religious controversies, in order artificially to divide this microcosm of the whole of Christian Europe from its close-knit unity into separate and independent parts, just as Europe had naturally divided itself over its shared spoils. They knew how to present these individual states that had thus grown up in the lap of a single nation, which had no enemy save for the foreign lands themselves and no interest save for the common interest of resisting foreign blandishments and perfidy with combined strength – they knew, I say, how to present these states to one another as natural enemies, against whom each had always to be on its guard, whilst representing themselves as natural allies against the danger posed by their own countrymen: the allies with whom alone they stood or fell and to whose enterprises, therefore, they likewise had to lend their wholehearted support. Only through these artificial ties did every quarrel that might flare up over some bone of contention in the old world or the new become the quarrels of the German tribes among themselves; every war that sprang up for any reason had to be fought on German soil and with German blood; every disturbance of the balance of power required an adjustment in that nation which was a stranger to the source of these troubles. And the German states, whose separate existence was already contrary to all nature and reason, had to be made, so that they might amount to something at least, into make-weights to supplement the larger weights in the scales of European power, whose movement they followed blindly and without a will of their own. Just as in many foreign states citizens are identified by their belonging to this or that foreign party, and having voted for this for that external alliance, but those who champion the patriotic party cannot be named; so the Germans, too, had for a long time held with some foreign party or other, and it was seldom that one came across anybody who might have espoused the cause of Germany and expressed the belief that this country should be allied only to itself.

This, then, is the true origin, import and outcome, for Germany and the world, of the notorious theory of an artificially maintained balance of power among the European states. If Christian Europe had remained one, as it ought to have and as it originally was, there would never have been any occasion to conceive such an idea. That which is one rests on and supports itself, and is not divided into conflicting forces that must be brought into equilibrium; only for a Europe that had become unlawful and divided did such an idea acquire an urgent significance. To this unlawful and divided Europe Germany did not belong. If at least Germany had remained one, she would have rested on herself in the centre of the civilised world, like the sun at the centre of the cosmos; she would have maintained herself, and hence her neighbours, in peace; and by her mere existence, without the need for any artificial measures, she would have kept everything in balance. Only the trickery of foreign lands entangled Germany in their unlawfulness and quarrels, and taught her that fraudulent concept as one of the most effective means of deluding her about her own true advantage and preserving her in this delusion. This aim has now been sufficiently achieved and the intended result lies perfected before our eyes. If we cannot undo it, then why should we not at least eradicate its source in our own understanding, which is almost the last thing left to our jurisdiction? Why should the old dream image still be put before our eyes after the evil has woken us from our slumber? Why should we not now at least see the truth and behold the only means that could have saved us? Perhaps our descendants will do what we perceive must be done, just as we suffer now because our fathers dreamt their dreams. Let us recognise that the idea of an artificially maintained balance of power might well be a comforting dream for foreign lands amidst all the guilt and ills that oppressed them, but as an utterly foreign product it should never have taken root in a German mind, and the Germans should never have found themselves in the situation where it could have taken root among them; that now at least we see through its vanity; that we must realise that universal salvation lies not in that balance of power, but only in the unity of Germans among themselves.

Just as alien to the German is that freedom of the high seas so often preached in our days, regardless of whether this freedom is really intended or merely the power to exclude all others from it. Throughout the centuries of rivalry among the other nations, the German showed little desire to take part to any considerable degree, and he never will. Nor does he need to. His richly endowed land and his own hard work provide him with all that civilised man requires for life; nor does he lack the skill to develop these resources for that same purpose, and his own scientific spirit will not let him want for a means of exchange to obtain the one true benefit that international trade brings, the expansion of scientific knowledge of the earth and of its inhabitants. O if only the German's auspicious fate had spared him from an indirect share in the plunder of other continents, as it spared him from a direct share! If only gullibility and the craving to live in the same fine style as other peoples had not left us dependent on the luxury goods produced in foreign worlds; if only, in respect of the more essential commodities, we had made conditions more tolerable for our free fellow citizens instead of drawing profit from the sweat and blood of some wretched slave beyond the seas; then at least we would not ourselves have furnished the pretext for our present fate, nor would we be under siege as purchasers, nor would we have been ruined as a market-place![81] Almost a decade ago, before anyone could foresee what has since come to pass, the Germans were counselled to make themselves independent of world trade and to establish a closed commercial state.[82] This proposal ran contrary to our habits, but particularly to our idolatrous worship of coined metal, and was passionately attacked and pushed aside. Since that time we are learning, in dishonour and under the compulsion of an external power, to do without that, and much else besides, which once we insisted we could not do without, though then we might have done so freely and with the greatest honour to ourselves. May we take this opportunity, when enjoyment of these things at least no longer corrupts us, to correct our notions forever! May we see at last that, although all those swindling theories of international trade and manufacture are fit for the foreigner and part of the arsenal with which he has waged war on us since time immemorial, they have no application for the Germans; that, besides the unity of the Germans among themselves, their internal self-sufficiency and commercial independence are the second means to their salvation and thereby the salvation of Europe.

Let us, finally, have the courage to behold in all its loathsomeness and irrationality the phantom of a universal monarchy, which is beginning to be offered as an object of public veneration in place of the balance of power that for some time has been growing ever more implausible![83] Spiritual nature was able to represent the essence of humanity only in highly manifold gradations of individuals and of individuality in general,

---

[81] On 21 November 1806 Napoleon issued the Berlin Decree forbidding the import of British goods into European countries allied with or dependent upon France, and installing the Continental System in Europe.

[82] By Fichte himself in his treatise *The Closed Commercial State* (1800).

[83] For example by Friedrich Buchholz in his *Rom und London, oder über die Beschaffenheit der nächsten Universal-Monarchie* (1807).

of peoples. Only as each of these peoples, left to itself and in accordance with its peculiar quality, develops and takes shape, and as every individual among that people, in accordance with this common quality as well as with his own, develops and takes shape, is the appearance of divinity reflected in its proper mirror, as it should be; and only he who either had not the least inkling of lawfulness and divine order or was a implacable enemy thereof could dare to interfere in that supreme law of the spiritual world. Only in the invisible particularities of nations, which are concealed even from their own eyes, as that which connects them with the source of original life, lies the guarantee of their present and future dignity, virtue and merit. If these particularities are dulled by adulteration and friction, then this flatness gives rise to a separation from spiritual nature, which in turn causes all men to become fused together in uniform and mutual ruination. Are we to believe those writers who console us over all our misfortunes with the prospect that we shall instead become subjects of the incipient new universal monarchy, when they say that someone has determined that all the seeds of what is human in humanity be ground down in order that the yielding dough may be pressed into some form or other; that such monstrous brutality or enmity against the human race is possible in our age? Or, even if we were resolved to believe this quite preposterous claim for the moment, then by what instrument is such a plan to be executed? What manner of people is it to be that, given the present level of European culture, will conquer the world for a new universal monarch? The peoples of Europe ceased many centuries ago to be savages and rejoice in destruction for its own sake. All seek beyond war a final peace; beyond toil repose, beyond confusion order; and all long to see their career crowned with the serenity of a quiet and homely life. For a while even a merely imagined national advantage may inspire them to war; when the summons comes again and again in the same way the dream image vanishes and so too does the fervour it produced; the yearning for peaceful order returns and the question arises: 'To what purpose am I doing and suffering all this?' A world-conqueror of our time would first have to expunge all these feelings and then, in an age that by its very nature brings forth no savages, breed such a people with deliberate art. But there is more. The man whose eye is accustomed from youth to see cultivated lands, prosperity and order takes pleasure in the sight of these things wherever he encounters them, if only he is able to enjoy a little peace. For they represent the background of his own longing, a longing that can never be quite eradicated; and it pains him to have to destroy them. Also, to offset the benevolent disposition that is so deeply ingrained in social man, and the sorrow at the evils that the soldier visits upon the conquered territories, a counterweight must be found. The only suitable one is rapacity. If to acquire treasure becomes the dominant motive of the soldier and if, as flourishing countries are laid to waste, he becomes used to thinking of nothing save what he may gain for himself amidst this general misery, then it is only to be expected that the feelings of pity and compassion fall silent within him. Apart from that barbaric brutality, a world-conqueror of our time would have to train his men in cool and premeditated rapacity; he would have to encourage rather than punish extortion. The shame, too, that naturally attaches to this activity would have to be washed away and robbery taken for an honourable mark of a refined intellect; it would have to be reckoned as an act of heroism and as paving the way to every distinction and dignity. Where is there in modern Europe a nation so devoid of honour that it could be drilled in this fashion? Even supposing that this transformation were successful, his purpose would be thwarted by the very means employed to attain it. Such a people henceforth sees in conquered men, lands and artefacts nothing more than a means of making money with the greatest speed, in order to go on and make yet more money; it extorts swiftly and casts aside those it has sucked dry, leaving them to their fate; it fells the tree whose fruits it seeks to gather. To whomever works with such instruments every art of seduction, persuasion and deception is rendered useless; only from a distance can they deceive; seen at close quarters, their animal brutality, and their shameless and brazen rapacity, are manifest even to the most stupid of men, and the revulsion of the entire human race raises its voice against them. With such instruments the earth can be pillaged and laid waste and ground down into a gloomy chaos, but it could never be ordered into a universal monarchy.

These ideas, and all ideas of this sort, are products of a thinking that merely plays games with itself and occasionally even gets caught up in its own web, a thinking that is unworthy of German thoroughness and seriousness. At best some of these images – like that of a political equilibrium, for example – are useful guides by which to orient oneself and bring order in an extensive and confused manifold of appearance; but to believe in the natural existence of these things, or to strive for their realisation, is no different than if someone tried to look for the pole, the meridian and the tropics, by which he finds his bearings on the earth, as if they were impressed and inscribed on the actual globe. May it become the custom in our nation to think not merely for amusement and, as it were, experimentally, to see what might come of it, but in such a way that what we think shall be true and have real validity in life! Then it would be superfluous to warn against such phantoms of a statecraft that is foreign in origin and has merely beguiled the Germans.

This thoroughness, seriousness and weight of our way of thinking will, when once we possess it, break forth in our life also. We are a defeated nation; whether at the same time we want to be despised and rightly despised, whether we want to lose our honour on top of everything else we have lost – that will still depend on us. The armed struggle is ended; now there begins, if we so will it, the new battle of principles, of morals and of character.

Let us present our guests with a picture of faithful devotion to friends and fatherland, of incorruptible probity and love of duty, of all civic and domestic virtues, as a hospitable gift to take home with them, whither one day they must return. Let us beware of inviting them to despise us; nothing would be more certain to achieve this than if we either feared them unduly or strove to abandon our way of life and imitate theirs. Far be from us the unseemliness of an individual challenging and provoking another to the fight; but as for the rest the safest policy will be to continue on our way, as if we were by ourselves, and not to enter into any relationship that necessity does not dictate to us. The surest means of doing this will be for each to be satisfied with what the old relationships in his fatherland can do for him, for everyone to shoulder the common burden to the best of his ability, but to consider any favour conferred by a foreigner to be a dishonourable disgrace. Unfortunately, it has become an almost universal European – and hence German – custom that, when faced with the choice, one prefers to debase oneself rather than appear to be imposing, as it is called, and perhaps the whole doctrine of what is accepted as the good life can be traced back to the unity of that principle. On the present occasion may we Germans offend against this mode of life rather than offend against something higher! May we remain as we are, even though this may constitute just such an offence; indeed, if we can, may we become more emphatically and decidedly what we ought to be! May we be so little ashamed of the faults that one is apt to find with us, namely that we are all too lacking in nimbleness and easy dexterity, that we become too earnest, too grave and too ponderous in everything: may we be so little ashamed of this that we endeavour to be ever more justly deserving of these reproaches and to an ever greater extent. Let our resolve be strengthened by the conviction, acquired without difficulty, that in spite of all our efforts we shall never do right by them, unless we cease entirely to be ourselves, which means the same as ceasing to exist at all. There are peoples who, while retaining their particularity and wishing that it be respected, recognise, grant and permit other peoples their own particularity also. To these the Germans undoubtedly belong, and this trait is so deeply grounded in their entire past and present earthly life that very often they have been unjust to themselves in order to do justice to foreign lands, both of their own time as well as of antiquity. Then again there are other peoples whose self-absorption never allows them the freedom of detachment to take a cool and calm view of the foreign; therefore they are obliged to believe that there is only one possible way to exist as a man of culture, and that is always the way which some chance or other has thrust on them at this moment; that the rest of humanity has no other destiny than to become just like them and would owe them a large debt of gratitude if they took it upon themselves to mould them in this way. Between peoples of the first kind there takes place an interaction of their culture and education, which is highly beneficial for the development of humanity in general, and an interpenetration, where each, with the goodwill of the other, nevertheless remains identical to itself. Peoples of the second kind are unable to cultivate anything, for they are unable to lay hold of anything in its present state of being; they want merely to annihilate all that exists and, beyond themselves, to create everywhere an empty space in which they can only ever reproduce their own form; even their apparent adoption of foreign manners to begin with is only the good-natured condescension of the educator towards the still weak yet promising student; even the figures of past ages do not please them until they have dressed these in their own garb, and they would, if they could, rouse them from their graves to educate them according to their own fashion. Far be from me the arrogance of accusing any actual nation of this narrowness of spirit wholly and without exception. Let us rather assume that here again those who say nothing are the better ones. However, if those who have appeared among us and have pronounced on these matters are to be judged according to their pronouncements, it would seem to follow that they must be placed among the class I have described. Such a statement would appear to demand proof, and, without commenting on the other emanations of this spirit that lie before the eyes of Europe, I shall adduce only one circumstance, namely the following: we have done battle with one another; we are the vanquished, they the victors; this is true and we admit it as such. With that they could doubtless rest content. Now, what if one among us continues to believe that we had right on our side, that we deserved victory and it is a cause for regret that victory did not come our way: would that be so very bad and could our conquerors, who from their point of view may think what they will, hold it against us? But no, we are not supposed to have the audacity to think such thoughts. We are supposed to recognise at once what an injustice it is ever to want something different than they and to resist them; we are supposed to bless our defeats as the most salutary event ever to befall us and to bless our conquerors as our greatest benefactors. It cannot very well be otherwise, and it is hoped that we will see sense. But why need I say at length what Tacitus, for example, said almost two thousand years ago with such succinctness in his *Annals*? The view among the Romans of the relationship between them and the barbarians they were fighting (which was based on a pretence requiring some apology, namely that to offer resistance to Rome was a criminal rebellion and revolt against the laws of gods and men, that Roman arms could bring peoples nothing but blessings and Roman chains nothing but honour) – it is this view that today has been formed about us, generously attributed to us, and assumed to be current among us. I do not put utterances such as these down to arrogant scorn; I can well understand how, as a result of immense conceit and narrowness of spirit, one might seriously think this way and sincerely impute the same opinions to one's opponent, just as I hold that the Romans, for example, really did think this way; but I only ask you to consider whether those among us for whom it is impossible ever to profess this belief can ever reckon on any kind of settlement.

We incur the profound contempt of foreigners if, in their hearing, we blame other German tribes, classes, individuals for our common fate and trade bitter and impassioned reproaches back and forth among ourselves. In the first place, all accusations of this kind are for the most part unfair, unjust and unfounded. We showed earlier what causes brought about Germany's recent fate; these have for centuries been native to all German tribes without exception and in the same way. Recent events are not the consequences of some particular error of a single tribe or its government; they had been in preparation for long enough and might just as easily have befallen us before now, had it solely been a matter of the causes lying within us. Here the guilt or innocence of all is equally great and no longer admits of calculation. When the final result came suddenly upon us, it transpired that the individual German states did not even know themselves, their own strength and their true situation; how, then, could anyone presume to step outside of himself and pronounce on the guilt of others a final judgement based on thorough knowledge?

It may be that, throughout every tribe of the German fatherland, a better-founded reproach is levelled at a certain class, not because it could see or do more than the others, for none is free of blame in that respect, but because it gave the impression that it was able to see or do more, and displaced all the other classes from the administration of each state. If such a reproach had foundation, then who should make it? And why is it necessary that it be made and debated now, more loudly and bitterly than ever before? We see that there are writers who do so.[84] If before, when all the power and authority was still in the possession of that class with the tacit consent of the vast majority of the human race, they spoke then as they speak now, then who can blame them for reminding us of what they once said, which has now been borne out by experience? We hear, too, that they summon before the tribunal of the people individual persons of name who once stood at the head of the state, expose their incompetence, their indolence, their ill will, and clearly demonstrate how such causes must necessarily lead to such effects. If before, when the accused were still in power and the evils that must inevitably result from their government could still be prevented, they had already perceived exactly what they perceive now and gave voice to it just as loudly; if even then they denounced the ones they hold guilty with the same vigour and left no means untried to deliver the fatherland from their hands, and their cries merely fell on deaf ears; then they are right to remind us of the warnings that once went unheeded. But if they are simply wise after the event, since when all the people have reached the very same conclusion, why should it be they who now say what everybody else knows just as well? Or in former days did they perhaps flatter out of a desire for private gain or stay silent out of fear of that class and those persons on whom, now that they have lost power, their immoderate words of censure rain down? O in the future let them not forget to include among the sources of our troubles, besides the nobility and the incompetent ministers and generals, the political writers, who, just like the common people, know only

---

[84] Polemicists against the Prussian ruling class included Friedrich Buchholz (1768–1843), author of *Gallerie Preussischer Charaktere* (Berlin, 1808), Julius von Voss (1768–1832) and Christian von Massenbach (1758–1827).

after something has happened what ought to have been done to prevent it; who flatter the powerful, but mock and gloat over the fallen!

Or do they reprove the errors of the past, which of course cannot be undone by all their reproof, merely so that these shall not be committed again in the future? And is it merely their zeal to effect a thorough improvement of human affairs that allows them to disregard considerations of prudence and propriety with such boldness? We would gladly credit them with this good will, if only their profundity of insight and understanding stood warrant for their good will in this department. Not only the individual persons who happen to have found themselves occupying the highest positions, but also the interconnection and complexity of the whole, the entire spirit of the age, the errors, the ignorance, the shallowness, the despondency, and the uncertain tread that must follow, all the manners of our time have brought about our misfortune; and thus it was less the persons who acted than the positions. Everyone, even the stern rebukers themselves, can assume with a high probability that, if they had found themselves in the same position, they would have been pushed by their surroundings towards more or less the same goal. Let us dream less of deliberate wickedness and treachery! Folly and indolence suffice in almost every case to explain the events; and this is one failing from which no one ought to absolve himself completely without a searching self-examination; especially since, where the mass has a very large amount of inertia, the individual would have to be endowed with an extremely high degree of activity to prevail. Hence, though the faults of individuals may stand out ever so sharply, the cause of our distress is still by no means revealed, nor is it abolished if these mistakes are avoided in the future. So long as men remain imperfect, they cannot but err; and, even if they flee from the mistakes of their predecessors, they will find new ones all too easily in the infinite space of imperfection. Only a complete regeneration, only the beginning of an entirely new spirit, can help us. If our political writers will work with us towards this same development, then we will gladly confer on them not only the glory of a good will, but also that of a just and salutary understanding.

As these mutual reproaches are futile and unjust, so they are extremely unwise and must bring us very low in the eyes of foreigners; especially since, to cap it all, we make it easy for them in all sorts of ways to learn of our bickering, even forcing the knowledge on them. If we do not grow weary of telling them how confused and tasteless everything was with us before, and how wretchedly we were governed, then are they not bound to believe that, however they might behave towards us, they are still too good for us and could never treat us too badly? Are they not bound to believe that, in view of our great clumsiness and ineptitude, we should accept with the most humble thanks everything they have already proffered us from the rich treasure of their arts of government, of administration and of legislation, or may think to bestow upon us in the future? Need we share their rather high opinion of themselves and their low opinion of us? As a result, will not certain of their utterances, which otherwise would have to be regarded as bitter scorn, become merely reiterations of what we say ourselves and the echo of our own words of flattery – as, for instance, their claims that it was they who first brought a united fatherland to the German lands where previously there was none, or that they abolished a slavish dependency of one person on another, supposedly enshrined in law among us? It is a disgrace we Germans share with none of the other peoples of Europe whose fate has been in other respects the same as ours that, as soon as foreign arms were brandished among us, we poured abuse on our governments, on our rulers, whom previously we had flattered in distasteful fashion, and on everything pertaining to the fatherland, as if we had long awaited this moment and wished promptly to do ourselves a good turn before the time for it had passed.

How do we who are innocent remove the disgrace from our heads and leave the guilty standing alone? There is one way. No more libellous pamphlets will be printed as soon as we are sure that none will any longer be purchased, and as soon as the authors and publishers can no longer reckon on readers attracted by idleness, empty curiosity and gossip or by the malicious pleasure of seeing humbled what once instilled in them the painful feeling of respect. Let everyone who feels our disgrace hand back with the proper contempt the pamphlet presented to him for his perusal; let him do so, even though he believes he is the only one who acts thus, until it becomes customary among us that every man of honour conducts himself in this way! Do this, and we shall soon be rid of this shameful section of our literature without the need for the forcible proscription of books.

Finally, we lower ourselves most of all before foreigners when we devote ourselves to flattering them. Some among us already in earlier days made themselves sufficiently contemptible, ridiculous and disgusting by taking every opportunity to offer the coarse incense of praise to the erstwhile rulers of the fatherland, sparing neither reason nor decency, neither good manners nor taste when they thought a fawning speech was in order. This custom has been abandoned in recent times, and these eulogies have been partly transformed into invective. However, so that we should not get out of practice, as it were, we sent our clouds of adulation in a different direction, towards where power now resides. Even the old way, the flattery itself, as well as the fact that it was not declined, was bound to pain every serious-minded German; but this remained our own affair. Do we now want to make foreigners witnesses of our base toadying, as well as of the great inelegance with which we bestow flattery, and thus add to their scorn for our baseness the laughable sight of our clumsiness? We lack in this matter all the refinement peculiar to the foreigner; and to ensure that we are not ignored we become crude and prone to exaggeration, beginning right away with deifications and raising our idol to the stars.[85] Moreover, we give the impression that it is above all fear and terror which squeeze our honeyed words from us; but nothing is more ridiculous than a fearful man who extols the beauty and grace of someone he in fact thinks a monster and merely wishes, through this flattery, to persuade not to devour him.

Or are these hymns of praise perhaps not flattery but a sincere expression of the veneration and admiration they are compelled to pay to the great genius who, they say, guides the affairs of men? How little they know the mark of true greatness! Greatness has been the same in all ages and among all peoples, in that it was not vain; whereas all who showed vanity have always been petty and base. Truly great men, who depend on themselves alone, take no pleasure in statues erected in their honour by contemporaries, or in the epithet 'the great', or in the clamorous applause and praise of the mob;[86] rather, they spurn these things with proper contempt and await judgement to be passed, first that of the judge within their own hearts, then the public verdict of posterity. Furthermore, it has ever been a characteristic of great men that they respect and dread obscure and enigmatic fate; they remain mindful of the ever-turning wheel of fortune, and refuse to be celebrated as great or blessed before the end. Thus those eulogists contradict one another and, by the very act of speaking their words, make them a lie. If they believed the object of their apparent adoration to be truly great, they would concede that he was above their applause and their praise, and honour

[85] Not hyperbole but the literal truth: in 1807 the University of Leipzig took the decision to name the Belt of Orion after Napoleon.

[86] Napoleon was frequently called 'the great'; after his victory at the Battle of Austerlitz in 1805 he gave orders for the construction of the Arc de Triomphe and the Colonne Vendôme, the latter of which is topped by a statue of the Emperor.

him with respectful silence. By making it their business to praise him, they show in fact that they think him petty and base, and so vain that their eulogies could please him, and that they hope thereby to avert some misfortune or obtain some benefit or other.

That enthusiastic cry: what a sublime genius, what profound wisdom, what an all-embracing plan! – what does it really mean when we examine it more closely? It means that the genius is so great that even we understand him perfectly, the wisdom so profound that even we see through it, the plan so comprehensive that even we are able to copy it perfectly. Accordingly, it means that he who is praised is roughly of the same degree of greatness as the dispenser of praise, but not quite, for the latter understands and surveys and consequently stands above the former; and, if only he made sufficient effort, could lift himself to even greater accomplishments. One must have a very high opinion of oneself to believe that one can pay one's court so easily; and he who is praised must have a very low opinion of himself if he accepts such homage with pleasure.

No! My honest, earnest, sober German men and compatriots – let such folly be far from our minds and let such pollution be far from that language of ours which is formed to give expression to the truth! Let us leave it to foreigners to exult at every new phenomenon with wonderment; to produce in every decade a new standard of greatness; to create new gods; and to utter blasphemies in praise of men. Our measure of greatness shall remain the old one: great alone is that which is capable of, and inspired by, those ideas which always bring salvation to the peoples of the earth; but let us leave it to posterity to judge men who are living now!

Note to p. 166
After I had waited a number of weeks for the manuscript of this thirteenth address to be returned to me from the censor's office, I finally received the following note in its stead:

'After it had been granted the imprimatur the manuscript of Professor Fichte's thirteenth address was accidentally lost, and despite our best efforts it has not been possible to locate it again.

In order not to cause the publisher Reimer any delay in printing, I ask Professor Fichte to complete this address from his notebooks and send it to me for the imprimatur.

Berlin, 13 April 1808

von Scheve'

Whatever the author of this missive may understand by a notebook I do not keep, and the loose leaves on which, in working out the text, I made my plans and preparations were consigned to the flames during a change of lodgings around this time. I was therefore compelled to insist that the lost manuscript be found and restored to me. This, I have been assured, was not possible, even after the most meticulous searches; at any rate it has not happened, and I have had to fill in the gaps as best I could.

Whilst I am required for my own vindication to bring this incident to the attention of the public, I ask you nevertheless to accept that the phenomena revealed in the incident itself, as well as in the above letter, are by no means a universal practice with us, but that this incident is an extremely rare and perhaps even unprecedented exception, and that it is to be expected that measures will be implemented to prevent such a case from ever recurring.

Conclusion of the whole

The addresses which I hereby conclude have directed their loud voice primarily at you, but they had in view the entire German nation; and in aim they have assembled about them, in the room in which you visibly breathe, all who might be capable of understanding the same as far as the German tongue extends. If I have succeeded in lighting a spark in any breast beating here before me now, a spark that will glimmer on and take life, then it is not my intention that they remain solitary and alone. Rather, I should like to gather to them, from across the whole of our common soil, men of similar sentiments and resolutions, and unite them, so that throughout the length and breadth of the fatherland, as far as its most distant frontiers, a single flowing and continuous flame of patriotic thought spreads out from this centre and ignites. Not for the amusement of idle eyes and ears have these addresses appealed to this age: I wish at last to know, and everyone of like mind shall know it with me, whether there are others besides us who share our way of thinking. Every German who still believes he is part of a nation, who thinks highly and nobly of it, who hopes in it, who dares, endures and suffers for it, shall at last be released from the uncertainty of his belief; he shall see clearly whether he is right or only a fool and fanatic; henceforth he should either continue his path with sure and joyful consciousness or else with a hearty determination renounce a fatherland here below and in the heavenly one find his only consolation. To you, not as such and such individuals in our daily and limited life, but as representatives of the nation, and through your ears, to the whole nation, these addresses call out thus:

Centuries have passed since you were last convoked as you have been today; in such numbers; in so great and urgent and communal an affair; so thoroughly as a nation and as Germans. Nor will you ever again be so bidden. If you do not now mark these words and examine yourselves, if again you let these addresses pass you by as an agreeable tickling of the ears or as a strange prodigy, then no man will count on you ever again. Hearken at last for once; for once at last reflect. Only this time do not go forth from here without having made a firm resolution; and let everyone who hears this voice make his resolution within himself and for himself, as if he alone existed and must do everything alone. If very many individuals think thus, then soon a great whole will stand there, merging into a single, close-knit power. If each exempts himself, relying on others and leaving the cause to them, then there are no others at all and they will all remain together as they were before. Make it on the spot, this resolution. Do not say: 'Let us rest a while longer, let us sleep and dream a while longer', until, perchance, improvement comes of itself. It will never come of itself. He who has once missed the opportunity of yesterday, when reflection would have been more convenient, cannot make up his mind today, let alone tomorrow. Every delay only makes us more indolent and lulls us yet more deeply into genial habituation to our wretched plight. Nor could the external impulses to reflection ever be stronger and more urgent. He whom the present does not arouse has surely lost all feeling. You have been summoned to make a firm and final resolution and decision: not to give commands and mandates to others, or place demands on them, but to place demands on yourselves. A resolution you shall make, a resolution that each can carry out only by himself and in his own person. In this connection the idle declaration of intent, the will to will at some future time, are not sufficient, nor is it enough lazily to rest content until self-improvement sets in of its own accord: what is required from you is a resolution that is at once both life and inner action, which endures there and continues to hold sway without wavering or cooling until it has reached its goal.

Or is the root, from which alone can spring a resolution that intervenes in life, perhaps completely eradicated and vanished within you? Has your whole being been thinned and washed out so that it is but a pale shadow, devoid of sap and blood, without its own motive power; a dream in which colourful visions are produced and busily commingle, but the body lies stiff and deathlike? For a long while the age has been flatly told that this is more or less how it is viewed, and the message has been repeated in every possible variation. Its spokesmen believed that such utterances were merely contumelies and saw themselves challenged to respond in kind, supposing that the natural order of things would thereby be restored. Yet there has not been the least sign of change or improvement. If you have heard this indictment, and it was able to rouse your indignation, then by your very actions give the lie to those who thus think and speak of you! Show yourselves to be otherwise before the eyes of all the world, and before the eyes of all the world they will be convicted of their falsehood. Perhaps they spoke so harshly of you with the very intention of forcing this refutation from you and because they despaired of any other means of provoking you. If so, then how much better they were disposed towards you than those who flatter you to keep you in sluggish repose and thoughtless distraction!

However weak and feeble you may be, clear and calm reflection has been made easier for you in this time than it ever was before. What really plunged us into confusion about our situation, into our thoughtlessness, into our blind easygoingness, was the sweet satisfaction with ourselves and our mode of living. That is how it was and how it has been ever since. If anyone challenged us to reflect, we triumphantly pointed out to him, in place of some other refutation, our existence and its continuance, which owed nothing to reflection on our part. But it has only been like this because we were not put to the test. Now we have passed through that trial. So should not the deceptions, the illusions, the false consolations, by which we all led one another into confusion, have collapsed and fallen by now? The inborn prejudices which, without proceeding from this point to that, spread like a natural fog and cloak us all in the same twilight – should they not have vanished by now? That twilight no longer obscures our eyes, nor can it serve any longer for an excuse. Now we stand naked and bare, stripped of all foreign vestments and draperies, simply as ourselves. Now it must become clear what this self is or is not.

One among you might step forward and ask me: 'What gives you, and you alone of all German men and writers, the special task, vocation and privilege of assembling us here and haranguing us? Would not any one among the thousands of writers in Germany have exactly the same right to do this as you have? And yet none does so; but you alone thrust yourself forward?' I answer that each one would indeed have had the same right as I; that I do it precisely because none among them has done it before me; that if another had, I would now hold my tongue. This was the first step towards the goal of a radical improvement; someone must take it. I was the first vividly to perceive this; hence I became the first to take it. After this, a second step will be taken; and thereto everyone has now the same right; but in actuality it will again be but one individual who takes it. Someone must always be the first; and whoever can be, shall be!

Without worrying about this circumstance, let your gaze linger for a moment on the consideration to which we have previously led you, namely how enviable a position Germany and the world would be in if the former had known how to utilise the good fortune of her situation and recognise her advantage. Fix your attention on what both now are and let yourselves be suffused with the pain and indignation that must hereupon lay hold of every noble soul. Then look to yourselves and see that it is you whom time can release from the errors of the preceding age and from whose eyes it will clear the mist, if you permit it; that it is granted to you, as to no other generation before you, to undo what has been done and to erase these inglorious pages from the annals of the German nation.

Let the various conditions between which you must choose pass before you. If you continue in your torpor and heedlessness, then all the evils of servitude await you: privations, humiliations, the scorn and insolence of the conqueror; you will be pushed from pillar to post because you belong nowhere and are everywhere in the way, until, at the sacrifice of your nationality and language, you purchase some lowly nook and your people is gradually wiped from the face of the earth. If, on the other hand, you rouse yourselves and make a stand, then you will endure, finding at first a tolerable and honourable existence; later you will live to see grow up among and all about you a race that promises you and the Germans the most glorious memory. In your mind's eye you will see the German name exalted by this race to the most illustrious among all the peoples, you will see in this nation the regenerator and restorer of the world.

It is up to you whether you want to be the end, the last of a race that is unworthy of respect, despised for certain by posterity even beyond its due, a race in whose history – if indeed there can be any history in the barbarism that will then commence – succeeding generations will rejoice when it perishes and praise Fate that she is just; or whether you want to be the beginning and the point from which a new age unfolds, magnificent beyond your every imagining, and to become those from whom your descendants will date the year of their salvation. Bethink yourselves that you are the last in whose power this great change lies. You have still heard the Germans called one people, you have seen a visible sign of their unity, an empire and an imperial federation, or at least been told of it; among you from time to time have still been audible voices inspired by this higher love of fatherland. Those who come after you will grow used to other ideas; they will adopt alien forms and take up a different walk and way of life. And then how long will it be until there is no one left alive who has seen or heard of the Germans?

What is demanded of you is not much. You are asked only to pull yourselves together for a brief while and to think about what lies clearly and immediately before your eyes. About this situation you are merely to form a firm opinion, remain true to it, and then voice it to your neighbours. It is our assumption, nay, it is our sure conviction that this thinking will produce the same result in all of you; that, if only you really think and do not stray back into your previous heedlessness, you will think as one; that, if only you acquire spirit and do not persist in your vegetable state, this unity of sentiment and concord of spirit will come of themselves. When once this point has been reached, everything else that we need will follow on its own.

This thinking is, moreover, demanded of each and every one of you who can still think for himself about that which lies before his very eyes. You have the time for it; the moment will not stun you and take you unawares; the records of your deliberations will remain before your eyes. Do not let them out of your hands until you are in agreement with yourselves. Do not, oh do not become lax by relying on others or on anything beyond yourselves; nor yet by the foolish wisdom of the age, namely that the epochs of history are made by the agency of some unknown force without the aid of humanity. These addresses have never tired of impressing on you that nothing can help you but you yourselves, and they find it necessary to repeat this point to the last moment. Rain and dew, fruitful and unfruitful years, may well be made by a power unknown to us and beyond our control; but the quite special time of man, human affairs, is made only by men themselves and not by any external power. Only when they are all equally blind and ignorant do they fall victim to this hidden power; but it is within their grasp not to be blind and ignorant. It is true that how far things may go badly for us depends in part on that unknown power, but even more on the understanding and goodwill of those to whom we are subject. But whether we shall ever again fare better is entirely up to us; and surely we shall nevermore enjoy a sense of well-being if we do not obtain it by our own efforts, especially if each individual among us acts and works in his own way as though he were alone and as though the salvation of future generations rested solely on his shoulders.[87]

That is what you have to do; and these addresses adjure you to do it without delay.

They adjure you, young men. I, who have for some considerable time ceased to belong among you, believe, and have expressed my belief in these addresses, that you are more capable of any thought transcending the commonplace and more easily aroused to all that is noble and good, because your age still lies closer to the years of childlike innocence and to nature. The majority of the older generation regard this characteristic of yours very differently. They accuse you of presumption, of rash and overweening judgement that races ahead of your abilities, of self-righteousness and a mania for the new. Yet they merely smile good-naturedly at these faults of yours. All this, they think, is due solely to your lack of knowledge of the world – that is, of universal human corruption, since they have eyes for nothing else on earth. You are supposed to have courage now only because you hope to find like-minded helpers and are unacquainted with the fierce and stubborn resistance that your schemes for improvement would encounter. When once the youthful fire of your imagination has burned itself out, when once you perceive men's universal selfishness, indolence and aversion to work, when once you taste for yourselves the sweetness of plodding along in the same old groove, then the desire to be better and cleverer than the rest will soon leave you. They do not simply pluck this fair hope out of thin air; they have found it confirmed in their own persons. They must confess that in the days of their foolish youth they too dreamed of improving the world, just as you do now; yet with increasing maturity they became as tame and docile as you behold them today. I believe them. In my own, not so very extensive experience I have already seen for myself how young men who at first raised other hopes, nonetheless at a later time fully met those well-meaning expectations of this riper age. Do this no more, young men, for how else could a better race ever begin? It is true that the bloom of youth will desert you, and the flame of your imagination will cease to nourish itself; but seize this flame and concentrate it by clear thinking, make the art of this thinking your own, and you will receive as an additional benefit the most beautiful appurtenance of men: character. Through this clear thinking you will preserve the fountain of

---

[87] The final clause that begins 'especially' was added at the behest of the censor.

eternal youth; though your body may grow old or your knees tremble, your spirit will be reborn in ever-renewed freshness and your character stand firm and unchanging. Grasp at once the opportunity offered here; think clearly about the subject presented for your deliberation; the clarity that has dawned on you in one point will gradually spread over the others as well.

These addresses adjure you, old men. You have just heard what others think of you and are prepared to tell you to your face; and this speaker adds frankly for his own part that, leaving aside the not uncommon and all the more admirable exceptions, they are perfectly right with regard to the great majority of you. Review the history of the last two or three decades; all are agreed save you (and even then each of you agrees only when it comes to a department that does not directly concern him) that – always discounting the exceptions and looking only to the majority – in all walks of life, in science as well as in the professions, greater incompetence and selfishness are found in men of advanced years. The whole world has witnessed that anyone who wanted something better and more perfect not only had to struggle with his own lack of clarity and with his other surroundings, but wage the bitterest battle with you; that you were grimly resolved that nothing must come forth which you would not have done and known likewise; that you regarded every stirring of thought as an insult to your intelligence; and that you strained every sinew in order to triumph in your fight against what was better – and triumph you usually did. Thus you were the retarding force holding back all the improvements that bounteous nature bestowed on us from her ever-youthful womb, until you were returned to the dust from whence you came, and the next generation, once at war with you, had become just like you and taken over your former functions. Now, too, you need only act as you have previously acted when confronted with every proposal for reform; you need only once again prefer to the common weal your idle boast that there is nothing twixt heaven and earth that you have not already fathomed; then, by this final struggle, you will be spared all further struggle; no improvement will come but only deterioration upon deterioration, so that you at least will have cause to celebrate.

Do not think that I despise and belittle old age as such. If the source of original life and of its onward movement is absorbed into life through freedom, then clarity grows, and with it power, for as long as life endures. A life like this is lived better; the dross of its earthly origins falls ever more away; it is ennobled to the life eternal and blossoms towards it. The experience of such years is not reconciled with evil, but only makes the means clearer and the art more practised by which we may prevail against it. Deterioration due to increasing age is solely the fault of our time, and wherever society is very corrupt the result must be the same. It is not nature that corrupts us, for we are born in innocence; it is society. He who once surrenders himself to its effects must inevitably become worse the longer he is exposed to this influence. It would be worth the trouble to investigate the history of other extremely corrupt ages in this regard and to see whether – for example, under the rule of the Roman emperors – those who were once bad did not become continually worse with increasing age.

You men of age and experience who are the exception! These addresses adjure you first of all to confirm, strengthen and counsel in this matter the younger generation, who respect and look up to you. You others, however, who are the rule, they adjure you: do not lend a hand, just this once do not interfere, do not again stand in the way, as you have always done previously, with your wisdom and your thousand objections. This matter, like every matter of reason in the world, has not a thousand aspects, but only one: that is one of the thousand things you did not know. If your wisdom could save us, then surely it would have saved us before; for you it was who advised us hitherto. Now, like everything else, this is forgiven, and you should no longer be reproached with it. Only learn at last to know yourselves, and hold your tongues.

These addresses adjure you, men of state. With few exceptions you have thus far been at heart hostile to abstract thought and all knowledge for its own sake, though you gave the impression that you held it only in gentlemanly contempt; you kept the men who engaged in such pursuits, and their proposals, as far away from you as possible; the charge of lunacy or the recommendation that they be committed to the madhouse were all the thanks they could usually expect to receive from you. They, in their turn, did not dare to speak of you with the same frankness because they were dependent on you; but their true and most heartfelt opinion was that, with few exceptions, you were shallow prattlers and puffed-up braggarts, half-educated men with but a smattering of knowledge, gropers in the dark, crawlers in the same old rut who neither could nor would do otherwise. Refute them by your deeds and seize the opportunity to do so that is now presented to you; lay aside that contempt for deep thought and thorough science; take advice, listen and learn what you do not know, or else your accusers will be vindicated.

These addresses adjure you, thinkers, scholars, writers who are still worthy of the name. In a certain sense that rebuke laid upon you by the men of state was not unjust. Often you went your way too unconcernedly in the realm of pure thought, without worrying about the real world and without examining how the former might be linked to the latter; you circumscribed your own world for yourselves and left the real one lying to one side, disdained and despised. All ordering and shaping of actual life must proceed from a higher regulating concept, and to continue down the same old track is of no use in this regard; this is an eternal truth and in God's name it strikes down with unconcealed contempt anyone who dares to go about his business without knowledge thereof. Yet between the concept and its introduction into any individual life lies a great gulf. To bridge this gulf is the task both of the man of state, who of course must first have learned enough to understand you, and of you yourselves, who should not forget life on account of the world of thought. Here you both meet. Instead of looking askance and disparaging one another across the gulf, let each party rather do his utmost to fill it from his side and so pave the way to union. Understand at last that both of you need each other, just as a head needs arms and arms need a head.

In other respects, too, these addresses adjure you, thinkers, scholars and writers still worthy of the name. Your complaints about universal shallowness, thoughtlessness and dissipation, about self-conceit and inexhaustible babble, about the contempt in which seriousness and thoroughness are held by all classes may well be justified; indeed, they are. But which class is it, pray, that has educated the others, turned all that pertains to science into a jest for them, and trained them from their earliest years in that same self-conceit and babble? Who is it who still educates those generations which have outgrown school? The most conspicuous cause of the torpor of the age is this, that it has been made torpid by reading what you have written. Why are you nevertheless still so concerned to entertain this idle rabble, though you know they have learned nothing and wish to learn nothing? Why do you call them the 'public', flatter them as your judge, incite them against your rivals, and seek by any means to win this blind and confused mob to your side? Why, even in your literary reviews and journals, do you furnish them with the material as well as with the model for their impetuous judgery [*Urteilerei*], by yourselves judging as inconsistently, as haphazardly and for the most part just as tastelessly as the least of your readers? If not all of you think thus, if there are still among you some who are better-minded, then why do they not unite to bring an end to the evil? As for those men of state in particular, they acquired their smattering of knowledge under your care; you say so yourselves. Why, then, did you not at least use their fleeting attendance at school to infuse in them some silent respect for the sciences and especially to break the self-conceit of the high-born youth and show him that rank and birth confer no favours in matters of thought? If perhaps even then you flattered him and singled him out undeservedly, then take responsibility for what you have done!

They mean to excuse you, these addresses, on condition that you had not grasped the importance of your task; they adjure you that, from this hour forward, you acquaint yourselves with its importance and no longer go about your work as if it were merely a trade. Learn to respect yourselves; show by your actions that you do so, and the world will respect you. You will give the first proof of this through the influence that you exert on the resolution we have proposed and through the manner in which you conduct yourselves regarding it.

These addresses adjure you, princes of Germany. Those who behave towards you as if no man were permitted to say aught to you at all, or had aught to say, are contemptible lickspittles, they are wicked slanderers of your person; send them away. The truth is that you were born just as ignorant as the rest of us and that you must listen and learn, as we must, if you are to escape from this native ignorance. Your part in bringing about the fate that has befallen you at the same time as your peoples has been here set forth in the mildest way and, we believe, in the only fair and proper way; unless you wish to hear only flattery, but never the truth, you can have no complaint against these addresses. Let all this be forgotten, even as the rest of us wish also that our share in the blame be forgotten! Now begins a new life, for you as well as for us. May this voice reach you through the crowds of hangers-on that are apt to make you inaccessible! With proud self-confidence this voice dares to say to you: you rule peoples, faithful, pliable, worthy of good fortune, such as no princes of any age or nation have ruled over. They have a love of freedom and are capable of freedom; but they followed you into bloody war against what seemed to them freedom because you willed it so. Some among you later willed otherwise and they followed you into what must have seemed to them a war of extermination against one of the last remnants of German independence and self-sufficiency; again because you willed it so.[88] Since

---

[88] A reference to the princes of the Confederation of the Rhine, allied with Napoleon.

that time they have endured and borne the oppressive burden of our collective misery; and they do not cease to be true to you, to cling to you with fervent devotion and to love you as their divinely appointed guardians. If only you could observe them without being seen and, free of the entourage that does not always present to you the fairest aspect of humanity, descend into the house of the burgher, into the cottage of the peasant, and observe the quiet and hidden life of these classes, in which the loyalty and integrity that have become ever rarer among the higher ranks seem to have taken refuge; then surely, oh surely you would resolve to ponder more seriously than ever how they can be helped. These addresses have suggested to you a remedy that they hold to be certain, far-reaching and decisive. Let your counsellors deliberate whether they also find it so or whether they know a better means; only it must be just as decisive. The conviction that something must be done, and done on the spot, something far-reaching and decisive; that the time for half-measures and for palliatives is over – this conviction these addresses would like, if they could, to engender in you personally, as they still have the greatest confidence in your integrity.

You Germans as a whole, whatever position you may occupy in society: these addresses adjure each and every one of you who can think, that you think first of all about the subject touched upon here and that each does whatever lies nearest to him according to his station.

Your forefathers unite with these addresses and adjure you. Imagine that in my voice are mingled the voices of your ancestors from the grey and distant past, who with their own bodies stemmed the tide of Roman world dominion, who won with their own blood the independence of those mountains, plains and streams which under your charge have become the spoils of strangers. They call out to you: represent us, pass on our memory as honourably and blamelessly to future ages as it has come down to you, and as you have gloried in it and in your descent from us! Until now our resistance was thought noble and great and wise; we seemed to be the initiates and votaries of the divine world-plan. If our race terminates with you, then our honour is turned to shame, our wisdom to folly. For if one day the German tribe is doomed to be swallowed up by Romanism [*Römertum*], it were better that it were the Rome of old than a new Rome. We faced the former and triumphed; before the latter you have been reduced to dust. Nor, since things are as they are, shall you conquer them with weapons of steel; your spirit only shall rise up before them and stand tall. Yours is the greater destiny, to found the empire of spirit and reason, and to annihilate completely the crude physical force that rules the world. Do this, and you shall be worthy of descent from us.

With these voices mingle also the voices of your later forebears, those who fell in the holy struggle for freedom of religion and of belief. Save our honour likewise, they call to you. To us it was not wholly clear what it was we fought for; besides our just determination to suffer no external power to dictate to us in matters of conscience, we were also driven by a higher spirit that never entirely revealed itself to us. To you this spirit is revealed, and, if you have but the ability to see into the spirit world, it now gazes at you with lofty, clear eyes. The confused motley of sensuous and spiritual impulses shall be deposed from its dominion over the earth, and the spirit alone – pure and divested of all sensuous impulses – shall take up the helm of human affairs. It was in order that this spirit might have the freedom to develop and to rise to a self-sufficient existence that our blood was spilt. It lies with you to give a meaning and justification to our sacrifice, by installing this spirit on the worldly throne reserved for it. Should this not be realised, as the final goal to which all the previous development of our nation has tended, then our struggles were but a fleeting and vapid farce, and the freedom of spirit and of conscience that we won an idle word, if henceforth spirit and conscience are to be no more.

Your as yet unborn descendants adjure you. You are proud of your forebears, they cry to you, and gloried in your descent from a noble line of men. See that the chain is not broken with you: make sure that we also may be proud of you, and through you, as through a flawless link, can join ourselves to this same illustrious line. Do not cause us to be ashamed of our ancestry as mean, barbarous and slavish; do not lead us to think that we must conceal our origin, or assume a foreign name or parentage, lest we be immediately tossed aside and trodden underfoot without further trial. According as the next generation that proceeds from you shall be, so shall be your memory: honourable, if it testifies honourably of you; ignominious even beyond your due, if your posterity has no voice and you leave it to the victor to write your history. Never yet has a conqueror had inclination or knowledge enough to judge the vanquished fairly. The more he degrades them, the more justified does he appear. Who knows what mighty deeds, what excellent institutions, what noble manners of many a people of antiquity have passed into oblivion because their off-spring were enslaved and the conqueror reported them as it suited his own ends and without fear of contradiction?

Even the foreigner adjures you, insofar as he still understands himself in the slightest and still has an eye for his true advantage. Indeed, among every people there are still souls who refuse to believe that the great promises made to the human race of a reign of law, reason and truth are vain and an empty phantom, and who therefore cherish the conviction that the present age of iron is but a transit to a better state. They, and all modern humanity with them, are counting on you. A large part of them trace their lineage from us, the rest have received from us religion and all manner of culture. The former adjure us by the common soil of our fatherland, the cradle of their infancy also, which they freely bequeathed to us; the latter by the culture they accepted from us as a pledge of a higher happiness, to maintain ourselves as we have ever been, for them and their sakes also, and not to suffer this so very important link to be torn from the ranks of the new-sprung race; so that when one day they shall need our counsel, our example, our co-operation, in pursuit of the true goal of earthly life, they do not sorely miss us.

All ages, all wise and good men who have ever drawn breath upon this earth, all their thoughts and glimmerings of something loftier, mingle with these voices and encircle you and raise imploring hands towards you. Even Providence, if we may venture so to speak, and the divine world-plan in the creation of a human race, a plan that exists only that it may be thought by men and by men made into reality, adjure you to save their honour and their existence. Whether those shall be proved right who believed that humanity must ever improve and for whom thoughts of its order and dignity were not empty dreams, but the prophecy and pledge of future reality, or those who slumber on in the indolence of an animal and vegetable life and mock every flight to higher worlds – this is the question which it has fallen to you to pass a final judgement on. The ancient world with its glories and grandeur, as well as all its shortcomings, has been sunk by its own unworthiness and by the might of your forefathers. If there is truth in what I have said in these addresses, then of all modern peoples it is you in whom the seed of human perfection most decidedly lies and to whom the lead in its development is assigned. If you perish in your essentiality, then all the hopes of the entire human race for salvation from the depths of its misery perish with you. Seek not comfort in the opinion, plucked from thin air and merely counting on history repeating itself, and trust not that, for a second time, after the fall of the old culture, a new one will arise from a half-barbarous nation on the ruins of the first. In ancient times such a people existed, equipped with the requisites for this vocation; it was well known to the civilised people and is described in its literature; and they themselves, had they but been able to imagine their own downfall, could have discovered in this people the means of their restoration. To us, also, the whole surface of the earth is well known and all the peoples who dwell upon it. But do we know one, like the ancestral people of the modern world, of whom the same expectations may be entertained? I believe that every man who does not merely give himself over to idle hopes and fancies, but who thinks thoroughly and searchingly, must answer this question in the negative. There is, then, no way out: if you sink, all humanity sinks with you, without hope of future restoration.

This, gentlemen, was what, at the conclusion of these addresses, I saw as my duty and desire to impress upon you, as my representatives of the nation, and, through you, upon the nation as a whole.

Glossary

Angelegenheit	affair, interest
Antrieb	impulse, motive
Ausland	foreign lands, foreign peoples, foreigners
Ausländerei	foreignism
ausländisch	foreign
Bild	image
bilden	to cultivate, form, train
bildlich	imageable
Bildlichkeit	imageability
Bildung	cultivation, culture, formation
Eigennutz	self-interest
Eigentümlichkeit	particularity
eingreifen	intervene in
ergreifen	seize
Erscheinung	appearance, phenomenon
fremd	alien, strange, foreign
Geist	spirit, mind
Gemüt	soul, mind, temper
Geschlecht	race, generation
Gesetzmäßigkeit	lawfulness
das Mehr	surplus
ein Mehreres	something more
Nachbild	copy
Schlechtigkeit	wickedness
Selbstbeständigkeit	self-subsistence
Selbstständigkeit	self-sufficiency, independence

Selbstsucht	selfishness
Selbsttätigkeit	self-activity
selig, Seligkeit	blessed, blessedness
Sinnbild	symbol
Sinnbildlichkeit	symbolism, symbolic character
sinnlich	sensuous
Stamm	tribe
Stammsprache	ancestral language
Stammvolk	ancestral people
Stand	estate, class, rank, order
Ursprache	original language
Urvolk	original people
vernichten	annihilate
Vorbild	pre-figuration
Weltplan	world-plan
Willensentschluss	decision of the will
Zustand	state, condition

Index

Index

CAMBRIDGE TEXTS IN THE HISTORY
OF POLITICAL THOUGHT

Titles published in the series thus far

Aquinas *Political Writings* (edited by R. W. Dyson) 978 0 521 37595 5 paperback

Aristotle *The Politics* and *The Constitution of Athens* (edited by Stephen Everson) 978 0 521 48400 8 paperback

Arnold *Culture and Anarchy and Other Writings* (edited by Stefan Collini) 978 0 521 37796 6 paperback

Astell *Political Writings* (edited by Patricia Springborg) 978 0 521 42845 3 paperback

Augustine *The City of God against the Pagans* (edited by R. W. Dyson) 978 0 521 46843 5 paperback

Augustine *Political Writings* (edited by E. M. Atkins and R. J. Dodaro) 978 0 521 44697 6 paperback

Austin *The Province of Jurisprudence Determined* (edited by Wilfrid E. Rumble) 978 0 521 44756 0 paperback

Bacon *The History of the Reign of King Henry VII* (edited by Brian Vickers) 978 0 521 58663 4 paperback

Bagehot *The English Constitution* (edited by Paul Smith) 978 0 521 46942 5 paperback

Bakunin *Statism and Anarchy* (edited by Marshall Shatz) 978 0 521 36973 2 paperback

Baxter *Holy Commonwealth* (edited by William Lamont) 978 0 521 40580 5 paperback

Bayle *Political Writings* (edited by Sally L. Jenkinson) 978 0 521 47677 5 paperback

Beccaria *On Crimes and Punishments and Other Writings* (edited by Richard Bellamy) 978 0 521 47982 0 paperback

Bentham *Fragment on Government* (introduction by Ross Harrison) 978 0 521 35929 0 paperback

Bernstein *The Preconditions of Socialism* (edited by Henry Tudor) 978 0 521 39808 4 paperback

Bodin *On Sovereignty* (edited by Julian H. Franklin) 978 0 521 34992 5 paperback

Bolingbroke *Political Writings* (edited by David Armitage) 978 0 521 58697 9 paperback

Bossuet *Politics Drawn from the Very Words of Holy Scripture* (edited by Patrick Riley) 978 0 521 36807 0 paperback

The British Idealists (edited by David Boucher) 978 0 521 45951 8 paperback

Burke *Pre-Revolutionary Writings* (edited by Ian Harris) 978 0 521 36800 1 paperback

Cavendish *Political Writings* (edited by Susan James) 978 0 521 63350 5 paperback

Christine De Pizan *The Book of the Body Politic* (edited by Kate Langdon Forhan) 978 0 521 42259 8 paperback

Cicero *On Duties* (edited by M. T. Griffin and E. M. Atkins) 978 0 521 34835 5 paperback

Cicero *On the Commonwealth* and *On the Laws* (edited by James E. G. Zetzel) 978 0 521 45959 4 paperback

Comte *Early Political Writings* (edited by H. S. Jones) 978 0 521 46923 4 paperback

Conciliarism and Papalism (edited by J. H. Burns and Thomas M. Izbicki) 978 0 521 47674 4 paperback

Constant *Political Writings* (edited by Biancamaria Fontana) 978 0 521 31632 3 paperback

Dante *Monarchy* (edited by Prue Shaw) 978 0 521 56781 7 paperback

Diderot *Political Writings* (edited by John Hope Mason and Robert Wokler) 978 0 521 36911 4 paperback

The Dutch Revolt (edited by Martin van Gelderen) 978 0 521 39809 1 paperback

Early Greek Political Thought from Homer to the Sophists (edited by Michael Gagarin and Paul Woodruff) 978 0 521 43768 4 paperback

The Early Political Writings of the German Romantics (edited by Frederick C. Beiser) 978 0 521 44951 9 paperback

Emerson *Political Writings* (edited by Kenneth S. Sacks) 978 0 521 71002 2 paperback

The English Levellers (edited by Andrew Sharp) 978 0 521 62511 1 paperback

Erasmus *The Education of a Christian Prince* (edited by Lisa Jardine) 978 0 521 58811 9 paperback

Fenelon *Telemachus* (edited by Patrick Riley) 978 0 521 45662 3 paperback

Ferguson *An Essay on the History of Civil Society* (edited by Fania Oz-Salzberger) 978 0 521 44736 2 paperback

Fichte *Addresses to the German Nation* (edited by Gregory Moore) 978 0 521 44873 4 paperback

Filmer *Patriarcha and Other Writings* (edited by Johann P. Sommerville) 978 0 521 39903 6 paperback

Fletcher *Political Works* (edited by John Robertson) 978 0 521 43994 7 paperback

Sir John Fortescue *On the Laws and Governance of England* (edited by Shelley Lockwood) 978 0 521 58996 3 paperback

Fourier *The Theory of the Four Movements* (edited by Gareth Stedman Jones and Ian Patterson) 978 0 521 35693 0 paperback

Franklin *The Autobiography and Other Writings on Politics, Economics, and Virtue* (edited by Alan Houston) 978 0 521 54265 4 paperback

Gramsci *Pre-Prison Writings* (edited by Richard Bellamy) 978 0 521 42307 6 paperback

Guicciardini *Dialogue on the Government of Florence* (edited by Alison Brown) 978 0 521 45623 4 paperback

Hamilton, Madison, and Jay (writing as 'Publius') *The Federalist* with *The Letters of 'Brutus'* (edited by Terence Ball) 978 0 521 00121 2 paperback

Harrington *A Commonwealth of Oceana* and *A System of Politics* (edited by J. G. A. Pocock) 978 0 521 42329 8 paperback

Hegel *Elements of the Philosophy of Right* (edited by Allen W. Wood and H. B. Nisbet) 978 0 521 34888 1 paperback

Hegel *Political Writings* (edited by Laurence Dickey and H. B. Nisbet) 978 0 521 45979 4 paperback

Hess *The Holy History of Mankind and Other Writings* (edited by Shlomo Avineri) 978 0 521 38756 9 paperback

Hobbes *On the Citizen* (edited by Michael Silverthorne and Richard Tuck) 978 0 521 43780 6 paperback

Hobbes *Leviathan* (edited by Richard Tuck) 978 0 521 56797 8 paperback

Hobhouse *Liberalism and Other Writings* (edited by James Meadowcroft) 978 0 521 43726 4 paperback

Hooker *Of the Laws of Ecclesiastical Polity* (edited by A. S. McGrade) 978 0 521 37908 3 paperback

Hume *Political Essays* (edited by Knud Haakonssen) 978 0 521 46639 4 paperback

Marx *Later Political Writings* (edited by Terrell Carver) 978 0 521 36739 4 paperback

James Mill *Political Writings* (edited by Terence Ball) 978 0 521 38748 4 paperback

J. S. Mill *On Liberty*, with *The Subjection of Women* and *Chapters on Socialism* (edited by Stefan Collini) 978 0 521 37917 5 paperback

Milton *Political Writings* (edited by Martin Dzelzainis) 978 0 521 34866 9 paperback

Montesquieu *The Spirit of the Laws* (edited by Anne M. Cohler, Basia Carolyn Miller and Harold Samuel Stone) 978 0 521 36974 9 paperback

More *Utopia* (edited by George M. Logan and Robert M. Adams) 978 0 521 52540 4 paperback

Morris *News from Nowhere* (edited by Krishan Kumar) 978 0 521 42233 8 paperback

Nicholas of Cusa *The Catholic Concordance* (edited by Paul E. Sigmund) 978 0 521 56773 2 paperback

Nietzsche *On the Genealogy of Morality* (edited by Keith Ansell-Pearson) 978 0 521 69163 5 paperback

Paine *Political Writings* (edited by Bruce Kuklick) 978 0 521 66799 9 paperback

Plato *The Republic* (edited by G. R. F. Ferrari and Tom Griffith) 978 0 521 48443 5 paperback

Plato *Statesman* (edited by Julia Annas and Robin Waterfield) 978 0 521 44778 2 paperback

Price *Political Writings* (edited by D. O. Thomas) 978 0 521 40969 8 paperback

Priestley *Political Writings* (edited by Peter Miller) 978 0 521 42561 2 paperback

Proudhon *What is Property?* (edited by Donald R. Kelley and Bonnie G. Smith) 978 0 521 40556 0 paperback

Pufendorf *On the Duty of Man and Citizen according to Natural Law* (edited by James Tully) 978 0 521 35980 1 paperback

The Radical Reformation (edited by Michael G. Baylor) 978 0 521 37948 9 paperback

Rousseau *The Discourses and Other Early Political Writings* (edited by Victor Gourevitch) 978 0 521 42445 5 paperback

Rousseau *The Social Contract and Other Later Political Writings* (edited by Victor Gourevitch) 978 0 521 42446 2 paperback